Cognitive–Analytic Therapy:
Active Participation in Change

WILEY SERIES ON
PSYCHOTHERAPY AND COUNSELLING

Series Editors

Franz Epting
Department of Psychology
University of Florida

Glenys Parry
Department of Psychiatry
University of Southampton

Self, Symptoms and Psychotherapy
Edited by
Neil Cheshire and Helmut Thomae

Beyond Sexual Abuse
Therapy with Women who were Childhood Victims
Derek Jehu

Cognitive–Analytic Therapy: Active Participation in Change
A New Integration in Brief Psychotherapy
Anthony Ryle

Further titles in preparation

Cognitive–Analytic Therapy: Active Participation in Change

A New Integration in Brief Psychotherapy

ANTHONY RYLE

St Thomas's Hospital, London

With Contributions from

Amanda M. Poynton

Guy's Hospital, London

Bee J. Brockman

West Midlands Regional Health Authority, Birmingham

JOHN WILEY & SONS

Chichester · New York · Brisbane · Toronto · Singapore

Other Wiley Editorial Offices

John Wiley & Sons, Inc., 605 Third Avenue,
New York, NY 10158–0012, USA

Jacaranda Wiley Ltd, 33 Park Road, Milton,
Queensland 4064, Australia

John Wiley & Sons (Canada) Ltd, 22 Worcester Road,
Rexdale, Ontario M9W 1L1, Canada

John Wiley & Sons (SEA) Pte Ltd, 37 Jalan Pemimpin 05–04,
Block B, Union Industrial Building, Singapore 2057

Library of Congress Cataloging-in-Publication Data:
Ryle, Anthony
    Cognitive–analytic therapy : active participation in change. A new
integration in brief psychotherapy / Anthony Ryle ; with
contributions from Amanda M. Poynton, Bee J. Brockman.
        p.   cm.—(Wiley series on psychotherapy and counselling)
    Includes bibliographical references.
    ISBN 0 471 92003 7
    1. Cognitive therapy.   2. Brief psychotherapy.   I. Poynton,
Amanda M.   II. Brockman, Bee J.   III. Title.   IV. Series.
    RC489.C63R95   1990
    616.89'14—dc20   89–22515
                                                               CIP

British Library Cataloguing in Publication Data:
Ryle, Anthony
    Cognitive–analytic therapy : active participation in change.
    A new integration in brief psychotherapy
    1. Medicine. Cognitive therapy
    I. Title   II. Poynton, Amanda M.   III. Brockman, Bee J.
    616.89'14

    ISBN 0 471 92003 7
    ISBN 0 471 93069 5 (pbk)

Typeset by Setrite Ltd, Hong Kong
Printed and bound in Great Britain by
Biddles Ltd, Guildford and King's Lynn

Contents

Preface

This book describes an integrated model for understanding neurotic and personality disorders and for conducting psychotherapy. The approach is called Cognitive–Analytic Therapy (CAT) to indicate its main derivation. It could be described as the application of psychoanalytic understanding and of some psychoanalytic techniques within a framework, and with additional treatment methods derived from cognitive psychology and psychotherapy. Time-limited therapy within the framework of this approach is an adequate treatment for a high proportion of patients attending primary care resources or hospital outpatient departments with neurotic disorders, and is a safe and useful first intervention for more seriously disturbed patients, including those with poorly integrated personalities. Trainee therapists from different theoretical backgrounds and of different primary trainings, some with little or no previous therapy experience, have been able to practise the method effectively under supervision. The form of the approach makes research evaluation of its effectiveness practicable and some such research has been carried out. For these reasons the method is particularly appropriate for psychotherapists with responsibility for providing services for populations— especially those who, as is usual, have minimal resources with which to meet the needs and demands facing them.

The book is intended as a guide to clinical work but the underlying theoretical issues will also be addressed. The ideas and methods are illustrated with a large amount of case description, with writing from therapists and patients, and with some directly recorded material from sessions. No claim is made to teach or describe all that a psychotherapist needs to know, but for somebody with a basic clinical training in one of the medical, psychological or associated fields, or for those trained or training in counselling or psychotherapy, it will give a guide to new ways of thinking about carrying out psychotherapy.

The single most distinguishing characteristic of the CAT approach is that patient and therapist are required to carry out jointly the tasks of reformulation in the course of the early therapy sessions. On the basis of this early work, patient and therapist share an agreed written description of those modes of thinking and acting which are repeatedly used by the patient and which are causing or maintaining his difficulties. These descriptions represent a working model of the restrictive or harmful modes of proceeding which it will be the aim of therapy to modify. The work involved in formulating these descriptions is often in itself therapeutic, for it can transform the patient's relation to his difficulty from one of passive suffering and confused powerlessness to one of active engagement and potential problem-solving.

Once the defining task of the early sessions is completed therapy can be carried out in a flexible, eclectic way, in which any skill available to the therapist and helpful to the patient can be employed. The reformulation can be seen as the scaffolding of the therapy within which the therapist can combine quite different interventions; it can also be seen as a tool, fashioned by patient and therapist, with which to do the work of transformation.

Whatever range of therapeutic methods may be utilized, emphasis is placed on teaching the patient to learn to recognize and modify his active contribution to his problems. This involves him learning to apply the high-level general descriptions which have been arrived at to his behaviour and experience. This feature of the approach is in contrast to both dynamic and behavioural therapies, in which relatively low-level interpretations of behaviour are utilized, the patient having the task of generalizing what is learned. These high-level descriptions are not dealing centrally with material which, in psychoanalytic terms, would be considered to be 'dynamically repressed', although the form of the patient's procedures often bears traces of defensive distortions and restrictions. Reformulation offers a form of self-description which can be understood and applied, in most cases, without resistance, in both neurotic and normal subjects. Most of us, while able to describe our 'tactics', are incompletely aware of the strategic assumptions expressed in them, but once these are recognized we can usually remember and apply this recognition. In the same way, the understanding and the application of these high-level strategic descriptions, applied to self-damaging procedures, can be quickly achieved by most patients. Such descriptions represent powerful conceptual tools which even severely beleaguered 'egos' can utilize, and once grasped they reduce the need for defensive restriction. In patients with poorly integrated personalities such descriptions form the basis upon which self-observing and integrating capacities can be developed: an 'eye' from which an 'I' can grow. And this result can be achieved in unsophisticated patients who enter therapy with uncertain motivation and devoid of 'psychological mindedness'.

The book will open with an overall description of the origins and main features of the approach (Chapter 1) and with an account of the reformulation process (Chapter 2). Although clinical interviewing remains the central source of information, a number of written paper-and-pencil procedures are used; these usefully engage the patient in the task of therapy in a co-operative way and can serve to speed up the early stages. Amongst the devices used at this stage is the 'Psychotherapy File'; this is reproduced in Chapter 1, where it can serve to introduce the reader, as it serves to introduce the patient, to some of the ideas underlying this approach. Chapter 3 consists of a discussion of general treatment methods and then Chapter 4 provides an edited transcript of a complete therapy. Following this the problems of achieving more complicated reformulations of patients' difficulties will be considered in more detail (Chapter 5), and the treatment of the more disturbed patient discussed (Chapter 6). In subsequent chapters the use of CAT procedures in long-term therapy, in couple therapy and in different work settings will be discussed, and the theory and practice characteristics of CAT will be discussed more fully and compared with those of cognitive and psychoanalytic approaches. Finally, the training, supervision and research evaluation of CAT will be considered.

Because of my medical background, the word 'patient' is used to describe those whom others may prefer to call 'client'. I regard the terms, in this context, as synonymous.

ANTHONY RYLE

Series Preface

This series of texts on psychotherapy and counselling is written for practitioners, teachers and advanced students. Some books in the series focus on a particular problem area and give psychotherapists the benefit of specialist experience, others will offer original thinking on theory and technique. Some, like this one, will given an authoritative account of a single approach.

There has been great interest recently in how best to integrate different theoretical approaches to psychotherapy. This is partly because research evidence suggests that no single method has a monopoly of effective technique and that all therapies achieve their results through common pathways as well as specific effects. There is also a search for brief, pragmatic approaches which offer the greatest good to the greatest number and in reality that is often a matter of economics. This is a criterion for both public health care delivery systems and private health insurance—the third party payment system demands that psychotherapy be not only demonstrably effective but also cost effective. In this sense, therapies will have to be needs-led rather than theoretically driven and this is another reason why integrationism is attractive.

Rather than find an integrationist approach odd and in need of explanation, perhaps we should ask why so few therapists have the ability to draw on the findings of psychoanalysts, cognitive psychologists, developmental theorists, constructivists and behaviourists. The answer is surely the absence of any shared language or overarching paradigm which allows one to build a coherent picture. In my view, one of Dr Ryle's most important achievements is in building such a picture by applying the concept of *procedural sequences* to human information processing and intentional action. By including a developmental perspective on emotional and interpersonal procedures and by accepting unconscious processing, he arrives, in effect, at a cognitive translation of Object Relations Theory. By emphasizing the ways in which action in the outer world produces contingent feedback which can modify 'procedures' he is firmly committed to behaviour having a central role in change. Finally, he is fundamentally Kellian in his account of the ways in which individuals actively construct their own reality, and how the structure of these realities prevents us learning from experience.

Dr Ryle has been passionately concerned to use these insights to develop an intervention which can be useful to a very broad range of people suffering mental health problems. The result is a therapy which is based on theoretical principles and has *reformulation* of the problem at its heart. It does not reduce the patient (or client) to an object to be treated or a child to be parented, but asserts again and again the importance of creating individual choice and promoting an adult, active learning process. It is designed as a collaborative venture in which the client participates fully but it does not deny the power and value of understanding transference and countertransference. It is a therapy with clearly stated goals and so is amenable to evaluation. Most of all, it provides a coherent framework in which various specific techniques can be accommodated without producing a mishmash eclecticism which has neither logic nor structure. Dr Ryle's book will be essential reading to those already engaged in Cognitive–Analytic Therapy and will introduce many others to the possibility of an effective and theoretically coherent integration of psychodynamics, cognitive and behavioural therapies.

GLENYS PARRY
Series Editor

Acknowledgements

In the case histories and other material reported, the names of patients described are, of course, fictitious; patients' permission has been obtained for the fuller accounts in most cases and in all instances details have been changed to ensure that recognition would be prevented. The therapists involved have not been identified in the text; they are listed below and I would like to thank them in particular, while also acknowledging the many others not so named who have also contributed to the development of CAT. Chapters 3 and 9 are largely the work of my colleagues, Drs Amanda Poynton and Bee Brockman respectively, early members of the weekly seminars in Room F of the Munro Clinic at the Guy's Hospital, to whom special thanks are due. The continued support offered by Professor J.P. Watson, chairman of the Division of Psychiatry at the United Medical and Dental Schools of Guy's and St Thomas's Hospitals, for what he likes to call 'sensible psychotherapy' is acknowledged with much gratitude. I would also like to thank Glenys Parry for being at once an incisive and supportive editor. I would like to thank Mark Dunn for his careful and patient preparation of the typescript, and Tereza Chrysostomos of the medical illustration department at St Thomas's Hospital for the figures.

The following documents incorporated in the text and also reproduced for convenience in the book's appendices, are in the public domain and may be copied for clinical use: due acknowledgement should be given if their use is reported or published. (1) The Psychotherapy File, (2) The Personal Sources Questionnaire, (3) The Relationship Test, (4) The Reciprocal Role Rating Sheet, (5) The TP/TPP Rating Sheet.

The following therapists provided case material:

B. Adam
A. Adamopoulou
B. Brockman
C. Boa
A. Curran
P. Carney
S. Donias
J. Fosbury
G. Garyfalos

L. Harvey
E. McCormack
A. Nehmad
K. Persaud
A. Poynton
A. Ryle
J. Smith
S. Taylor
F. Wray

CHAPTER 1

The Origins and Main Features of Cognitive–Analytic Therapy

The development of Cognitive–Analytic Therapy (CAT) reflects my professional biography. My first 12 years after qualifying in medicine were spent in general practice. In the course of that time I became increasingly interested in common psychiatric problems. This interest led me in two directions; on the one hand, into a great deal of informal counselling, and some more sustained therapeutic work with individuals and couples on my general practice list, and on the other hand, to my first research, consisting of epidemiological studies of my practice population (Ryle, 1967). These experiences made me aware of the high prevalence, persistence and personal cost of the common neuroses, and of how they were inseparably bound up with the social context and problems of living for my patients, and with their family structure and personal relationships.

My next 15 years were spent in a university health service, which offered students direct access to psychotherapeutic help. This experience confirmed the high prevalence of psychological and emotional disturbance, and also served to make me an optimistic therapist. In this context I was able to develop a research interest in the neuroses and in psychotherapy. The basis of my psychotherapy was psychoanalytic (the object relations school in particular), and later on group analytic, although I remained unhappy about many aspects of the theoretical structure of psychoanalysis. My research work relied increasingly on the application of Kelly's (1955) essentially cognitive repertory grid technique. These parallel experiences, my exposure to personal construct theory and the developments occurring in behavioural and cognitive psychotherapy, generated an increasing interest in integrating the diverse theoretical and practical approaches competing for the psychotherapeutic field. At the same time, the research requirement to define the goals of psychotherapy faced me with the difficulty of converting psychoanalytic formulations into operationally reliable descriptions or measures. In time, it became clear that the descriptions of my patients' problems in

1

terms derived from repertory grid testing often produced more precise, acceptable and useful descriptions of the patients' difficulties than did those derived from hypotheses based on psychoanalytic theory. Psychoanalytic formulations require the therapist to use a language relating to early development and to postulated unconscious processes. Grid data, on the other hand, express more directly the evident possibilities and choices and implications of change resulting from a patient's construction of himself and his life. For example, concepts like 'castration anxiety' or 'latent homosexuality' might or might not be true descriptions of the unconscious fantasies operating in a science student in academic difficulties, but it proved more useful to say 'It seems that, for you, the choices open to you seem to be confined to being *either* like your insensitive, authoritarian brigadier father, *or* like your sensitive, creative and artistic mother. Perhaps this is the reason why you spend your time playing your guitar and not turning up for your engineering practical classes. Could we perhaps explore how far the way in which you see your options might be unnecessarily restrictive?'

The problem of defining research goals for psychodynamic therapy was, to my mind, quite satisfactorily solved by articulating patients' problems and the aims of therapy through descriptions of this sort, descriptions which did not require developmental hypotheses or complex constructions of unconscious events. This does not mean that the importance of developmental and unconscious factors was denied, and the descriptions might sometimes include postulates about such processes, for example, by saying of a patient's behaviour that 'It is *as if*, because of your father's death, you feel guilty and cannot allow success.' The definitions of problems arrived at in this way, as well as facilitating outcome research, also began to play an important part in the therapeutic process, as these descriptions were worked out in discussion with the patients. It turned out that the redefinition of the problem was an important stage in its solution, something well known in the problem-solving literature.

A useful description of a neurotic is that he is someone who continues to act in ways that work badly for him, but is unable to revise his ideas or behaviour in the light of the adverse outcomes. Psychotherapy is designed to overcome these blocks on re-learning. The most helpful description of a neurotic problem is one which both describes it accurately and which embodies in the description an understanding of this inability to learn and identifies how it is maintained. By looking through a series of case notes of patients I had treated psychotherapeutically, I derived three main patterns of neurotic repetition. Extensive further practice and supervision suggests that these three categories do satisfactorily account for a wide range of neurotic phenomena. The three patterns were labelled, 'traps', 'dilemmas', and 'snags' (Ryle, 1979). The essential features of these three patterns are as follows:

1. *Traps* — Negative assumptions generate acts which produce consequences which reinforce the assumptions.
2. *Dilemmas* — The person acts as though available action or possible roles were limited to polarized alternatives (false dichotomies) usually without being aware that this is the case.
3. *Snags* — Appropriate goals or roles are abandoned (a) on the (true or false) assumption that others would oppose them, or (b) independently of the views of others, as if they were forbidden or dangerous. The individual may be more or less aware that he acts in this way and may or may not relate this to feelings such as guilt.

At this point it may be helpful for the reader to go through the psychotherapy file. This file, which has evolved over the years, combines instructions for self-monitoring with descriptions of a range of traps, dilemmas and snags. It is normally given to patients at the end of their first assessment interview. The descriptions represent somewhat unfamiliar but usually recognizable ways of understanding the determinants or limits of one's behaviour. It may be useful for the reader to go through the file both with him- or herself in mind or with a particular patient in mind. (The file is reproduced in Appendix A in a form suitable for administration.)

The Psychotherapy File

An Aid to Understanding Ourselves Better

We have all had just one life and what has happened to us, and the sense we made of this, colours the way we see ourselves and others. How we see things is for us how things are, and how we go about our lives seems 'obvious and right'. Sometimes, however, our familiar ways of understanding and acting can be the source of our problems. In order to solve our difficulties we may need to learn to recognize how what we do makes things worse. We can then work out new ways of thinking and acting.

These pages are intended to suggest ways of thinking about what you do; recognizing your particular patterns is the first step in learning to gain more control and happiness in your life.

Keeping a Diary of Your Moods and Behaviour

Symptoms, bad moods, unwanted thoughts or behaviours that come and go can be better understood and controlled if you learn to notice when they happen and what starts them off.

If you have a particular symptom or problem of this sort, start keeping a diary. The diary should be focused on a particular mood, symptom or behaviour, and should be kept every day if possible. Try to record this sequence:

1. How you were feeling about yourself and others and the world before the problem came on.
2. Any external event, or any thought or image in your mind that was going on when the trouble started, or what seemed to start it off.
3. Once the trouble started, what were the thoughts, images or feelings you experienced.

By noticing and writing down in this way what you do and think at these times, you will learn to recognize and eventually have more control over how you act and think at the time. It is often the case that bad feelings, such as resentment or depression or physical symptoms, are the result of ways of thinking and acting that are unhelpful. Keeping a diary in this way gives you the chance to learn better ways of dealing with things.

It is helpful to keep a daily record for 1–2 weeks, then to discuss what you have recorded with your therapist or counsellor.

Patterns That Do Not Work, but are Hard to Break

There are certain ways of thinking and acting that do not achieve what we want, but which are hard to change. Read through the list that follows and mark how far you think they apply to you.

Traps

Traps are things we cannot escape from. Certain kinds of thinking and acting result in a 'vicious circle' when, however hard we try, things seem to get worse instead of better. Trying to deal with feeling bad about ourselves, we think and act in ways that tend to confirm our badness.

Aggression and assertion. People often get trapped in these ways because they mix up aggression and assertion. The fear of hurting others can make us keep our feelings inside, or put our own needs aside. This tends to allow other people to ignore or abuse us in various ways, which then leads to our feeling, or being, childishly angry. When we see ourselves behaving like this, it confirms our belief that we shouldn't be aggressive. Mostly, being assertive, asking for our rights, is perfectly acceptable. People who do not respect our rights as human beings must either be stood up to or avoided.

Examples of traps.

1. *Avoidance* We feel *ineffective and anxious* about certain situations, such as crowded streets, open spaces, social gatherings. We try to go

back into these situations, but feel even more anxiety. Avoiding them makes us feel better, so we stop trying. However, by constantly avoiding situations our lives are limited and we come to feel increasingly *ineffective and anxious*.

2. *Depressed thinking* — Feeling *depressed*, we are sure we will manage a task or social situation badly. Being depressed, we are probably not as effective as we can be, and the depression leads us to exaggerate how badly we handled things. This makes us feel more *depressed* about ourselves.

3. *Social isolation* — Feeling *under-confident* about ourselves and anxious not to upset others, we worry that others will find us boring or stupid, so we don't look at people or respond to friendliness. People then see us as unfriendly, so we become more isolated, from which we are convinced we are boring and stupid, and become more *under-confident*.

4. *Trying to please* — Feeling *uncertain about ourselves* and anxious not to upset others, we try to please people by doing what they seem to want. As a result (1) we end up being taken advantage of by others, which makes us angry, depressed or guilty, from which our uncertainty about ourselves is confirmed; or (2) sometimes we feel out of control because of the need to please, and start hiding away, putting things off, letting people down, which makes other people angry with us and increases our uncertainty.

Dilemmas (false choices and narrow options)

We often act as we do, even when we are not completely happy with it, because the only other ways we can imagine seem as bad or even worse. These false choices can be described as dilemmas, or either/or options. We often don't realize that we see things like this, but we act *as if* these were the only possible choices.

Do you act as if any of the following false choices rule your life? Recognizing them is the first step to changing them.

Choices about yourself.

I act as if:

1. *Either* I keep feelings bottled up, *or* I risk being rejected, hurting others or making a mess.
2. *Either* I feel I spoil myself and am greedy, *or* I deny myself things and punish myself and feel miserable.
3. If I try to be perfect, I feel depressed and angry; if I don't try to be perfect, I feel guilty, angry and dissatisfied.
4. If I must, then I won't (other people's wishes, or even my own, feel too demanding, so I constantly put things off, avoid them, etc.).

5. If other people aren't expecting me to do things, look after them, etc., then I feel anxious, lonely and out of control.
6. If I get what I want, I feel childish and guilty; if I don't get what I want, I feel angry and depressed.
7. *Either* I keep things (feelings, plans) in perfect order, *or* I fear a terrible mess.

Choices about how you relate to others.

I behave with others as if:

1. If I care about someone, then I have to give in to them.
2. If I care about someone, then they have to give in to me.
3. If I depend on someone, then they have to do what I want.
4. If I depend on someone, then I have to give in to them.
5. *Either* I'm involved with someone and likely to get hurt, *or* I don't get involved and stay in charge, but remain lonely.
6. As a woman, I have to do what others want.
7. As a man, I can't have any feelings.
8. *Either* I stick up for myself and nobody likes me, *or* I give in and get put on by others and feel cross and hurt.
9. *Either* I'm a brute, *or* I'm a martyr (secretly blaming the other).
10. *Either* I look down on other people, or I feel they look down on me.

Snags

Snags are what is happening when we say 'I want to have a better life but . . .', or 'I want to change my behaviour but . . .'. Sometimes this comes from how we or our families thought about us when we were young; such as 'she was always the good child', or 'in our family we never . . .'. Sometimes the snags come from the important people in our lives not wanting us to change, or not being able to cope with what our changing means to them. Often the resistance is more indirect, as when a parent, husband or wife becomes ill or depressed when we begin to get better.

In other cases, we seem to 'arrange' to avoid pleasure or success, or if they come, we have to pay in some way, by depression, or by spoiling things. Often this is because, as children, we came to feel guilty if things went well for us, or felt that we were envied for good luck or success. Sometimes we have come to feel responsible, unreasonably, for things that went wrong in the family, although we may not be aware that this is so. It is helpful to learn to recognize how this sort of pattern is stopping you getting on with your life, for only then can you learn to accept your right to a better life and begin to claim it.

You may get quite depressed when you begin to realize how often you stop your life being happier and more fulfilled. It is important to remember that it's not being stupid or bad, but rather that:

(a) we do these things because this is the way we learned to manage best when we were younger;
(b) we don't have to keep on doing them now we are learning to recognize them;
(c) by changing our behaviour, not only can we learn to control our own behaviour, but we also change the way other people behave to us;
(d) although it may seem that others resist the changes we want for ourselves (for example, our parents or our partners), we often underestimate them; if we are firm about our right to change, those who care for us will usually accept the change.

Do you recognize that you feel limited in your life:

(a) for fear of the response of others;
(b) by something inside yourself.

Difficult and unstable states of mind. Indicate which, if any, of the following apply to you:

1. How I feel about myself and others can be unstable; I can switch from one state of mind to a completely different one.
2. Some states may be accompanied by intense, extreme and uncontrollable emotions.
3. Other states are accompanied by emotional blankness, feeling unreal, or feeling muddled.
4. Some states are accompanied by feeling intensely guilty or angry with myself, wanting to hurt myself.
5. Or by feeling that others can't be trusted, are going to let me down or hurt me.
6. Or by being unreasonably angry or hurtful to others.
7. Sometimes the only way to cope with some confusing feelings is to blank them off and feel emotionally distant from others.

Integration of Interpretive and Cognitive Methods

During the time spent in the development of trap, dilemma and snag descriptions, and in preliminary research into the effectiveness of brief therapy focused in this way, I had also become more concerned with the issue of theoretical integration (Ryle, 1978). During the same period, my clinical work shifted from the university context to a National Health Service setting. As a consultant psychotherapist, I became responsible for the provision of psychotherapy to a population of 165,000 people, and for the training and supervision of trainee psychiatrists and members of other professional groups. In this role, I was once more sharply confronted with the issue of the level of need in relation to the level of provision, having to provide treatment for a large population with minimal resources and needing to rely, to a large extent, on relatively untrained and inexperienced therapists. CAT proved applicable within this setting, and it was from this experience of teaching and supervising therapy, and the research associated with it (Brockman *et al.*, 1987), that the now more-or-less formalized but still evolving characteristics of CAT developed.

The theoretical roots, as indicated above, are mostly to be found in object relations theory, Kelly's personal construct theory, in cognitive and behavioural psychotherapies and in developmental and cognitive psychology. Psychoanalysis is the dominant clinical influence both for the theoretical understanding it offers of the link between infantile development, personality structure and patterns of relationship, and for the crucial focus it lays upon the therapy relationship, that is to say upon transference and counter-transference and their use in therapy. While many patients can be helped by therapists paying no regard to these issues, many *cannot*, and I believe every therapist needs to be able to understand and to use the phenomena described in this way. However, research has shown no overall exclusive virtue for any one psychotherapeutic approach and the narrow orthodoxies of competing schools do not deserve too much respect. Faced with the demonstrated efficacy of many behavioural and cognitive methods, it seemed appropriate to abandon some of the abstentions prescribed to psychoanalytic therapists, and to combine other methods with a basically analytic technique. Naturally, the therapeutic relationship is altered by this, for the therapist who emphasizes joint work, offers concepts, prescribes reading, suggests homework assignments, and so on, will evoke different responses from those evoked by the more impassive, reflective or inert therapist. Such differences do not, however, make working with the transference impossible. Indeed, experience has shown that transference issues are frequently thrown up sharply and early in more active therapies, in ways that bring the patient's problems very directly into the room, and this can be of value, particularly in time-limited therapy. If patients are able to work effectively on the conceptual tasks given them, such as reading the Psychotherapy File, carrying out paper-and-pencil tests, and so on, and if they carry out self-monitoring in the context of developing a positive relationship with the therapist, the basic transference is positive, and there is an early loss of defensiveness, with therapeutic change often beginning in the earliest sessions. In such cases, further transference issues may arise in the middle of therapy, as some disappointments and setbacks are encountered, or as some Target Problem

Procedures become manifest; an example would be a snag in which the improvement experienced as a result of therapy is opposed by others or sensed as forbidden. In many cases, termination will provide an occasion for experiencing feelings derived from the past, especially in those cases where past losses have been incompletely mourned. In other patients, however, the work asked of them, and agreed by them, will not in fact be done. They will fail to self-monitor, will leave their psychotherapy file on the bus or will present the familiar late arrivals or missed appointments of passively resisting patients. In such cases, the reformulation arrived at must incorporate an understanding of these behaviours, and the work of therapy will depend on identifying and challenging them, as well as demonstrating their relation to the life difficulties being complained of. This is helped by the fact that the same reformulation will be applied to the behaviour in and out of the therapy context.

The Procedural Sequence Model

Although psychoanalytic ideas are central to CAT, they appear in forms which will be unfamiliar and perhaps unacceptable to many readers. It is therefore necessary to spell out the basic theory from which the language of CAT is derived. The traps, dilemmas and snags listed in the Psychotherapy File are particular examples of the kinds of procedure involved in the general organization of intentional, aim-directed action. The underlying model is the Procedural Sequence Model (PSM), which represents the theoretical base of CAT. This model gives a general account of the sequence of mental and behavioural processes involved in the carrying out of aim-directed activity. The model is one of *procedures*, how things are organized, and *sequences*, the order in which the stages follow one another. A given procedure will be defined by its aim, and will, of course, be but one part of the individual's complex life enterprises. A procedure will normally be part of an hierarchical structure representing a sub-procedure of a higher-order one, and being effected in turn through lower-order sub-procedures. For example, if a higher-level procedure is 'to enjoy my life', one intermediate-level procedure could be 'to take care of my health', and one low-level procedure could be 'not to smoke cigarettes'. Because of this hierarchical structure, changes at one level are likely to have effects on procedures at higher and lower levels. This enables one to understand, for example, the often indistinguishable outcomes achieved by very different therapeutic inputs (Ryle, 1984). The procedural sequence serving a given aim will normally operate repeatedly, perhaps with modification and making use of alternative sub-procedures. In this sense the sequence is to be understood as a circular process with both anticipation ('feed forward') and feedback mechanisms being integral to it. The stages are as follows (note: stages 1−4, 6 and 7 are mental; stage 5 is external, an action in the world, but can be carried out in imagination):

1. Define aim (maybe in response to external event).
2. Check aim for congruence with other aims and values, i.e. for personal meaning.
3. Evaluate situation, and predict one's capacity to affect it, and the likely consequences of achieving the aim.
4. Consider the range of means or roles (sub-procedures) available and select the best.
5. Act.
6. Evaluate (a) the effectiveness of the action and (b) the consequences of the action.
7. Confirm or revise (a) the procedure and (b) the aim.

In terms of this model, neurosis is understood as the persistent use of, and failure to modify, procedures that are ineffective or harmful. Snags represent, for example, the inappropriate abandonment of aims (stage 7), due to a true or false perception or prediction of negative outcomes. Dilemmas represent undue narrowing (false dichotomization) of the possible sub-procedures (stage 5). Traps represent the reinforcement of negative beliefs and assumptions (stages 2 and 3) by acting, (stage 5) in ways that evoke consequences which are, or are seen to be, confirmatory of negative assumptions (stages 6 and 7).

It will be clear that the PSM is a cognitive theory in the broadest sense, that is to say, one that is concerned with higher-level mental procedures, and in no way excludes the affective. Meanings and dispositions are actively involved throughout the sequence, and emotions are understood as subjective experiences signalling directions and discrepancies within the procedural system. Stage 2 of the PSM can be understood in terms of recent developments in the field of the emotions. These suggest that a partially separate system is involved, concerned with a particular 'type of information processing about the self in interaction with the environment' (Greenberg and Safran, 1987). This system is involved in wide scanning of the environment, processed in ways that have clear implications for action. It represents right hemisphere, tacit, as opposed to left hemisphere, explicit, functioning (Guidano, 1987) The articulation of this affective processing with cognitive processes is clearly involved in other stages of the PSM, notably 3 and 6. (See Chapter 11 for a fuller discussion of these issues.)

Certain procedures may involve diminished awareness of feeling, for example, dealing with threat by acting as if it were absent. In this model the 'ego defences' of psychoanalysis are understood as the 'editing' of procedures to diminish conflict or anxiety at the cost of a diminished experience of self and of reality. Patients with a personality disorder fail to maintain a coherent relation between alternative procedures, and may manifest both ineffective action and extreme inappropriate emotion. Horowitz (1984) has edited an up-to-date debate between cognitive and psychoanalytic writers on the converging understanding of these processes.

The PSM produces an overall model of sequences which can be applied to procedures at different levels in the procedural hierarchy. Semner and Freese (1984) suggest four levels, as follows:

1. The sensorimotor, concerned with consistent, stereotypical sequences.
2. The perceptive-cognitive, concerned with the basic array of action patterns.
3. The intellectual, concerned with complex analysis and problem-solving.
4. The abstract, concerned with the detection of regularities and laws and the identification of contradictions.

The CAT therapist is operating at level 4, mobilizing the patients' level 3 and 4 capacities with the aim of modifying ineffectual procedures at levels 2, 3 and 4; effective intervention will demand recognition of the way in which action tendencies are determined by emotion and by systems of personal meaning.

CAT: The Treatment Plan

CAT, within a time-limited frame, will have a clear form and rhythm. The task of the earliest sessions is to establish a working relationship, to maximize the powerful and non-specific effects of therapy on morale and to convert passive suffering to active engagement in problem-solving. This phase usually lasts for the first four sessions, during which more-or-less undirected listening will be supplemented by the setting of, and receiving back of, particular homework tasks to be carried out between the sessions. These tasks are all directed towards the issue of reformulating, and will lead to the therapist and patient agreeing upon a written account of the patient's past and of how this past is reflected in the list of current problems and problem procedures, the Target Problem (TP) and Target Problem Procedures (TPPs) list. This list provides the agenda and framework for therapy. During the assessment phase, transference issues may have already become apparent, and provisional interpretations or reformulations will have been discussed. In its final form, each TPP should be a *clear, succinct, accurate, generally applicable and specifically adequate* description of a patient's repeatedly used maladaptive procedures. In addition, an account of the patient's past and how this has led to the present problems serves to flesh out and emphasize the origins and manifestations of the processes being described in a way which takes account of the original need for these procedures. These reformulations, written as a letter to the patient, or in the patient's own voice, identify the patient's 'chronically endured pain' (Mann and Goldman, 1982), and represent a powerful way of strengthening the therapeutic alliance.

On the basis of an agreed list of TPs and TPPs, therapist and patient will usually conclude a time-limited contract. The various aids to reformulation used during the assessment phase will be considered in Chapter 2, and their use illustrated in the case history in Chapter 4. The main skill of the CAT therapist is the ability to arrive at good reformulations and TPP descriptions. This involves hard focused thinking. This thinking is, however, of extreme relevance to the therapeutic task; the reformulation often plays a large part in mobilizing denied emotion and restoring meaning to the past, while the TPPs, if well developed with and understood by the patient, make subsequent therapeutic work accurate and effective.

Although therapeutic change may well have started during the assessment phase, once reformulation is agreed and written down (usually at session 4), the emphasis shifts from the identification and description of TPPs to practice in their recognition and, in due course, revision. It is crucial that these new descriptions, which represent redefinitions of hitherto accepted automatic procedures, are not just understood in the clinic, but are applied in the patient's life. Learning to recognize the recurrent use of these procedures is, therefore, an important part of this phase of the therapy. This learning takes place within two contexts—in the consulting room and in the work during the week between sessions.

If TPPs are well thought through, they will, in nearly all cases, anticipate transference issues that may arise in the course of therapy. The availability of these descriptions to the therapist enables her to recognize and use this recognition quickly, and it is often the case that good use of transference–counter-transference issues can be achieved by inexperienced therapists. As a supervisor, when confronted by a therapy which seems to be stuck, it is my regular habit to ask the therapist to read out the TPPs in full. In most cases, this makes it clear that what has happened is that the therapist has been drawn into a collusion with one of the patient's procedures. For the patient, learning to recognize the operation of TPPs in action in the world is assisted through focused diary-keeping. During the assessment phase, self-monitoring is applied to spontaneously occurring events, like symptoms or mood changes, but during the treatment phase, monitoring should be directed towards the identification of these newly described and recognized problem procedures. This explicit task forces patients to take the descriptions and concepts out into the world, and develops in the patient a new capacity for self-observation. Initially TPP diaries will record 'I did it again ...' (details should be noted), but after quite a short period, often one to three weeks, patients may begin to be able to report 'I noticed I was beginning to do it again, but was able to stop and think ...'.

Transference work and diary-keeping in relation to the TPPs is the central therapeutic input during the treatment phase, with the issue of termination being kept in focus by always numbering the sessions. This, however, is not done mechanically; there are wide variations between patients and therapists in how they work together, and the form of sessions remains largely unstructured, except in respect of the setting and receiving back of the diary assignments and other tasks. At the end of each session, the patient is asked to rate change on the list of TPs and TPPs; this provides an opportunity for gathering all the reported material and the events of the session, and relating them to these descriptions. In this way, diverse experiences within and outside the therapeutic hour are consistently referred back to these defined problems. Changes in any one area where a TPP is operating can be related to other areas where the same pattern is occurring, which is likely to aid generalization.

Where these basic tactics do not lead to change, other specific methods may be called for; for example, the patient whose conceptual understanding remains divorced from feeling may be helped by role-playing, or by being given provocative behavioural tasks which expose him to avoided situations. The patient who recognizes patterns, but is unable to change his behaviour, may need detailed help with planning gradual programmes of change, perhaps combined with rehearsals or role-playing in the session.

In general, patients' and therapists' imaginations and skills are not restricted in the CAT model, as long as what is done and experienced is discussed in relation to the agreed problems defined by the TPPs. A fuller description of a range of methods of keeping therapy moving will be found in Chapter 3.

Reformulation in general and TPP descriptions in particular can be seen, therefore, to generate accurate descriptions and crucial redefinitions of patients' procedures, offering a new tool for self-reflection. They anticipate issues likely to arise in the transference. They are the basis for the patient's learning a new ability to identify and consciously revise hitherto automatic and maladaptive procedures. For the therapist, they provide a conceptual scaffolding within which brief, intensive therapy using a wide range of therapeutic methods can be carried out coherently. Finally, being brief and memorable, they are 'portable' by the patient, who can take them away as a reminder of the work of therapy between sessions.

At the end of a brief therapy, both therapist and patient may agree to write an account of what has been achieved, and the therapist can indicate areas where further work is needed; this 'goodbye letter' serves to keep the work of therapy in focus during the follow-up period, and often thereafter too.

It will be seen that CAT utilizes a 'threefold way' to therapeutic change: new understanding, new experience and new acts can all initiate change and influence each other. But new understanding, as incorporated in the reformulation of the patient's problems, is the most powerful agent of change, for using this new tool of self-understanding, the patient can often initiate new acts and discover new experiences for herself.

By the end of a satisfactory 12–16-session therapy, it is usual for the patient to have become aware of the operation of her main TPPs and to have begun to use this awareness to alter her behaviour in some respects. Brief therapy does not allow 'working through', and the patient's subsequent progress will depend upon her ability to hold on to her newly learnt understanding, and apply it in her daily life; the 'goodbye letter' from the therapist, highlighting what remains to be done, can be helpful here. Research evidence suggests that, on average, the changes achieved in therapy are stable, but are not much further extended. Patients need to be followed up after 2–3 months, and at that time some patients (about one in four) may be offered further top-up sessions, further follow-up, another brief therapy, group therapy or some other intervention.

CHAPTER 2

The Reformulation Process and the Uses of Writing

The initial sessions in CAT are devoted to the gathering of the history and to the joint task of reformulation. Patients will normally have been selected for referral, but how this is done will depend upon the setting in which the patient is seen and on the sources of referral. In the context of the NHS or other public provision of services, or where limited insurance cover is available, time-limited CAT is a suitable first intervention for the great majority of patients with either neurotic or personality disorders, except for those who might be considered for couple or family therapy or for group therapy. Patients with any dependency on, or abuse of, alcohol, prescribed drugs or minor illegal drugs will be required to record and rapidly control their intake; more severe abuse would be a contraindication for therapy. Patients with symptoms of a major depression will be advised to take antidepressant medication. For those reluctant to do this, progress will be carefully monitored; in most cases likely to respond to psychotherapy, change will probably have begun by the fourth or fifth session (DiMascio et al., 1979). If it has not, then psychotherapy is unlikely to be effective unless the depression is treated.

It is usually best to leave the final decision as to the aims, form and duration of therapy until the fourth session, for these will depend upon the understandings reached and upon the development of TP and TPP descriptions. By this time the therapeutic process will usually be under way and the patient's ability to work and change will be becoming apparent. At this point some patients may be referred for other kinds of treatment, but the great majority will be offered a specific number of further sessions; the number will be clearly defined at this stage. In general, CAT has been offered in 12–16-session contracts, but shorter intervention of 6–8 sessions, followed by homework and follow-up, are currently being researched. In settings where research is not taking place the offer could be variable, and it might sometimes be appropriate to offer longer therapies of up to 24 sessions, but it is always important to set and adhere to a fixed, finite number.

The first three sessions with the patient will consist largely of semi-structured and unstructured interviewing. If patients are not previously screened, a psychiatric assessment will be included during these sessions. In the course of this time a full life history and a detailed account of the patient's problems will be acquired, and the patient's interaction with the therapist and his ability to carry out the tasks assigned and to make use of any comments or provisional reformulations offered will be noted. This interviewing will be of a general form familiar to dynamic psychotherapists, leaving most of the initiative and selection of topics to the patient, while prompting and elucidating the meanings accorded to reported experience, and noting remembered and elicited or apparently avoided emotional responses. In the therapist's mind this history will be scanned for events likely to have made particular adjustments difficult or particular solutions necessary, and an attempt will be made to explore what conclusions the individual may have drawn from his experience about himself and in terms of his values, assumptions and strategies. Often it will be apparent that the present complaint or difficulty is the result of the strategies adopted of necessity in early life. In some cases the early experience and the survival tactics adopted may bear the mark of the distorted or simplified framework of perception and judgement of the child. In other cases, a major distancing from the emotional importance of the events discussed may be apparent. The CAT therapist, however, will be concerned above all to identify and describe the repetitively used harmful or restrictive procedures for self-care and control and for relating to others operating in the patient's life, and often manifest in the 'here and now' of the session. The particular flavour of the CAT reformulation derives from this emphasis on achieving such descriptions at this early stage, aiming to make the highest-level, most generally applicable descriptions possible.

The Psychotherapy File and Self-Monitoring

The unstructured clinical interview is supplemented in all cases by giving the patient a Psychotherapy File to read. This is usually given at the end of the first therapy session but can be given along with other suggested paper-and-pencil exercises at the end of the initial assessment interview as part of a 'waiting-list' package. Any patient who has an intermittent or variable mood disorder (depression, anxiety, anger) or psychologically provoked symptoms should start monitoring these as instructed in the file. It is important to emphasize that this self-monitoring needs to note (1) the occurrence of a symptom or mood change, (2) the context in which it occurs and (3) the preceding and accompanying thoughts and images. For some patients it may be best to start with a simple symptom diary and add later the requirement to consider thoughts and accompanying images. Diary-keeping of this sort frequently modifies the symptoms and is always of diagnostic interest. Careful analysis of self-observed inner and outer events associated with symptoms usually makes it clear that the symptom has replaced a feeling or behaviour that the patient cannot allow. These are commonly concerned with assertion and aggression or with need and abandonment. This recognition will play a part in the formulation of TPPs. Where symptoms persist, they can be used as signals drawing attention to the fact that the problem procedure is operating and in this respect can operate consciously to serve the same function as would have been served by the repressed emotion.

This form of self-monitoring is a development of that suggested by Beck (1976) for depressed thinking. In CAT, particular emphasis is placed on the interpersonal context of the phenomena being monitored and on issues of self-care and control; such monitoring is applied to a wide range of symptoms, emotions and behaviours. An indirect effect of involving patients in this activity is that their relation to their distressing symptoms or behaviours is altered from a passive to an active one, and they are therefore, from the beginning, participants in the therapeutic work. A second effect is that the way in which the patient carries out or fails to carry out the allotted tasks frequently makes manifest his interpersonal procedures, that is to say transference is evoked and becomes another source of understanding. It should be emphasized that diary-keeping for its own sake is of little value; as the Spanish proverb says, it is like blowing one's nose and then looking in the handkerchief. During the reformulation phase diary-keeping needs to have a highly specific aim, namely to identify the procedures lying behind passively experienced symptoms or uncontrolled behaviour, and the patient should be given careful instructions to focus on these issues.

The Psychotherapy File: Recognizing TPPs

Most patients, even those with little sophistication or education, will also benefit from reading the remainder of the Psychotherapy File, which consists of descriptions of common patterns of problem procedures. Patients are usually able to identify accurately which of these descriptions apply to them. Discussing these traps, dilemmas and snags with the patient contributes to the formal focusing of the fourth session. During these early meetings particular illustrative examples will have emerged. With experience, therapists will be able to identify TPPs from the clinical material, but this form of description will be unfamiliar to start with to many, and it is sometimes helpful for the therapist to go through the file in between sessions with the particular patient in mind. In some cases obsessional patients or nervous therapists may go through the file together, exploring which procedures apply. This will also be necessary for illiterate patients. Although this may seem an artificial approach, in fact it often produces much relevant understanding as the patient identifies and fleshes out her particular problems. In all cases patients should be asked to illustrate why they feel a particular description applies to them. Some patients will find themselves reflected in every description, in which case questions of degree of importance must be considered. Others will deny that the descriptions have any relevance or meaning; these latter patients may be rejecting a too mechanical use of the file or may be manifesting one of the dilemmas described in it, such as 'I act as if, "If I must then I can't or won't"'. In many cases of this sort, the file may be usefully reintroduced at a later date. Even though the dense abbreviated descriptions offered in the file may be acceptable, it is usually best to make up a patient's TPP list with her in as individual a way as possible, drawing upon the patient's own language and metaphors.

It is possible to carry out CAT using clinical interviewing, self-monitoring and the file with no other special procedures. Later in this chapter some other devices that can be useful both clinically and in research settings will be considered, but at this point the nature of the work to be done in the fourth session will be described more fully.

The Reformulation Process

The aim of the assessment period is to engage the patient in therapy, to set up an effective therapeutic alliance and to define accurately the processes which therapy will seek to modify. To achieve this requires that the therapist possesses listening skills and a capacity to communicate clearly in terms appropriate to each patient, and that he initiates a co-operative relationship which mobilizes the patient's own capacity for work. There is no place in CAT for the opaque therapist or, for long, for the entirely passive patient. At the start, the nature of therapy and of the particular procedures employed will be spelt out, and the therapist's questions and comments will be clear and direct. The patient will be told that he will be expected to work between sessions and the actual work to be done (the 'homework', such as the self-monitoring, reading the file and other tasks) will be discussed and agreed with him and usually recorded in writing. As the therapist begins to see the underlying patterns emerging she will offer her tentative descriptions of them to the patient for comments and for modifications. Hence, by the fourth session there is already an experience of joint work, and a provisional reformulation has been considered by the pair. This work is formally brought to fruition in the fourth session, in which the therapist will offer a written draft of her reformulation which she will modify where necessary after discussion with the patient, after which she will produce a written record of it, giving a copy to the patient and retaining a copy for her own use.

There are two parts to this reformulation, the letter or description and the listing of TPs and TPPs. These crystallize out the understanding developed over the first meetings and are a powerful means of cementing the therapeutic alliance. The descriptive part may be written in the form of a letter to the patient, or in the patient's own 'voice', the choice depending upon preference or on the clinical picture. For example, for a patient who feels easily intruded upon, a tentative letter from the therapist may be the best, whereas for other patients the experience of someone else being able to help them speak accurately in the first person can be particularly reassuring. Generally speaking, these reformulations will give an account of the patient's key past experiences, will describe how these were coped with and will demonstrate how present problems are maintained by the procedures developed during the patient's past. The account will describe both the person's sense of his relationship with himself and his way of relating to others. The emotional significance of events will be clearly and directly named and the individual's inability in the past to acknowledge fully such feelings may also be indicated. The information recorded is that given by the patient, but the therapist shapes the account to highlight meanings and connections, confirming with the patient sentence by sentence that the final account is felt to be correct. When this final version is read back to the patient and a copy handed over, patients are often very thoughtful and many cry. It is clear that this process does more than record; it serves also to validate and deepen the person's sense of his own history. The prose account is followed by a list of TPs and TPPs similarly agreed with the patient; the suggested exits or aims for each of these will also be discussed and recorded. This TP/TPP list serves to underline the fact that therapy is concerned with the modification of *current, repetitively used, harmful procedures*, and all subsequent therapeutic work will be carried out in relation to these. This list will also provide the basis for a rating of change at the end of all subsequent sessions using a simple visual analogue scale.

Carrying out this reformulating task is very demanding on the therapist. Those with a psychodynamic training often feel rushed (as indeed they are) and will wish to postpone the process 'in order to get a fuller history'. In fact, if full use is made of all the sources, namely the interview, transference and counter-transference events, the patient's use of the file, the patient's self-monitoring and perhaps some of the other paper-and-pencil test procedures (discussed below) it is very rarely impossible to arrive at a powerful and accurate reformulation within the three to four sessions normally allotted. Issues obscurely or incorrectly framed by the therapist will be clarified through discussion with the patient, and in so far as the final version is accurate and meaningful patients will feel safely understood and will thereafter remember and describe their histories, present problems and feelings more freely. Later revisions or extensions of reformulations are only rarely called for.

The effect of this process is to 'reach through' the patient's defences, as

Mann describes (Mann and Goldman, 1982), in relation to his spoken descriptions of the central issue, forging a working alliance in which the therapist's empathic presence is linked firmly with the jointly achieved conceptual understanding. Therapy proceeds thereafter using this shared instrument.

At this point some examples of reformulation will be provided. After this the use of other paper-and-pencil procedures of value in this process will be described. These are not essential to the practice of CAT but can contribute to the process and are also ways of guiding patients towards helpful forms of introspection.

Case Example: Catherine

Catherine had for years complied with her husband's need to control all aspects of her life, and had also submitted to various forms of perverse humiliating sexual control. At work and with work colleagues she was capable and competent, however. The reformulation read as follows:

> It is as if from childhood on I have had to earn and be grateful for any care and affection received and must accept limitations and restrictions on my own energies and desires, being unable to trust my own feelings. In my marriage I have gone along with my husband's prescriptions and definitions of who I am, as if I was ineffective and without separate needs or rights, and I have tolerated his control over my body, my time, my friendships and my future. My children's energy and aggression alarms me, perhaps because I recognize what is so hard to accept in myself, perhaps seeing in them some of the liveliness of my mother which I lost touch with when she died. I often side with my husband in restricting the children but do not feel I am seen by them as having any independent authority, and my own spontaneity and needs only find expression away from home.
>
> It is as if in relation to others I must be *either* tied up, restricted, giving in to others plans and pressures, being a doormat, *or* I will feel guilty and be rejected.

Case Example: William

William, aged 26, presented with general feelings of anxiety and depression and an inability to relax and enjoy himself; he was also troubled with sadistic imagery and thoughts which were most active when under stress. He found these thoughts at some level comforting, although he also felt very guilty about them. He felt he had a core of anger embedded in him and this could take the form both of anger with himself and also of intense anger with people seen as worthless or inferior to him. His reformulation was as follows:

The basic problem in your life began in early childhood when you learned that to get love from your parents, particularly from your mother, you had to be a 'good boy'. You learned that to be good meant having to hide your feelings, to do well and to do as you were told. For example, you loved your mother and you wanted to please her. She invited you to play 'sexual games' with her (to meet her own needs). You succeeded in being a 'good boy' on their terms so well that it became impossible for you to become a 'bad boy' who could feel jealous, angry and destructive. Instead of showing this side of you, you began being 'naughty' in secret, teasing and bullying other children, being extremely careful not to get caught out. You became competent at masking your true feelings, keeping them buried inside instead. Though you were still very young, you were not sure that what mum did was OK and you began to feel very guilty, as though you were responsible. This irrational belief makes you feel even more guilty and frightened, and you have tried even harder to please in order to control these feelings of guilt and fear. You feel that if you were to lose control you would hurt and destroy others around you. As a consequence of this need for complete control, you have thoughts that surface in hurtful and destructive ways. Thus your anger is directed inward, in terms of your destructive thoughts, and projected outwards in the form of hatred for others—for example, people whom you see as inferior to you. You continue to try to please people as if you were a 'good boy'. This invites people to take you for granted or abuse you, and this makes you feel very angry and starts the whole trap off again.

This repeated pattern is of being a 'good boy' bottling up feelings and a tightly controlled self, versus 'bad boy', out of control, furious and destructive. In present relationships, such as the one with your girlfriend, you continue to repeat these patterns learned in childhood. You try very hard to be the perfect partner (perfect friend, perfect brother, perfect son, perfect client) to please others, yet deep down you feel angry and resentful. Or you are a 'bad boy' and feel deeply guilty, expecting rejection, anxious and afraid. The strength of these feelings inside you is so powerful that you feel as if you might 'go mad' or become a 'criminal' and this strengthens your fear that you are dangerous, evil and destructive. This terrifies you, so you try to render yourself harmless by becoming a powerless dependent 'child', ignoring your own needs and giving in to others' demands.

The exit from this lies in learning to integrate the 'good boy' and the 'bad boy' and in releasing yourself from the need to be perfect and in control all the time. In doing so you will begin to free yourself from this irrational belief. Another exit is to become more assertive (distinguishing *aggression* from *assertion*) about your own needs and those of others, thus preventing the continuing cycle of suffering.

Your problem can be summarized as follows:

1. It is as if I am *either* a 'good boy', bottling up feelings in a tightly controlled self, *or* I am a 'bad boy', out of control, furious and destructive.
   Exit: To accept and integrate both the 'good' and 'bad' boy to create a safe middle ground.
2. It is as if I am *either* independent, responsible, isolated and needy, *or* I am dependent, irresponsible and guilty.
   Exit: To recognize that neediness and independence are both possible without loss of self.
3. It is as if I am *either* pleasing others and being taken for granted, *or* I am aggressive and being rejected, hurt and abused.
   Exit: To assert my own needs appropriately.

Case Example: Marjorie

Marjorie was a 26-year-old graduate, currently working as an unpaid voluntary worker, who came with depression. The main feature of her history was the way in which she always seemed to have 'arranged' to fail one part of every enterprise, often the part at which she was most competent. The following is the prose reformulation.

Dear Marjorie,
Over the first weeks of therapy I feel you have become more aware of the pain and anger you feel at being the 'beach baby' [the beach baby was a character in a song with which her sisters used to tease her]. It was your beach-baby image which determined the choices that you make which give rise to the difficulties in your life. I feel that this core of pain should be addressed at this stage in your therapy so that we can focus on the work to be done. As the beach baby, you were the most unwanted daughter and sister, the image of the song being how you were left on the sand and no one cared for you. Your mother actually feared your birth as she suffered

from toxaemia during her pregnancy with your sister Angela. How-ever, as the doctor said 'worse things come in the post' and you were allowed to come into the world very much against your mother's wishes. In your family a high premium was placed upon you to be successful, your mother in particular letting you know that you could be loved and wanted if you were a wonderful bright and shining star. Also, however, you *weren't* allowed to succeed, as that would hurt Angela who was frail and vulnerable with her heart condition; she wasn't to be disturbed by your outgoing nature. Angela had to be spared from envious feelings towards you and so you had to arrange to avoid pleasure or success. When your successes did come, in exams for example, you had to sabotage them in some way, failing at least one out of the set you had taken. You still feel restricted and out of control, as if you have been told that you cannot have what you want, and have remained confused about what you are allowed to have. You act as if your success will be envied and will hurt other people so you fail and feel excluded and dissatisfied. Your other two sisters, Mary and Sue, were also rivals to you, it was they who sang the beach-baby song and would laugh at you when it made you cry. This song seems to address the hurt you felt at being unwanted and devalued; you feel your mother condoned Mary and Sue's treating of you in this way because she resented having another daughter who took up your father's atten-tion. She made you feel you deserved to be excluded, you were certainly not to be compared with Angela who was obviously lovable and also required, and still requires, the protection of your mother and sisters. Now you have chosen work that reflects your low status at home — a volunteer amongst paid employees, with no status, at the bottom of the ladder, an employee who doesn't deserve the benefits that other employees receive. You did feel your father was sad about your beach-baby image, but this too makes you disappointed, because he was not able to protect you from the rivalry of the others; in fact you had to protect him, for you saw him as old and frail compared to your mother, so, although you loved him, this felt like a sad love. Similar pains underlie many of the uncertainties you feel with your boyfriend now; you do feel he cares for you but the fact he can't always remember what you are doing in your life makes you feel he's not really strong enough to meet your needs. In relation to him you act as if he must give in to you, but you've chosen somebody who is actually quite fearful of your anger and sadness, and shuts off when you present them to him.

Out of the jealousy and anger you feel with Angela you've come to reject many of the aspects of her which your mother admired and to see them as vain and disgusting. It's as if nice things belong to Angela and to have them yourself would be like stealing.

Two core issues resulting from this story could be described like this:

1. I act as if my success would be envied and would hurt others so I'm unsuccessful but feel excluded and dissatisfied — the aim here must be to confront and to become free of this fear because you are not responsible in this way for the lives of other people.
2. I act as though if I care for somebody they must give into me — the aim here must be to relate mutually.

Patients' Written Material Supplementing the History

In addition to the history and use of the psychotherapy file and self-monitoring, some other devices can be helpful in the assessment phase. One of these is the life chart. This basically requires three columns, on the left the date, in the middle the significant events and on the right evidence of distress, symptoms or previous treatment. These charts provide a check on the history and a basis for further enquiry, hence they increase accuracy and save time. They should be carefully read through with the patient and amplified in discussion, with particular attention paid to the possible influences of life events on symptoms.

Another useful device is that originally described by Kelly (1955). The patient is asked to write an account of herself described in the third person from the vantage point of a knowing but basically sympathetic friend.

A third device is the Personal Sources Questionnaire (PSQ) (reproduced in Appendix B). The PSQ is a simple paper-and-pencil exercise which serves to draw the attention of people to ways in which they may be maintaining difficulties and discomforts. The reader might find it useful to complete the PSQ, to get some sense of how it operates (and perhaps to enlarge self-knowledge). Completion of the questionnaire involves two stages. In the first, important sources of self-esteem are identified on a provided list, to which the patient may add his own sources. These sources may represent dependency on self or on others, and the pattern of choice should be noted. In the second phase of the test, the consequences of the ten most important sources are explored, the patient rating each of them against a set of descriptions according to how they feel when the source is available or operating. The 'cost–benefit' score for each source can be identified by a simple sum. It is to be noted that outcomes in lines one and four on the outcome rating are positive and those in lines two and three are negative.

The value of some of these devices is exemplified in the following case example:

Case Example: Gavin

Gavin was a 24-year-old man who consulted because of anxiety about his proneness to outbursts of aggressive behaviour with occasional physical violence. He was given a 'waiting-list package' [Psychotherapy File, Personal Sources Questionnaire and suggestions for a third-person description] to work on after assessment. From the Psychotherapy File he identified as the main dilemmas the following: 'If I must then I won't', 'If other people aren't expecting me to do things, look after them, then I feel anxious, lonely and out of control', 'If I get what I want I feel childish and guilty; if I don't get what I want I feel depressed', '*Either* I stick up for myself and nobody likes me, *or* I give in and get put upon by others and feel cross and hurt'. He also recorded that he felt his life limited both by fear of the response of others and by something inside himself (a snag).

In completing the PSQ, three sources had negative outcomes, No. 10 (to 'criticize or undervalue others'), No. 26 (to 'give myself treats'), and No. 28 (to 'show I don't have to do what others want or expect'). Commenting on this he wrote:

> It seems that I score highly on being dependent on others and I seem to depend on those who may be less assertive than myself, weaker maybe, because I can get away with it.

About source No. 10 (criticizing others) he wrote:

> Envy is the cause of this being a negative source; my father always criticized people and undervalued my mother, I have done the same to appear to be stronger than the other. I get into confrontations with people as a result of always thinking that I am better at everything. Instead of being pleased for people's achievements I have been upset by them and subsequently undervalued and undermined their pleasure at their experiences.

In relation to source No. 26 (to 'give myself treats') he wrote:

> I simply don't reward myself at the right time. I don't take pleasure from a break because I feel that I don't deserve it. I find it difficult to appreciate things that are done for me, for example crying with sadness and embarrassment at one of my birthday parties as a child, I had to pretend to be happy. It becomes almost natural for

me to pretend to be happy; unhappiness sometimes feels artificial
as if I have never learnt how to smile or be happy naturally. I feel
like an alien, and I don't want to be an alien, I want to learn to be
happy and deal with my sadness and depression and anger. I have
never been able to appreciate treats. I feel that I don't deserve
treats, pleasure or happiness because my father never allowed
happiness for either myself or my family.

In his third person self-description he wrote as follows:

Gavin is a fun, outgoing person. He dresses quite differently and
changes his appearance quite often. He is a perfectionist with an
obsession for detail. Sometimes he says hello to people in the street
and amuses them and makes them smile. He feels it is very important
not to do anything by half measures and quite often he loses
control through drink or drugs. He doesn't like this as he physically
reacts to the drugs and subsequently feels paranoid. He has a lot of
anxiety about his life being out of control. He is a very precise
worker and not afraid of hard work. Because part of him wants to
be seen as an outrageous character he often feels he is not taken
seriously enough. He entertains people in order to please them but
sometimes that doesn't please him and he finds it difficult to make
a decision to get away from people he doesn't want to be with. He
has the feeling that when he has created something or that when
things are going well he tends to destroy them.

One other aid to reformulation which may be used is the Relationship Test,
a semi-standardized dyad repertory grid. The use of this is described in
Chapter 4 and the test itself is reproduced in Appendix E.

Writing at the Termination of Therapy: the Goodbye Letters

The purpose of all the written material described above is to create, record
and make available for reference the best understandings and transformations
of the patient's difficulties. As therapy nears completion it is usually helpful
to repeat this exercise, noting now what has been achieved in the therapy
and highlighting what still requires to be attended to. Normally at the
penultimate session a draft therapist letter will be presented to the patient
for discussion, the revised final copy being handed over at the last meeting.
It is often of value also for the patient to bring her own written evaluation to
the fifteenth session, as this provides her with an opportunity to review what
has been achieved and experienced and to express any continuing uncertainties or unresolved feelings. Examples will be found in the next chapter.

The purpose of this chapter has been to describe and illustrate the basic reformulation process. For many therapists, the idea of being involved in written work and the setting of homework is unfamiliar and can seem too mechanical and too intellectual — or too much like work! It is hoped that the examples given in this chapter and later in the book will illustrate how, in practice, this method can generate important understandings and allow for the expression of deep feelings.

CHAPTER 3

Basic Treatment Procedures

AMANDA M. POYNTON

The second phase of therapy in the CAT model begins when the description of Target Problems (TPs) and Target Problem Procedures (TPPs) has been mutually agreed by patient and therapist. Reformulation is usually completed by the end of the fourth session and is written down, together with the corresponding aims. This is duplicated, so that both patient and therapist can retain a copy. From the fifth session onwards the focus of therapy is this agreed reformulation, and the therapist's activity is directed at enabling the patient to understand his own maladaptive procedures, to recognize when, where and how they are occurring and influencing his daily life, and to help him develop new, more flexible and adaptive ways of thinking, feeling and acting.

In order to achieve this, the therapist combines specific CAT procedures with techniques from various schools of psychotherapy with the aim of revising the TPs and TPPs in different but complementary ways. Therapeutic techniques are derived mainly from cognitive and psychoanalytic approaches, but this does not preclude the use of interventions from other models. CAT places an emphasis on the integration of these different methods in that all are related to the TP/TPP formulations; reformulation having described clearly what is to be changed, a range of therapeutic methods can be applied in concert towards the achievement of this change. The techniques incorporated may include, for example, behavioural strategies, gestalt methods, and the use of role-playing and paradoxical injunctions. These techniques serve to destabilize habitual maladaptive procedures by aiding introspection, by provoking novel direct experience and by mobilizing affects.

The blend of psychoanalytic, cognitive, behavioural and other techniques in a given therapy is decided by the therapist, and is tailored according to the patient's problems and to his response to early interventions. The precise blend of therapeutic techniques which are combined in any particular therapy depends on a variety of factors, which of course include the therapist's personality, training and supervision, in addition to patient-related factors. The therapist's task is to be alert and flexible, to note what the patient makes of the different methods and to 'push where it moves'. In considering the strategy with a particular patient, the major determinant of the therapeutic method is the patient; some patients work best when there is a strong cognitive-behavioural component, whereas others, especially those with poorly integrated personalities, may be impossible to help without actively relating the formulations to transference and counter-transference issues.

How much time and attention are devoted to the 'here and now' and how much to early experience is also variable. As has already been discussed, both aspects are usually explored during assessment and reformulation. Thereafter the emphasis of therapy will vary, but as the central aim of the therapist is to help the patient recognize the way in which he continues to use maladaptive procedures which perpetuate the currently unsatisfactory state for which he has sought help, there is a tendency to concentrate on contemporary events in preference to long and detailed delving into the past. Nevertheless, as the TPPs are hypotheses about or descriptions of habitual patterns of thinking and feeling, they provide a framework within which therapists can make links between current and past experience, which can be shared with the patient whenever this seems appropriate. There are many patients who respond to the safety offered by the therapist and the reformulation by remembering and 'revisiting' their histories, by dreaming actively and by experiencing long-suppressed emotion.

Transference and counter-transference issues are usually addressed in therapy. However, the way in which these phenomena are approached differs somewhat from traditional psychoanalytic therapy. Reformulation usually includes statements (TPPs) that encapsulate repeated difficulties in relationships, for such problems are almost invariably apparent in those entering therapy, and these TPPs anticipate the issues likely to arise in the therapist's relationship with the patient. Hence the therapist should be able to recognize transference issues quickly and avoid collusion, using them appropriately as a learning experience, that is to say, as a living demonstration of the TPPs which therapy aims to change. This aspect of reformulation may be particularly helpful for inexperienced therapists and those without any analytic training. Interpretation of transference made in terms of the identified TPs and TPPs directly links the behaviour in the session with life problems, and this aids generalization of what is learned.

Homework

In common with some other brief therapies, in particular cognitive-behavioural therapies, an important feature of the CAT model is that patients are given homework assignments to complete between sessions, with the aim of maximizing the progress which can be made in a short period of time. This represents the enlistment of the patient as her own co-therapist and serves to promote self-awareness and self-control and to minimize regression. Such homework is related to the reformulation task and to the recognition of TPPs, as explained in the previous chapter, or may involve exposure to new situations or attempting new activities.

Supervision

Trainee therapists are usually supervised on a weekly basis in small groups, comprising four or five members, carrying one case per group, or fewer members if their case load is greater. More time is devoted to a particular case in the first four sessions when it is important to ensure that the most powerful reformulation possible is made, but each case should be discussed each week whenever possible. As in other forms of psychotherapy, supervision is an opportunity to learn, both directly and vicariously, and it also provides a safeguard against inappropriate therapist responses based on counter-transference. Such problems are nearly always recognizable in terms of the therapist's involvement in one of the patient's relationship dilemmas. The supervisors role combines a concern with the therapist's correct use of therapeutic procedures with attention to the process of the therapy and how this reflects both the patient's procedures and those of the therapist. The responses of other seminar members to case presentations may be similarly illuminating.

Content of Sessions

There is no strict protocol for the content of therapy sessions, although there are certain requirements for therapists in terms of what should be addressed in each session. This varies to some extent according to the stage of therapy, with some features being common to all sessions, while others are usually limited to a particular phase of therapy, e.g. reformulation during sessions 1–4. There are some discrete prescribed activities which are usually given attention near the end of a session, in particular the completion of weekly ratings of TPs and TPPs and the allocation of homework assignments. In general, therapists are discouraged from taking notes during sessions, although joint paperwork may be called for. Full process records should be written up by trainees, and audio-taping for playback by the therapist is a useful learning tool.

Generally, the therapist should allow the patient to initiate the session, as his particular preoccupation or silence will be a valuable guide to his current state. The therapist may explore this issue as seems appropriate, and relate it to the TPs and TPPs.

If the patient is late for a session the meaning needs to be investigated. An appropriate moment to raise this issue is when a natural gap arises, after any interchange associated with the patient's opening remarks. At the start of therapy a contract will have been made and the implications of this will have been made explicit to the patient. These would normally include the forfeit of a whole session where the patient failed to give advance warning of his inability to attend, or shortening the session by the number of minutes that the patient was late. Nevertheless, it is not uncommon for a difficulty to arise; this may consist of a failure of either party to adhere to the previously agreed arrangement or of an unanticipated need to alter practical details. It may be necessary to change the schedule of times or dates of sessions to take account of holidays or to enable either party to fulfil other obligations. Obviously the nature of the practical difficulty will determine the need for attention, but if the problem is patient related, or if it is likely to provoke a response in the patient, the therapist should explore the problem further and may relate it to the TPPs. In this and in other respects therapists can, of course, be flexible, but departures from the normal 'rules' should always be discussed at supervision, as in many cases counter-transference is involved. In discussion of such issues, the therapist might remind the patient of the number of that session and the total number of sessions that he has been offered; this relates to the issue of termination which is discussed in more detail below. Sometimes these considerations may not seem appropriate near the beginning of the session. It is up to the therapist to choose a moment that feels right. However, it is important that the matter be addressed at some stage during the session.

The initiative for most of the rest of the session lies with the patient. Frequently he will mention events which have occurred since the last session of the therapy or his progress with the homework assignments, although some patients may bring up significant events in the distant past, or reports of material from dreams or mental imagery. Some patients remain silent; very long silences are unlikely to promote active change and possible meanings, often related to the TPPs, should be explored.

Sessions normally finish at an agreed time, with each session having an agreed duration; most therapists find that 45 or 50 minutes is convenient for their schedule. Under exceptional circumstances, the therapist may feel it is inappropriate to end the session at exactly the agreed time, but such a decision should be carefully considered at the time and should be discussed in supervision. Therapists should devote some time immediately after each session to making notes of the main points of each session, and to considering what should be discussed at supervision and the issues which may present at the next session. This process is likely to take at least 15 minutes and will be longer during the reformulation stage.

Therapist activities

Sessions should proceed in a largely unstructured fashion, but the therapist will use his therapeutic skills to focus on areas of relevance to the TPs and TPPs. The therapist must also attend to a number of 'prescribed' activities; as a reminder these are listed on the Therapist Activity Sheet, which indicates the essential agenda and a number of optional therapist activities for each session. The Therapist Activity Sheet (which is checked at the end of each session) is reproduced in Appendix C. The activities listed upon it are as follows:

1. History, patterns, feelings, meanings.
2. Rules, arrangements of therapy.
3. Assigning self-monitoring of any variable moods or symptoms.
4. Discussing self-monitorings and the Psychotherapy File.
5. Formulating TPs and TPPs with the patient.
6. TPP recognition homework assignment.
7. TPP homework discussed, TP/TPP ratings done by patient.
8. Other homework assignments.
9. Interpreting transference (+/− counter-transference) in relation to TPPs.
10. The fact and meaning of termination.
11. Role-plays, gestalt, etc.

The use of this checklist might suggest a rather rigid and directive approach on the part of the therapist, but in practice in most sessions only a minority of the time is spent on the predetermined semi-structured tasks and the bulk of each session is devoted to consideration of current life situations, historical events and the relationship between the patient and the therapist. The activities of the therapist during the session might include: active listening, exploration, reflection, guidance, challenge, empathy, explanation, interpretation and description. Although the broad range of possible therapist activities reflects the different approaches from which CAT has arisen, in CAT all of these activities are aimed at promoting the recognition by the patient of his TPPs and at encouraging his efforts to achieve their revision. Aspects of therapist activity which differ somewhat from other therapies are considered in more detail below.

The TPs and TPPs are a unique feature of CAT and all aspects of CAT are related to them. As has been explained in earlier chapters, the first four or so sessions are principally directed towards developing an accurate description of the patient's problems in these terms. The function of the sessions, after a reformulation has been made, is to engage the patient in the task of becoming more aware of his use of these maladaptive strategies and enabling him to find more appropriate alternative ways of acting. In a sense this can be considered as a two-stage process, with the first stage being recognition and the second stage being revision. The TPPs are repeatedly considered in every session by the therapist, with a view to achieving the objective of recognition/revision. This is done in several ways. The therapist will explore with the patient the statements which he makes and may examine in detail any event which exemplifies one of the TPPs, considering with the patient ways in which he might have modified his thoughts/feelings/ behaviour and how this might have affected the final outcome of that situation. Extension of this process can be achieved by asking the patient to self-monitor TPs and TPPs outside sessions so that recognition in the field is encouraged and the time devoted to efforts to change by the patient is maximized.

The principles of TPP self-monitoring are similar to those of self-monitoring of symptoms described for the first four sessions. The patient is asked to keep a written record, usually in the form of a diary, of the occurrences of one or more TPP. In relation to each such episode, the patient should note preceding and possibly precipitating events, details of the TPP or TP itself and subsequent outcomes. Monitoring internal thoughts and feelings as well as external factors is a crucial element of this task, and this is specified in the instructions to the patient. Therapist and patient may usefully construct a format for recording this information, as this will clarify the task for the patient and avoid wasting time through misunderstanding of what is required.

In requesting that the patient keep a TPP diary, the therapist should consider the practical implications of the task in hand as this makes compliance more likely. Some patients are embarrassed by illiteracy or poor writing skills, and will be given simpler forms of recording; while others will practice, at home initially, the task of writing. It is probably best to start monitoring a TPP which the patient is aware occurs comparatively frequently. Monitoring is easier and may be more useful for TPPs whose occurrence is clearly episodic rather than continuous but variable, as the former are easier to identify. It is important not to overburden or confuse the patient by giving him too many tasks. It is always important to explain the rationale for the monitoring and to be explicit about the therapist's desire to read the material at the next session. The patient should be asked to record each episode as soon as possible after it happens, but if this is impracticable then it is usually acceptable to reflect on the TPP each evening and write the account for the whole day at once. An account written the evening before the therapy session covering the whole of the previous week is likely to be much less satisfactory, as even though it might be entirely accurate it undermines an important facet of the task, which is to encourage the patient to adopt an 'on-line' self-monitoring system, that is to say one operating quickly as the procedural system is initiated. Only with such on-the-spot recognition can the patient introduce change into previously stereotyped patterns of thinking and behaving.

Case Example: Angela

Angela, an immature 22-year-old with a previous history of anorexia nervosa, came to seek help for her inability to make appropriate peer-group relationships. Her TP and TPP reformulation included the placation trap. In the first few weeks after reformulation, she carefully monitored episodes of placation, at first only reporting one or two such episodes each week. However, as she continued with the task more and more episodes of placation were noted. She and her therapist repeatedly discussed the detailed records which she made and explored each situation, considering how Angela could have acted differently on each occasion and what, for her, were the feared consequences of a change of behaviour. As therapy progressed, she became able to act in a range of new ways and her placation diminished. The therapist considered that the initial low rate of placation reported by this patient was the result of poor recognition, with the subsequent increase reflecting an improvement in this and the later decrease corresponding with revision of this TPP.

Case Example: Simon

Simon, a 20-year-old man, presented with depression and felt very uncertain about what he wanted to do in his life. He felt he could not communicate with people and described feeling nervous and blocked with friends, worried that they were bored with him or feeling bored himself.

Reformulation included two important TPPs as follows:

1. When I meet someone, my lack of confidence makes me afraid to speak freely and this makes any conversation difficult. Since I am not talking, only listening, I soon feel bored and when he/she stops talking, I feel it is because they have become bored with me. I then feel that I have failed, which in turn makes me feel even less confident.
   Aim: To become more aware that this vicious circle is happening, to recognize that it is not inevitable and to find ways to interrupt the cycle.
2. If I must do something then I question the value of it. This negative attitude does not allow me to put much effort into anything. Lack of effort ensures lack of results which reinforces my belief that the action was worthless in the first place.
   Aim: To recognize that there are alternative attitudes which can be more productive.

Once reformulation was complete Simon was given the homework of keeping a TPP diary, being asked to monitor both the TPPs detailed above. At first, he produced rather little homework. This seemed to be because he had relatively few social contacts, but in addition the therapist surmized that the TPPs themselves were hampering his progress in this respect. She raised these issues with Simon during sessions and pointed out that he was self-sabotaging, as in the second TPP, by not allowing himself to self-monitor and by tending to see the whole activity as pointless. There also seemed to be another issue, related to the first TPP, which involved his failure to produce homework for the therapist for fear of being boring to her. When these issues had been aired during the session, Simon became much more able to produce appropriate TPP homework and he also became much better able to express his feelings in the sessions. The TPP monitoring in turn led to the identification of a highly destructive chain of negative automatic thoughts, which led to the previously inexplicable sense of depression. Having recognized this pattern he quickly changed and no longer experienced such profound, long-lasting mood changes.

This example illustrates how the therapist's attention to the TPPs enabled this patient's resistance to change to be overcome. This was achieved by the combination of making explicit the role of the TPPs in the therapist—patient interaction and by TPP self-monitoring.

Case Example: Julia

Julia, a 32-year-old separated woman who was working full time as a secretary, sought help for feelings of inability to cope at the time of divorce from her second husband. Her life was further complicated by involvement with another man and an unsatisfactory housing situation for herself and her two children.

Reformulation included target problems of 'feeling bad about myself' and 'difficulty in relationships' and three TPPs as follows:

1. In relationships it is as if I am *either* playing games, disarmingly, excitingly in control but not feeling understood, *or* vulnerable, likely to get hurt, out of control and not feeling understood.
   Aim: To give others clear messages and to be prepared to take risks in relationships.
2. *Either* placation, *or* aggression.
   Aim: To be appropriately assertive.
3. It is as if I cannot hold on to my adequacy, my success, my decisions, because I feel I do not deserve them or feel guilty.
   Aim: To be able to claim my life.

The TPP of placation was the first that the therapist asked Julia to monitor. Julia had already been able to recognize that this was a basic pattern in both of her marriages, and during discussions in early sessions she had come to see that she had been behaving in this way because she had believed that this was the only way to stay in a relationship. This assumption seemed to be linked to her early life in a broken home where her mother had spent a good deal of time in trying to keep the peace. The diary which she kept helped her to identify many instances of giving in to others, followed sometime later by being very angry when the moment for standing up for herself had passed. She related this to the incident which had broken up her last marriage. She talked of these matters in a rather humorous way, as if designed to make the therapist laugh. She was very reluctant for the therapist to see what she had written. The therapist pointed this out to her, suggesting that what was happening in the therapeutic relationship was that she was behaving as described in the first TPP — being somewhat playful, remaining in control and perhaps preventing herself from being understood by being secretive and mistrustful.

As therapy progressed she focused on the aim of 'clear messages' in her homework, noting both instances where she had successfully achieved this, and others where she would have liked to but failed. During the sessions, much of the work centred around the first TPP, rephrased as '*either* powerful caregiver and disarming troublemaker *or* weak, vulnerable, non-coping and abandoned (like mother)'. She recognized that both these roles had been responses to the 'uncaring authority' role adopted by her father. At first she tended to present herself to the therapist as the former, then broke down in a session and then, after missing a session due to the therapist being sick, felt lonely, hopeless and stuck. The therapist explained her view of what seemed to be happening in the sessions, i.e. that Julia was oscillating between her two habitual roles and that the way forward was frightening as it involved abandonment of these two familiar positions and also greater trust in the therapist. Explicit reference to the operation of this dilemma seemed to be a turning point and accelerated change occurred in the few remaining sessions.

Interpretation and the Use of TPPs

Therapists offer understanding to their patients in many ways; usually these involve links between the present and the past. However, in CAT the emphasis is essentially descriptive rather than genetic. TPPs have been negotiated jointly with the patient already, and these enable the patient to recognize the persistent and pervasive nature of her maladaptive procedures. This is in contrast to traditional psychodynamic therapy, where a model of the patient's problems is developed gradually on the basis of repeated interpretations, without a central hypothesis being made explicit to the patient. It might be considered that CAT operates in a 'top down' fashion, allowing rapid generalization of new learning, whereas traditional dynamic psychotherapy utilizes a 'bottom up' approach. It follows from this that in CAT, accurate reformulation is the lynchpin of effective therapy.

In psychoanalysis, the timing of interpretation is considered crucial, premature interpretation (for example, of unconscious hostility) being considered dangerous. TPPs represent, on the other hand, a description of what the patient is doing habitually, and such descriptions are not threatening — they refer to current strategies, including defensive ones, rather than to hypothesized destructive impulses. This issue is further discussed in Chapter 12. In CAT, therefore, the therapist should use every opportunity to refer to the TPPs and should work hard in the sessions to monitor actively both the patient's communications and his own reactions to the patient in order to identify their manifestations. These may be evident either in reports of external events, internal thoughts and feelings on the part of the patient, or may be enacted in the patient—therapist relationship. If the therapist can maintain a high level of vigilance he will be able to relate the process of therapy to the reformulation, and share this understanding with the patient. This high level of activity by the therapist helps both parties concentrate on the stated focus. This can, in some therapies, engender some situations similar to a teacher—pupil relationship, but in contrast to the classroom the therapy session also applies understandings to the therapy relationship. There may be occasions when the agreed reformulation does not describe fully what is happening in the therapy. In such cases, which are relatively rare, the therapist or the patient may suggest a revision of, or addition to, the agreed reformulation.

Rating Sheets

At the end of every session, after reformulation, the rating sheet of TPs and TPPs is completed. The rating sheet consists of a series of visual analogue scales, one for each TP and TPP. An example of a rating sheet is given in Appendix D. The mid-point of each scale represents the patient's condition at presentation, while the two extremes represent 'aim achieved' and 'worst state possible'. Thus, week by week, the patient is asked to reflect on his condition and to compare it with how things were before therapy started, and this builds up a chart of the patient's subjective state.

The completion of these rating sheets serves several functions and there are benefits for both patient and therapist. The rating sheets serve as a reminder of the task in hand and their use in every session provides an opportunity to gather the material of the session together, and to reinforce the idea that the aim of therapy is to reach a set of identified goals. The goals are specific, namely the revision of habitual maladaptive procedures, and this emphasizes the patient's part in dealing with his perceived problems. The aims do not just comprise 'getting better' nor simply achieving relief from symptoms; the rating sheets maintain a specific awareness of what is to be changed. In most cases, whether due to specific or non-specific therapeutic efforts, ratings show improvement, which serves to promote optimism, increase self-awareness and improve self-control.

The rating sheets also act as a guide for the therapist in several ways. Firstly, of course, use of the rating sheets is as much of a reminder for the therapist as it is for the patient and hence can help the therapist relate all that happens to the focus of the therapy. For inexperienced therapists, the necessity of considering the TPs and TPPs every week may provide a welcome structure which will help them to work effectively, to concentrate on relevant issues and to remind them of areas of possible difficulty in the therapist–patient relationship. Although the ratings are intended to be subjective, the process of marking the rating sheet often involves some discussion, and allows patient and therapist to review their interaction, the homework, historical material, dreams or any other events in terms of the TPPs.

The ratings are, of course, by no means an objective measure and may be subject to bias. They are not meant to be valid or to act as research measures. In some cases, patient's procedures are manifest in the ratings, for example in placatory or depressed ratings or in negative ratings representing passive resistance. Ratings also indicate areas in which the patient feels progress is not being made. This is of most potential use when there is a marked discrepancy between the changes in the ratings of different identified problems. In these and other circumstances, the weekly ratings may help to prevent over-optimism on the part of the therapist and may draw the therapist's attention to issues which have been forgotten or avoided, or which might be more appropriately tackled in a different fashion.

Case Example: Gladys

Gladys, a middle-aged divorcee from a devout Roman Catholic background, presented with depression and suicidal feelings several years after separation from her husband. The reformulation included 'apparently unjustified feelings of depression' as a TP and the placation trap as a TPP. Often during the first few minutes of sessions, she reported feelings of sadness, but when asked to rate her mood at the end of sessions her ratings suggested that her aim of 'being content to be myself' had been nearly achieved. Her therapist raised this seeming inconsistency with her and suggested that it might indicate that her need to please was influencing her ratings; by producing 'good' ratings she was reacting towards the therapist in much the same way as had already been identified in relationships with her ex-husband, her mother, her teenage son and her colleagues at work. In this case, the act of completing the ratings provided the therapist with an opportunity to highlight the pervasive nature of the patient's placatory behaviour and to make links between her behaviour towards the therapist and towards significant others in her past and present life.

Homework

At the end of the session, the therapist may assign a task for the patient to do between that session and the next. The therapist may have planned the homework assignment before the session, perhaps as a result of discussion in the supervision seminar, or she may decide to base the homework on something which has come up during the current session. The homework may consist of one or more tasks; there is a wide range of possibilities, of which the TPP diary, already mentioned, is the most common. Behavioural homework assignments might include the use of relaxation techniques, either based on instruction during sessions which could then be practised at home, or involving the use of an audio-cassette recording of a programme for relaxation. In some cases, a programme of graded exposure to feared or avoided situations may be suggested, or planned behavioural change as part of a series of graded tasks designed to revise a problem procedure may be negotiated. More cognitively orientated tasks might include, in depressed patients, a coping and pleasure diary, recording for each part of each day what was done, how well it was achieved and how much pleasure was experienced. This can provide accurate information to the therapist and often helps correct the selectively negative recall of the depressed patient. Other patients may be encouraged to avoid exposure to difficult situations until prior rehearsal of anxiety management techniques has been done.

Therapists can use their ingenuity to devise tasks with the aim of helping their patients to revise their maladaptive strategies and they may wish to capitalize on the individual talents and propensities of their patients. Some people may be enabled to explore their feelings by self-expression in prose, poetry or art. This exercise may also provide new material for discussion and interpretation in the next session. Occasionally, homework instructions may take the form of a paradoxical injunction, but usually this technique is reserved for situations where there has been failure of the other techniques described above and the manoeuvre has been well planned and preferably discussed beforehand in the supervision seminar.

It should not be assumed that the setting of homework assignments is a rigid or authoritarian activity on the part of the therapist. As in other aspects of CAT there is normally a negotiation between patient and therapist before the details of the homework task are decided. Careful study of the task and situation is essential, and preparatory work in sessions is necessary before a specific homework task can be undertaken. In the following case, rehearsal in imagination and role-playing were explored in this way.

Case Example: Emma

Emma, a 45-year-old civil servant, had a lifelong history of being placatory. She was able to identify her unassertive behaviour but could not manage to change this, except to a certain extent with her immediate family. In situations involving strangers in which it would have been appropriate to stand up for herself she felt very anxious and reverted to her habitual pattern of placation. In order to help her overcome this, some time during sessions was spent examining such situations in detail and in considering different possible ways of reacting and their likely results. However, whilst she could appreciate that her own pattern of activity was not the only possible course of action, the patient said that she could not imagine herself being able to act in any other way than her habitual fashion. She was asked by the therapist to rehearse in her imagination being assertive, at which she became visibly panicky. The automatic thoughts which accompanied this were explored. The patient was asked to continue to rehearse in her imagination appropriately assertive behaviour for situations which cropped up in her daily life between sessions and to try to examine the thoughts and feelings which this produced. It turned out to be a task she found difficult and which continued to give rise to considerable anxiety. When she reported this at the next session, the therapist suggested a role-play, during the session, of an everyday situation in which the patient thought she could be more assertive, but had so far been unsuccessful in practice. Her marked anxiety was immediately apparent in the role-play; at the first attempt she was unable to continue. The therapist then adopted the role of the patient and modelled appropriately assertive behaviour. This then enabled the patient to role-play herself in the feared situation, and her anxiety diminished with practice and with further exploration of the irrational thoughts which accompanied the anxiety. By the end of therapy, she had begun to be more assertive in her dealings with strangers.

Outcome and Functions of Homework

The patient's homework, if completed, serves to indicate to the therapist how far the patient has begun to understand the ways in which maladaptive strategies are responsible for restricting his life and whether he is making progress in revising these. If the homework tasks are not carried out (provided the work was clearly agreed), the failure will be related to the patient's TPPs. Sometimes patients are unwilling to co-operate in homework assignments. Therapists should not be rigid and should try to find alternative ways of maintaining the thrust and focus of the work. Where some patients are unwilling to do homework, others (especially obsessional patients) produce an enormous volume. In such situations it is appropriate to ask the patient to summarize the content verbally. The therapist may read the homework after the session but thereafter it is best to set a limit of two to three pages for written work.

The following case example describes a difficult patient who was reluctant to co-operate with TPP diary-keeping (this failure could be understood in terms of his TPPs) but who did bring dream material to each session. The therapist decided to concentrate on this rather than engaging in a battle over other forms of homework.

Case Example: Martin

Martin, a 64-year-old divorced artist on the verge of retirement, came to seek help for his bitterness at feeling perpetually undervalued and his fear that his whole life would amount to nothing. He was much the youngest of a family of three children and had always had a sense that he was an afterthought, that he did not count or belong. He had had therapy on and off over a period of about 20 years before having CAT. Recently he had developed arthritis. He felt that the Psychotherapy File was too dry and simplistic and could not encompass his problems. Reformulation identified the social isolation and placation traps, and two dilemmas: (1) *Either* being assertive and rejected, *or* compliant and abused; (2) *Either* being beautiful and idealized, *or* damaged, crippled and undervalued. His failure to use the Psychotherapy File seemed to be an act of self-sabotage relating to the first of these two dilemmas, and this was pointed out to him by the therapist.

In the fourth session he reported a dream in which he was driving along a road and saw a young man disappear into a manhole. He felt alarmed but did nothing. Then a woman walked past carrying the body of a child. He offered her a lift, but feebly, and the offer was not accepted. Then he was surrounded by severely disabled people, felt unable to cope and experienced some revulsion, but was also aware of his inhumanity. Then he wished to defaecate but found all the lavatories full. The therapist understood this dream as referring to his sense of lost manhood, and his sense of not being heard or noticed. In addition, she related this to a fear of the therapist not meeting his needs. The second half of the dream she understood to refer to his revulsion at his own disablement and his sense of being unable to rid himself of unwanted material.

This dream helped him to recognize his tendency to view his whole life in terms of the second dilemma. The next few sessions were spent in exploring various aspects of this dilemma, and the issue as to whether he would be able to renounce this view, particularly of himself. He brought more dreams which the therapist worked with. For example, at the seventh session he brought a dream in which he was straining at stool, with a sense of being in a hurry; he then defaecated in his trousers, but felt that he was able to contain it, and was glad that he had managed to. The therapist interpreted this as a positive step, suggesting that he was now trying to rid himself of the rubbish of the past, in particular of his own view of himself as crippled, damaged and undervalued. The next couple of sessions were spent discussing what he described as the 'middle place' (representing the recognition of his dilemma) and his fear that his needs would not be satisfied. He brought another dream in which small plastic bags were blocking the flow of water in a gully, and he fished out the bags. The therapist again saw this as conveying his sense that something was changing; the 'rubbish' was still there but contained. Subsequent sessions concentrated on his feeling of depression, his tendency to feel an outcast, his sense of guilt because of his neediness, and his past abuses of himself. He brought a dream to almost every session. In the dream of session 13 he found himself confronting a man in uniform who wouldn't tell him his identity. He asked the man to go, but the man argued. Martin became furious and told the man he wouldn't be spoken to like that, and shoved him out of the house. The therapist suggested that the figure represented his 'crude and angry' side, which needed acknowledgement and valuing.

In session 14 he talked about his difficulty in knowing what talent really is. Part of him saw it as wanting to be admired and recognized (the old pattern) while another part felt that talent was a gifted ability to do the job in hand, whatever that might be. He reported a dream in which he followed objects as they flowed in a stream downhill, with his family following happily, and was surprised but joyful when the stream passed by a familiar, much-loved place. Later he came across the remains of a big, grey head; he felt as if he had made it. It belonged to a woman. He told her it was valuable, and that he would cast it in bronze because the clay that it was made of was fragile. It would be a marriage to save the object from further damage.

Martin felt pleased with the dream; he felt the stream represented his own life force moving positively with his family. He felt that something valuable had come out of it which could now achieve a state of permanence. The sense that the head was very ancient, but also made by him, and claimed by a woman (the woman in him, or his therapist, or both) enabled him to feel that art was timeless and allowed him to give up the anger he felt against his early family and himself. The last two sessions were spent reaffirming this 'middle place' and actively reclaiming his crude, crippled side as basic to his needs and creativity, rather than as a source of self-sabotage.

Termination

As can be seen from the therapist activity sheet, discussion of termination is considered essential. The issue of termination is considered in both a structured and an unstructured way. Firstly, in every session the patient is reminded of the session number and the number of sessions remaining. Secondly, as termination approaches more time during each session is devoted to issues of separation, relating these to TPs and TPPs where relevant. In the last few sessions this is combined with the review of the process of therapy and progress made. The relative importance of termination obviously varies considerably between different patients. It will have to be handled with especial care where the issue of separation is of central importance, as in unresolved grief reactions, or where there has been little evidence of change during therapy. It is common for the patient to experience some exacerbation of symptoms in the last few sessions, and this may be reflected in a drop in the TP and TPP ratings. It is often helpful for the therapist to predict this and to relate it to the forthcoming termination. The work of therapy and the issues raised by termination are also summarized in the goodbye letters written by the therapist and, often, by the patient.

These represent another example of the use of written material. One or two sessions before the last the therapist will express his intention of offering the patient a goodbye letter and will invite the patient to produce his own account for discussion. The therapist produces a draft account of the therapy, including a restatement of the reformulation and a summary of the progress made, with suggestions for further self-help. This will be discussed with the patient. Patients are invited to write their own summary and review. The reading aloud and discussion of these two goodbye letters allows a recapitulation of the themes of therapy and may take up most of the last session. When possible, both letters should be photocopied so that both patient and therapist can retain copies. Examples of goodbye letters are given below. It is felt that this procedure keeps the person of the therapist and the tools of therapy active in the patient's mind through the follow-up period and beyond.

Case Example: Ingrid

Ingrid had been referred from the sexual dysfunction clinic.

> Dear Ingrid,
> Looking back at the time when you first came to therapy, you may recall your expectations of some miraculous cure for the frigidity both you and your husband put forth as being the major obstacle to your joint pursuit of happiness. Well, no miracles have taken place, yet now you feel like a sexually capable person — a far cry from feeling finished or burnt out and desperately seeking for miracles. More importantly, you have gained a sense of independence and of being very worthy to be respected by others. How were these changes brought about? The essential thing was

that you gradually came to realize that frigidity was only the 'tip of the iceberg', the final expression of a whole constellation of pressures within the context of your important relationships. It both reflected the existence of a crucial problem in your life and a 'solution', however awkward or self-defeating the latter was. The problem consisted in establishing your independence while at the same time resentfully and placatingly committing yourself to your parents and to your husband without risking a choice. Frigidity, as a solution to this, enabled you to postpone making a choice without feeling responsible for this postponement. Now you don't need this any more; you have become your own agent, you have seen that you can be both tender and caring, and assert your own needs. What cut across the stalemate you were in, not daring to make any move, was the reinvestment in the positive aspects of yourself. You identified and worked upon the false dilemmas, the unobtrusive traps, the subtle snags which, you came to see, had dominated your way of dealing with yourself and the others, and had kept you enmeshed in that wasteland of inertia, dissatisfaction, guilt and anger. Now you feel confident enough to renegotiate the terms of your relationship with your mother and with your husband. Perhaps this is what makes me, on my part, feel happy and optimistic about your future, whatever it may be.

Case Example: William

This is the goodbye letter to the patient William whose reformulation was presented in Chapter 2.

Dear William,
This is a letter summarizing the main themes you have worked on in your therapy. It acknowledges the achievements and hard work that you have invested in our sessions together and makes some suggestions about how you can continue to build on these achievements.

You came to therapy feeling depressed, anxious and worried about what was in store for you in the future; whether you would be able to cope with the stresses and strains of life when, at that time, you were feeling insecure in yourself. You talked of the thoughts you had which disturbed you immensely and which you felt powerless to control.

In the early weeks of your therapy you shared with me the story of your life and the events in your childhood which made you feel angry, frightened and hurt, feelings you felt unable to express openly to your family, in particular to your mother. These feelings remained hidden within you, getting stronger and stronger whilst you continued to play the part expected of you, the 'good boy'. As you grew older it became more and more difficult even to display your feelings; you thus maintained tight control over your life, terrified that the powerful feelings inside you would destroy all those around you.

Over the weeks of therapy we began to understand the patterns in your life which have caused you such pain and distress, and which have restricted your life. On several occasions, both in therapy and in your own life, you have taken risks believing that your worst expectations might be realized. For example, you told your friend Sue you were having therapy and you feared rejection by her. This did not happen and your fears were not confirmed. You have also been able to challenge different family members without 'losing control' as you feared you might and also without accepting total responsibility for your family as you used to. Thus you have begun to experience boundaries and are practising applying them appropriately. This was something you previously found difficult.

You have also begun to recognize your own needs as differing from your family's and are beginning to integrate the 'good' and 'bad' parts of yourself. This process must have been very frightening and painful for you, yet despite this you have shown immense courage in continuing to come each week and working very hard both in and out of therapy. The assertiveness skills you have been working so hard on have begun to pay off for you. I know at times that you have felt extremely hopeless about your future, believing that nothing will change. Much of your anger has been directed at your parents for bringing you up in the way that they did. This recognition has been a painful process but I have every faith that you will continue to work on these issues, perhaps enabling you one day to reinterpret your past and change the way that you think about it. You have already started this process by noticing how your life is different now, how you are now in control of your own destiny (as a child you did not have this power).

More recently I have seen you rationalize why people may respond to you in particular ways, rather than irrationally assuming that any act or word spoken that is perceived by you to be negative implied that you were worthless and that they were not worth knowing. For example, in a recent diary entry (when talking about an unsympathetic friend) you state 'he is selfish, maybe he just doesn't want to know about my problems *at this time*'. This shows a really positive step where you are recognizing the needs of others, separating them from your own needs and realizing that one's needs cannot always be met all of the time, but that it is a gradual process.

Endings are very important and the emotions experienced can be very painful. We have been exploring these feelings; however, it may be in the weeks ahead that you experience a return or an increase of some of your fears. I trust in your ability to continue with your assertiveness in expressing your needs and in beginning to express your feelings. In doing so, you will continue to build on the potential friendships and support you have around you.

At times when things get particularly difficult, it may be helpful to read this goodbye letter, the Psychotherapy File, the written summary of your personal issues and your diaries. This will help you re-establish contact with your own strength which you carry within you.

Finally, I would like to acknowledge and appreciate the warmth, determination, humour and courage which I have encountered within you in our sessions.

Case Example: Marjorie

Here is the goodbye letter to Marjorie, whose reformulation was given in Chapter 2.

Dear Marjorie,
Over the past four months I feel you've worked hard to understand the ways in which the pain of your beach-baby experience led you to choices that prevented you from claiming a better life. You now do feel you deserve more, you've embarked upon study for a new career, you feel more satisfied in your personal relationships and have accepted to some degree that people you love don't have to give in to you to show that they care. As a consequence you have been less angry and disappointed with your boyfriend and your time with him has been less quarrelsome and more enjoyable. You are even less angry with your mother, you understand that Angela will always be the prime focus of her concerns, but you realize that you must still be her 'bright shining star'. You've recently been surprised to discover a sharing of values with Mary and an increasingly fulfilling relationship with Sue. For Angela, there are still many conflicting feelings but you have begun to realize in therapy that you are allowed success in your own life and that there is no need to sabotage that for fear of hurting Angela.

I feel that these revisions of attitude will enable you to recognize and therefore control the negative patterns that have been maintained by your 'beach-baby' image. Of course, there may be times when the old feelings and fears re-emerge, but undoubtedly the beach baby has left the beach for a new environment. Goodbye and good luck.

Marjorie wrote as follows:

These weeks of therapy have not been what I expected, I was worried that there would not be time enough to sort things out. I wanted the opportunity to talk exhaustively about all the things that had upset me in the past. It took a while for me to realize that this was not necessary and perhaps not even desirable. I found the middle sessions very difficult and felt quite discouraged about failure to get in touch with my hurt about my childhood. For me, the real revelation, the unexpected, was learning about self-sabotage. Before commencing therapy I wrote a list of some things I wanted to understand. The first point was why I was never properly prepared for examinations; it is really quite shocking to realize that one deliberately hurts oneself because fundamentally one feels unworthy. A related point was why I feel that I respect myself, and am confident in spite of evidence to the contrary. My major worry is that I will continue to spoil my chances. I feel that self-sabotage is deeply rooted and that it will take tremendous, sustained effort to combat it. I think it may be a long and uphill battle. The very positive thing that has emerged from therapy is the re-emergence of a 'lust for life'. There are so many things I want to enjoy, I have recovered a feeling of leaving therapy. Last week I felt ready for it, this week the fear that I may backslide is more prominent. If I'm honest I would like to have the continuous support of regular sessions until I feel more confident that I'm not going to undo the good work. Having said this though, I do not feel I am about to be abandoned, the three-month follow-up session is a considerable solace. My relationship with my boyfriend still needs improving. As regards to the future I want to continue to feel good about myself, to feel increasingly confident and to feel secure with this confidence, i.e. to know that it is a solid base and is not dependent upon props such as other people's opinions of me, or my career, etc. In brief, I want to be happy and autonomous and to feel that I have taken life in both hands. Perhaps I need some structured means of monitoring my progress by myself so that any backsliding can be arrested at the early stages.

Thank you, you've really helped me cut through the crap and to feel good and excited again.

The follow-up in three months in fact showed continuing growing confidence in the changes achieved during the therapy.

Case Example: Ian

Ian, a man in his thirties, had a life characterized by many unsatisfactory relationships and enterprises and his therapy often felt destined to repeat this pattern. His assessment of his experience of therapy was therefore an encouraging surprise:

> In a way difficult to define, the course was not what I expected. The difference was in its mood more than in its content; the subject matter, particularly the questions about early childhood experiences and the relation of these to my adult emotions, was what I expected. But the mood was at once low-key and severe. There were to be a few isolated moments of triumphant discovery, setting in motion again the violent swings of expectation and disappointment. These rhythms were to be avoided, like the traps enumerated in the lists.
>
> I feel now that this was a good thing, but it has made the effect of the course difficult to pin down or make tangible. I can't recall decisive moments, or sum up the content in more than very general insights, but these insights are having, I hope, a cumulative effect rather than an instantaneous one; they are working underground. It would be better for me not to expect too much of them or wait for them to work; rather I should be surprised by their achievement, or realize belatedly that they have worked. A general principle has been that I should inhabit the self and the life I have rather than fretting after another one; that I should live more in the present and that I should greet my rushes of feeling with equanimity, as if they were acquaintances or familiar sights, rather than struggling to resist them and wish they were otherwise.
>
> This itself can be a trap, if I turn it into a vigorous programme, like a deadline, for me to demoralize myself by not living up to it.
>
> I realized that early on in the course I was very resentful of the imbalance in the conversations we were having. I was producing very personal information, in long confessions, while my interlocutor was not reciprocating (of course he wasn't). Although I know that this was probably desirable or inevitable, I think I was unconsciously quite angry about it. I was more assertive in the earlier sessions, and found the lack of reaction to my peremptoriness

exasperating; particularly when the effect seemed to be that I was being caught out in what I laboriously said. I found the idea that I was at some level deliberately sabotaging my own intentions through panic and depression, deliberately bringing about my own illness, a very exasperating one; at times, in its recurrence, a glib one. I then came to accept it, and to see the possibility of being grateful for it, and this coincided with more submissive behaviour towards my psychotherapist. I sometimes felt that childish submissiveness was a kind of appeasement of him, like an alternative to argumentative resistance to being told off as a child. I also felt at this point that I was growing into the picture of myself that the conversations had created, and that my acceptance of it was both beneficial and a kind of obedience. This idea was set up by the very suggestive discussion we had had of my childhood responses to other people, and the continuing patterns derived from those responses.

I think the childishness is another way of distancing myself from events rather than committing myself to them; because it is a childish reaction, it is not really me; it is something I am doing to please while the real me skulks and observes on the sidelines. This was a pattern which was applying itself to the psychotherapy sessions even while they were making me aware of it.

And therefore I've often had the feeling that I've not been taking full advantage of this course, that I am somehow missing out on it and it is my own fault. The weekly session looms up ahead of me. When it is a long way off I have all kinds of thoughts about what might be achieved in it, and how it might be the decisive confrontation, but when it gets nearer I worry about being prepared for it, and then preparation is inevitably a rushed job. When it comes, I 'get by', using my spontaneous initiative, and afterwards I feel it was a chance missed. I'm treating the sessions like jobs or interviews, things I can botch together with a surprising amount of inspiration, but which could be so much better if I'd only prepared for them properly. Even in this context, I still have this notional other self, my fantasy self, but also my potential self, who does everything well, who is the same as me, but with the weaknesses and the evasions and time-wasting cut out so that the rest is purified.

But the course is, I think, counteracting this view, this polarization between fantasy success and actual life as missed opportunity. I do think it is untrue that I have failed to take advantage of this course, fobbed it off or day-dreamed through it, as I often do with people. I do at times feel strengthened in my ability to accept the immediate context life offers me, rather than setting aside in favour of a postponed or lost one (the one that the endless postponement of which became to me, in the end, a kind of death; so that I became obsessed with the fact and thought of actual death). With this I feel that I was there in that room having those conversations; I did not somehow miss them. That is a way of expressing what they have achieved.

Case Example: Paula

This had been a very difficult therapy extended to 26 sessions, Paula was a deeply unhappy and very withdrawn young woman who had had three unsuccessful previous therapies and who avoided eye contact throughout this therapy. Here is Paula's letter.

> One of the hardest things about therapy for me has been my inability to see myself. I feel a blank and cannot describe my feelings. Similarly I find it hard to recall the content of sessions, even immediately afterwards it disappears from my mind. To help define what I feel I have learnt I have used the device of re-reading a book which I flicked through earlier this year and found quite interesting, but no more than that. A good friend had bought it for me, *Families and How to Survive Them* by John Cleese and Robin Skinner. I now find on re-reading it that passages seem to have been written with me in mind. Since I find it easier to recognize myself than find words of my own I am including many passages from this book, not just the bits I think are clever, but to try to show those extracts which before therapy had no special meaning for me but which now seem to put what I have learned into words. [The following summary of what she had learnt had cross-references to sections of the book which for reasons of space are not reproduced here.] Three key ideas come to mind which had not specifically occurred to me before this therapy.
>
> 1. Dilemmas as detailed in the Psychotherapy File; these hopeless insoluble situations which leave me feeling trapped. Now I can see how I create these dilemmas for those close to me. Not only am I forcing them without realizing it to feel how I feel in not being able to do the right thing, but I am also perpetuating a chain in doing so. I feel this is explored in the Psychotherapy File but it was most interesting for me to see how I forced others into the dilemmas too, i.e. my boyfriend, my therapist, for example — nosy or uncaring, unsympathetic or weak and overindulgent, hostile and silent or intrusive and pushy. The hardest dilemma for me to cope with has been that posed by

therapy itself; to go for a limited period for a short time once a week with a stranger and unburden a quarter of a century of deeply hidden and frightening feelings that have to be denied before they can be examined. The therapist, a person who will not be shocked or offended or betray the confidences offered, and then to go out into the real world of uncaring people and difficult situations, feeling worse, with the raw edges revealed, wounds opened, partly stitched up and healed in 50 minutes.

2. Parental influence. I knew it was important but had not realized how it was the key, and how I am following a pattern. For example, I criticize as the only valid way of showing affection (as in not 'Darling, how lovely to see you' but 'What on earth have you spilt down your shirt?'). One reason it has been difficult is that though I complain superficially about my parents, I find it very hard to blame them for my bad state of mind. Opening your family life to a stranger and being disloyal to parents who have made very great sacrifices and tried very hard for their children, this brings out a strong feeling of being bad — not just an ungrateful daughter, but also a bad patient who has seen four specialists and three therapists, been to a day hospital and pestered the GP, but won't co-operate, won't talk. It's my own fault I feel bad, I refuse to do what will help me. I'm bad in relationships, messy, demanding, clinging, giving no real love or support, the ivy that throttles and kills the host. I was a bad pupil at school, naughty, disruptive, rude, argumentative, and at university, where I did no work, wasted my parents' and the tax payers' money.

Not only do I make myself unhappy, I am cruel about others. I notice their spots, their excess weight or whatever and I expect to be judged in the same way by them. As children we were constantly reproved for our own good. What makes me feel so tired is the fact that my life is a constant search for approval. I work till late so that no one can call me lazy. I don't like to be seen eating forbidden food. I am afraid to say I like a person, a film or a book in case this does not fit in, and yet if you asked me I would say that I don't care at all for what people think. I know I can't let my parents or my friends know that I'm not strong and not coping. I won't allow them to feel any guilt for that, I must keep all the pain for myself. I've realized that my father's own barren childhood made it impossible for him to express love easily. I understand more clearly my mother, who had grown up in a family which placed little value on girls, where she too was the eldest girl. I did not realize before how, since she struggled for further education and wanted the best, this made her want the same for me. I saw how she split me up into acceptable parts. She genuinely wanted me to have intellectual equality with boys, but as I grew older she couldn't accept my use of make-up, my teenage clothes and my talking to boyfriends. Did she want to keep me as a child, to keep me pure and respectable, to stop my studies being disrupted by emotions, or did she find a growing girl a threat to her own shaky sexuality ...?

3. The baby inside. This was a totally new theme to me before this therapy. For someone who would like to feel mature and adult to be told that one is really very immature and indeed has missed out on a stage or stages of development is very shameful. 'Grow up!' you say to an annoying person, 'act your age'. However, the more I read and think, the more this explains and this links into the previous theme of parental influence on a very young baby and how bad childhood experiences come out in this. Several comments stick in my mind; for example, a baby has no words or concepts to describe feelings, they are frightening and anomalous. A baby needs constant and infinite care, this is impossible and they learn to accept this; somewhere inside I didn't learn this. A baby is helpless to control his environment, only by rage can he have some impact but this is exhausting. Babies are intelligent and intuitive and pick up powerful vibes whose implications they don't understand and yet which make an indelible mark. The baby inside me is trying to override that part of me which is pretending to be capable, sabotaging my college career, making mistakes at work, because capable people don't get taken care of. Babies don't like change, they attach themselves to inanimate objects which won't argue or talk back; that's why I buy and surround myself with objects which I can take back to my room and carry around with me. A baby, however, is honest about its feelings. He throws his teddy bear out of the pram, is not polite or tactful. A baby has to learn that the mother he loves is also the one he hates for neglecting him, and join these two together. Although I manage this on a conscious level, I don't think it works unconsciously. If I am angry with people I really badly want to hurt them and can't bear to speak to them or be near them. I feel any compromise is dishonest so I go back into myself and sulk.

Follow-up

It is customary to offer patients a follow-up appointment at about three months after completion of therapy. This meeting serves the function of re-assessment where full resolution of the patient's problems had not occurred during therapy, and at this stage possibilities for further therapy can be considered. For those patients who have made good progress, the follow-up meeting may allow further consolidation of gains already made. Most patients, including those who have seemed to make adequate progress during therapy, lack confidence in their capacity to cope without weekly sessions; the prospect of a further meeting with the therapist in three months helps them to continue to use what they have learnt in therapy and to realize that they can cope alone. Decisions about further therapy or follow-up will be made at this meeting with about three-quarters of all patients being discharged.

CHAPTER 4

Twelve Sessions: An Edited Transcript

Introduction

What follows is an account of a brief therapy. The patient agreed at the end of the assessment meeting that her the py sessions could be audio-taped. The account below consists of edited excerpts from these tapes linked with summaries and comments to bring out tne issues related to Cognitive–Analytic Therapy. Many details are altered to preserve anonymity, both in the excerpts and the summaries, as are the names of people mentioned.

The patient was an intelligent 38-year-old graduate referred by a colleague who was familiar with the model of therapy, and hence was informed about, and favourable to, the idea of a time-limited approach. The main 'cast' consists of the patient Maggie, her boyfriend Stuart, her husband Ralph, her 2½-year-old daughter Helen, her colleague and friend Diana and her mother.

Following her first assessment session, Maggie was given the Psychotherapy File, and the Personal Sources Questionnaire; she had also been sent a copy of the summary of the assessment interview. (At this stage prose reformulation had not become part of the method.) This summary reads as follows:

> Maggie is a 38-year-old graduate who has sought help on account of her unhappiness following the break-up of the relationship with the father of her daughter. She has been quite seriously depressed following this, which took place four months ago, although she is now feeling better. She was anxious to understand more clearly the pattern of her relationships with men. She came across as a pleasant-looking young woman, able to speak forthrightly and directly, who had clearly done quite a lot of thinking about herself.
>
> She was brought up as the only child in the family, although her mother had had two sons, 10 and 12 years previously, from the marriage to her first husband. Maggie's father also had a previous marriage with two sons, with whom she had no contact. Her father committed suicide before her birth. She was therefore brought up essentially by her mother as an only child. Her mother was an

English woman, but her father was an American and she was born and spent her early life in America. Her mother explicitly decided that she would 'devote herself to the care of her daughter' and would not seek any further relationships. They lived in America until Maggie's graduation from an American college, whereupon they moved to London and Maggie became a post-graduate student in an English university. Early in her school career, Maggie was sent to a private school specializing in dance and drama, which initially she enjoyed, but in which she felt the odd one out, feeling physically awkward, and not being able to afford the kind of clothes the other girls wore. By her teens, she had become aware of her mother's depression and vulnerability; her mother would often depend on her when she was feeling depressed. She became increasingly oppressed by this, as they had no contact with other family members, and she was thus very pleased to leave home and go to college at the age of 17½. At that time she had her first relationship with a young man, a rather eccentric character of whom her mother disapproved quite strongly. During the early part of her post-graduate studies in England, she met and married her husband Ralph. Over the following years, Ralph, who was a university lecturer, had a series of affairs, some with other staff members and some with his students. He surrounded these by a complex web of deception, which for a long time Maggie believed in the face of much evidence about what was going on. After she discovered the deception, she still continued the relationship for a time, but finally insisted on him moving out. Looking back, she feels that he never showed very much interest in her own individual interests, in particular literature and writing. None the less, she feels her own horizons were much expanded by the relationship, and she described Ralph as a very interesting and amusing person. After the end of that relationship she had a brief, not very emotionally significant, relationship before meeting Stuart, 15 years her junior. She felt very flattered by his interest in her and wonders whether there was not some element of revenge on Ralph, to show that she too could attract younger partners. She had always felt somewhat anxious about her attractiveness. The original relationship with Stuart seems to have been based upon a sexual connection, combined with a good deal of 'maternal' tolerance on her part. Stuart was a musician, not working professionally, who mixed with younger fringe music friends whom Maggie did not find of particular interest. Three years before the consultation, she had decided to move to get herself retrained in a different job, but just before the move was about to take place, she discovered she was pregnant.

She decided she would never stop regretting it if she did not have the child, as this might be her last chance. To her surprise, Stuart did in fact take on a fairly strong parental role in the first year of the child's life. During that time, however, he was involved in a road traffic accident and was concussed, and, possibly related to this, some months later began to be irritable, prone to outbursts of anger, and then became manically overactive for a time. Their relationship became marked by increasingly painful rows and disagreements. Stuart then met a girl in a pub and decided very quickly to move off with her. Although she had been quite looking forward to the end of the relationship during the time of conflict, she was surprised to feel quite desolate when he did in fact go.

Maggie had been doing her present job for nine years, and had begun to feel quite stale in it. She was also beginning to feel 'middle-aged anxieties' about her daughter's needs and her own economic security, and by a sense of closing in of horizons. In recent weeks, Stuart had visited irregularly, and she felt annoyed that he had not made more stable arrangements to stay in touch with the child. His family were quite supportive of her and play a part with the child which is clearly important.

It seems that in this story there is first of all a history of men who go away, starting with the father before she was born, and that may have added to the pain of this recent relationship. Secondly, it was through her relationships with men that she freed herself from her mother, and there seems to have been some underlying lack of confidence in herself as a woman, which has not been remedied by the experience of being able to attract several men during the course of her life. Thirdly, and most importantly, in these relationships with men she has chosen men who were, in some sense, childish or weak. In these relationships she has not been able to demand or ask for her own needs to be met, and in this she seems very much to be caught in a repetition of the intense care-giving relationship she had with her mother from late childhood onwards. This model seemed acceptable to her; she said she had a lot of it worked out for herself, but she was particularly keen for therapy to clarify the history further, so in future she would be able to make better choices of men, and feel better about herself. It was agreed that she would start time-limited therapy in about three months' time.

Session 1

The first session took place eight weeks after the assessment. Maggie described how after a couple of meetings Stuart had moved back with her.

TH What did you want to happen?

PT What did I want? I guess I really deep down ... I probably wasn't admitting it to myself, but I was saying to myself on the surface, that I wanted just to have a friendly, happy relationship, but I reckon, probably underneath, I was saying 'Well, I want us to get back together.' I was hoping for that. He stayed the night that night, downstairs sleeping on the sofa, and then ... that was on Wednesday, and then on the Sunday he rang up and said he had been missing us both very much and he was getting depressed and very lonely, and so on, and then I saw him again on the following Wednesday, when he again stayed the night. He stayed overnight on two nights, and on the second night we slept together. Then another phone call on Sunday saying he was really missing us, and was very low indeed, and could he come back and stay for a few days. So he did, on the Monday, and he has been back ever since.

TH What account did he give of his departure when he came back?

PT Well, all he could say about it was that it was something ... partly why he feels so alone, I think he feels very ashamed about it. He is too ashamed to actually want to see anybody really, and that is why he stays in the house all the time. It was, he says (which doesn't really mean very much at all), it was all some sort of crazy romantic fling which was over in a few weeks.

TH What about you? What have you made of the story so far?

PT For him, I think it is ...

TH No, for you!

PT For me? I put it where I can try and understand it. But every now and again I feel very angry and upset, because it feels to me as though I am the one who stays at home, if you like, and I'm the sort of solid, reliable boring one, and that's not what I want to be. I suppose I fantasize about being the exciting vivacious one who rushes off and does crazy things, and was attractive for that reason. I suddenly felt a surge of anger about Stuart's running off, it had been almost like a reliving of those feelings. But I think I have been able not to feel overcome and overwhelmed by it, but to actually think about that feeling of anger more constructively, and that is based on feeling a little clearer about myself really, I think.

TH When you and Stuart started, was that the 'dazzling you', or the 'domestic you'?

PT When the thing with Stuart started? [*TH* Mmm.] Oh, that was the dazzling me.

TH So, do you have any hesitation in your life about what is going to happen next? Are you just pleased that he is back, or are you saying 'here we go again', or half way between the two?

PT Half way between the two. I am pleased that he is back. I don't understand myself actually, I don't understand how (when I step back and look at the way he is at the moment, and the fact that he is very inside himself, so he is not able to respond at all) how I can actually feel I care about him. That really worries me actually, because since he has been back I have jotted down just a couple of occasions when I did feel suddenly desperate, but most of the time I felt fine. I felt I cared about his being back, but also anxious about it; that I feel OK about that now, but very anxious about the future, and about whether I can go through the same pattern again. It is nice having him back, and it is very nice to see that Helen is thrilled and obviously very happy that he is back and making a bit of fuss of him and so on, but are we going to go through the same thing again, and am I going to ... am I also going to very quickly become disillusioned with the whole thing, and how am I going to cope with that, particularly given that Helen is involved? You know it was back to a situation where there was a sort of plea for help. I suppose I felt that he was really something I wanted, but it was also a plea for help that was just impossible to refuse, but although I ...

TH   Rather than 'make me an offer I can't refuse', its make a request I can't refuse ...

PT   Yes.

TH   Which is *you*.

In the above passage, we see the emergence of two patterns which were to become identified as Target Problem Procedures; Maggie's contrasting of the boring and dazzling roles, and her recognition of the way in which the need to be care-giver (which had been identified in the assessment session) was operating in the terms on which Stuart had returned. In the next part of the session, Maggie corrected some details in my assessment summary, a copy of which she had seen, and included the following comments:

TH   Was it odd, reading about yourself?

PT   Yes, very. Another revealing thing about myself, which ties in with the things I put down as sources, a reference to the Personal Sources Questionnaire, was about needing to be attractive. You have a description of me as a 'pleasant-looking young woman'. I thought about this, and I thought 'Mmm, I don't want this, I don't like this' and I decided that I would have preferred not to have been described at all physically. I thought 'pleasant looking' was a kind of downward praise, and that was a very interesting revelation, for me anyway.

TH   That was probably one of the few moments I was aware that you might read what I wrote down actually. I think you are very pleasant looking, so you needn't worry.

PT   Ha!
TH   That's the same division isn't it. Dazzling or domestic.

A bit later, Maggie referred to the theme of her feelings on the second
occasion that Stuart had stayed over, referring to some diary-keeping from
that time, and indirectly to the Psychotherapy File.

PT   And because this time, when he arrived, he was very depressed and
     confused, and made me feel helpless. Because I wanted to be someone
     who he wants to stay with, and I want him to feel that my house is his
     house, and I ought to be able to make him feel relaxed and happy, and
     sort of centred here. I have this feeling that I ought to be superhuman
     and able to remove the cares from him and give him all that he wants,
     although neither he nor I know exactly what that is. This actually was
     written after he had come back, and I had been really hooked in by
     then, hanging around and waiting for a phone call like the one I had
     the previous week, and just sort of waiting for it to happen. Helplessness
     with waiting for the phone call, I think that ties in with the dilemma
     that I made notes on too. I want to be perfect for whoever I am
     strongly and emotionally involved with, and I feel guilty when I can't
     be the perfect person. This is the crazy and disastrous exchange
     which I have written down here. On the second night that he stayed on
     that visit, when we were sitting on the sofa together, and we had a
     little bit to drink, and I was just sort of relaxed, and no more than
     that, I had half-jokingly said something about marriage. Stuart's re-
     sponse was 'I will never marry you!' That really shocked me and made
     me feel rejected and inadequate, and then I tried to think, when I was
     writing this, how would I have felt if he had said, 'Yes, I really want to
     marry you'? I have written that I suspect I would have felt much more
     detached again and back in control. So the pendulum swings between
     my either being in control and detached or more attached and depen-
     dent, and feeling sort of helpless and rejected at times.
TH   The form of your dependency is very much your need to be the person
     providing the perfect care. You require a need in him before you can
     be involved in that way. [PT Yes.] And not wanting anything except
     the right to be that sort of person [PT Yes.].

Following this, Maggie discussed how her relationship with her mother
always diminished when she was involved with a man, and then went on to
report a recent example of her mother involving her unnecessarily in some
minor legal and financial problems. She also recalled an earlier example
when, unusually, she had felt really angry with her mother and had actually
physically shaken her.

TH   What do you feel about that now?

PT   I still feel very angry about that really.

TH   In a sense, she made you her husband, didn't she? You know, a sort of
       barrier against the rigours of the world. I also feel your need to be the
       perfect provider in that. You were made to feel guilty if you weren't,
       and still are. [*PT* Yes.] So in a sense there is a kind of stream that is
       running out towards Helen, or Stuart or towards your mother, that is
       all rather one-directional.

In the next part of the session, Maggie talked about an older woman friend
Diana, realizing as she talked how she had felt that Diana had chosen her
for being exciting, and she was perhaps disappointed in her. She then
contrasted recently happy times with Stuart and Helen with her resentment
of Stuart's consistent vegetarianism.

PT   When he first came back, one of the first things I said to him was 'I
       have been giving Helen fish while you were away, and I have been
       eating fish myself, and I have been enjoying it. Fine, I won't eat meat
       while we are eating together because I realize you don't like it and it
       upsets you and disturbs you, but I really do want to carry on eating
       fish.' But it hasn't been possible, or else I gave up because of the
       confrontations it caused. I had it twice, and there were so many
       comments about how I stunk of fish, and he sort of recoiled away from
       me, and how it really upset him, so I just ceased to eat either fish or
       meat again except when I am on my own. When we were on holiday,
       we ended up living on omelettes, which was awful because there was
       all this delicious fish around, and most of the time I accepted that, but
       it blew up one evening, when we were looking for a restaurant,
       looking for somewhere where they would be prepared to serve some-
       thing else rather than the same old omelettes, and we couldn't find
       one anywhere, and I felt I was just doing the seeking, and that Stuart
       was just trailing along behind me, and I suddenly felt absolutely,
       furiously angry and very depressed about this. I actually just left him
       with Helen, and went back to the hotel. I was so angry about it. It was a
       feeling of being taken over, and having colluded with this, and having
       gone along with the very little bit of pressure which had been put on
       me to always be a vegetarian when he was around.

TH   So again you always have to be what is required of you.

Maggie then went on to discuss how she had probably lost the chance of
getting some writing published through procrastination.

PT   I mean, you know, that rationally I could have done it earlier, so we would have to look at some irrational forces which would determine that I didn't do it. What happens when Stuart is around is that I have to spend time with him in the evenings, particularly at the moment when he is so entirely dependent on me, so that is a good excuse for not doing any work. I mean, I feel quite bad if I actually sit down and say, 'You know, I have to concentrate, I can't talk to you for a couple of hours', or whatever. It's very difficult, I find it very difficult to do that. But I didn't have that excuse for some considerable amount of the time that I was supposed to be doing this writing. It is actually something that I want to do for myself you see, it's not something that other people are wanting from me, it is my loss if I don't send them the synopsis, it is no skin off their noses, so it is sabotage of myself really.

Having suggested a possible link between needing to please other people and sabotaging herself as being a related passive resistance to demands, the following recapitulation was suggested:

TH I have the sense of you being re-engulfed in the pattern of relationship with people who are ultimately non-supportive of you, and demanding of you, and to whom you grant the right to stop you eating fish or doing anything else you want to do. You hand it over to them and it is justified because 'he needs you' (he or she or whoever). 'Well, he is depressed, he's there, therefore I must!' You really do something to maintain your own structure, which has been there for a long time. You *could* say he needs you like a hole in the head! It could be more that you need him. Put it another way—the fact that you have always done this seems to me to be a function of the fact that to be a demanding or a needy person didn't get you very far as a child, but this doesn't necessarily mean that you weren't needy. I think it is just that you learnt to deny that aspect of you.

The session ended with the discussion of some professional care that Stuart was currently receiving (something of importance, given the story of a possible manic episode in the past and his current depression), and also with the suggestion that it was very important at this stage to consider very carefully the terms of the resumed relationship.

Session 2

PT I made a few notes during the week before I came here. One of the things I feel at the moment is very blocked and very confused really, like, er, like 'where do I go from here?'

TH How did you feel immediately after you left last time?

PT Oh, well, that was one of the things I made a note about, because I felt guilty. I felt disappointed with myself and I felt I had let you down. I was walking over the bridge and I was trying to think what this feeling of disappointment was about, and that is what it seemed to come down to. I felt like I had let you down.

TH Do you know what I wrote down as my preliminary reformulation after I left you last time?

PT No!

TH 'Either anxiously and sensitively attending to the needs of others, or being manipulative.' I mean, from your history, that is what you do, and now even with your therapist you worry whether you have done the right thing for his needs!

PT That's right, yes, that's exactly right. Perhaps that is what I had realized, that perhaps, in a sense, I had not fulfilled the brief, having come back with the situation changed and Stuart back.

TH Did you manage to get past that and forgive yourself for 'failing' me?

PT I think I did, yes. It took me quite a long time, but over the week I have thought about that feeling quite a lot and I think I felt that that was not my responsibility, and I felt that it was quite useful really because I was able easily to identify what was going on now.

The conversation then turned to Stuart's mother.

PT I feel she is not really able to cope with his depression, and is very pleased that he has returned to me. She is still wanting to retain the good mother role with him. She is very frightened of losing both her children, I think, and is intensely maternal and not really able to let them grow up. I think that she thinks that growing up is synonymous with losing them. Quite a lot of comments have been coming my way about, 'You must push Stuart into getting a job', 'You mustn't let him do this', and 'You mustn't let him do that', 'You must tell him', and 'You must lay down the law', and so on, which I feel very angry about, because I am being dumped ...

TH You are being dumped with all the fierce part of it.

PT That's right, and the good part remains with her, so I have been quite deliberately not doing that, because I feel very angry, but then another bit of me feels 'Well, he is kind of depressed at the moment, perhaps I am actually just opting out, perhaps I should just give him a push to initiate the change, which would be good for us both, and would enable us both to change.'

TH I think I hear you talking very much about what is good for him.

PT Yes, I was. You see, that goes with thinking, 'Well, what is good for

him if he changes will be good for me, and will enable me to change',
and feeling sort of helpless really. I am not allowing myself the possibility of changing. I am very frightened about a change, although I
don't know what that change would be.

TH A change in you do you mean by that?

PT Yes, but it would affect the relationship. I am just thinking about
change in the abstract now. Just thinking of the word, and not tying
anything specific on to it. It makes me feel quite frightened about what
would happen to the relationship.

TH But are we treating the relationship, or are we treating you?

PT Me.

TH They are not necessarily the same. Well, they may be, in fact they are
the same, because if it is going to survive as a relationship then it has
to survive on terms that are all right for you. If we look back on your
history, it is very easy to see why that is so. I mean, underneath your
mother's hovering focus on you and only you, which was your early
experience, you detected, by your teens anyway, that that was *her*
need, not your need. I am sure by that time you had already been
trained to be the daughter your mother required. Your training was
exquisite, as though all the discomforts were part of the virtues, so
that to feel good about yourself, you had to do that—you had to be
this person who is not just being nice, but who is tuned in even better
than the other person is to what they need.

PT Yes, oh yes!

TH You are responsible for what they need and want, and there is no
place for you at all, except on those terms.

PT It is as you say; knowing more than the person themself knows is in a
sense very true. I have quite often felt bad about Stuart. I have done
so much thinking and detective work on his behalf: 'Why is he like
that, what does it stem from?' Remembering things that the family
have said about him, and when the problems first started ...

The content of the session so far can be seen as providing some confirmation
of the provisional Target Problem Procedures. The issue of the control
vested in Maggie's chosen role was now proposed.

TH The only other thing to say about this is that, quite apart from having
been groomed to this role, it also gives you power. It is the strongest
place to be in, to know one is both powerful and good. Right?

PT Yes, I was also thinking about that on my way here, and trying to
imagine. I was giving myself a model of an extreme, which is perhaps
deliberate. I was trying to imagine myself in a relationship where I
was, if you like, much more in a sort of childlike role, where I was

much more dependent on somebody else. When I was thinking about it, the dependence was more financial. Now that is interesting, but thinking about a very strong emotional dependence in terms of my being the child in a relationship plus perhaps being financially supported, I find actually terrifying. At the moment, I guess, that is one of the blocks on envisaging a balanced relationship. I find that very difficult.

TH   Well, right, if you are stuck in a dilemma with opposing poles, you stay where you are because the opposite pole is a lot worse.

PT   Yes, and the block is actually trying to get that into focus. Coming back to being so tuned in to the needs of others, our present relationship sets up all other sorts of guilts and anxieties really. I know (well I have actually been told), that my friends think it is an inappropriate relationship, and people find it very difficult to issue invitations just to me, because of the couples thing. It is quite tricky if they say, 'just you come to this'. They feel an obligation to invite us both, but they don't really have any interest in Stuart, and therefore that is a very tricky one for them to handle. If they do extend the invitation to us both, then, you know, there is always a sort of an edge, and they don't issue invitations very often. I think I am slowly overcoming that, but I do feel a lot of anxiety, due, I suppose, to the attitude of my friends. So much so, that when Stuart returned to me, I didn't tell anybody for quite a long time, and I actually gave the impression that I was going on my own on this vacation, and I didn't tell anybody that I was going with Stuart.

After describing some friendships which had been preserved successfully, there was a pause, after which Maggie continued with the discussion of her relationship with her daughter, one in which both guilty placation and resentment was to some extent acknowledged, but with a sense of a better balance being achieved.

PT   She is very vulnerable and very emotional, and that used to worry me a lot. I used to worry a great deal that it was something that I was doing, that it was something about how I had been with her when she was a tiny baby, and so on, and I am now able to get away from that feeling quite a lot, and to feel, well ...

TH   That she is all right the way she is?

PT   Yes, exactly. This is the sort of person she is, and she needs to have a tantrum every now and then, or to get very upset about what seems to me to be a very small thing, and not for me to feel terribly anxious or over-protective, or whatever.

After further discussion of Stuart's state and his search for treatment, and

the problem of sorting out the relationship while he was in this depressed
state, a piece of homework was suggested.

TH I think one thing you could try and start doing is to force yourself to
begin a few sentences with 'What Maggie wants is . . .', right? Actually
put yourself rather firmly at the beginning of the sentence in that way,
and just try and see where it leads. The other thing is the dilemma.
You know perfectly well in your head that there are 405 ways of
having a relationship, the balances are of all sorts.

PT So what are you saying I should do?

TH I am saying that you should do some homework, that you should give
yourself some time every day apart from Helen and apart from Stuart,
and apart from work, and take a blank piece of paper and write down
what Maggie wants. She can have anything, right? [*PT* Yes.] And
secondly, on another piece of paper, write down some version of this
dilemma which we haven't quite worked out yet, about attending and
responding perfectly to the needs of others etc. (which is the preferred
pole) or helplessly depending. Right?

PT Yes.

Following this, Maggie agreed to do the Relationships Test, and also asked
for some feedback from the Personal Sources Questionnaire.

PT Was there anything that came out from what I gave you last week?

TH Yes. In fact, I thought it was quite interesting. The same sort of things
are emerging. Basically the two sources which produce the most mixed
outcomes for you are 'to be a helpful and caring person', and 'to be
tolerant and forgiving'. Out of all the sources that you chose, those
two are the ones which, on balance, produce almost as many negative
as positive outcomes. Suprise, suprise.

PT Actually I haven't read through it myself, so it is a surprise if that is
what I did.

TH The thing that worked very well for you was 'to feel confident in your
work', and that has obviously been one very important source throughout your life.

The session concluded with some recapitulation from the therapist about a
related possible dilemma between the idea of competence versus being a
'dolls' house' wife, and this led on in turn to Maggie talking about her
relationship with her husband Ralph.

PT I mean intellectually, and in a lot of ways, he is my superior, he is
much quicker on the uptake, and much quicker in argument.

TH   Very quick on the uptake wasn't he? But in that relationship you were
       still the person who was aware of the needs of the other, so you were
       forgiving, and not so aware of your own needs. Wasn't it a rule that
       you had to have partners who were incompetent in some way? That
       you had to be the one who was in charge emotionally, in the sense of
       being the one who understands and provides and meets the needs of?
       And if the need was to have seven girlfriends then that was all right
       too?

PT   I think part of it is actually the fear that 'If I don't do this in a
       relationship, what else have I got?' I can sense that if I don't play it by
       these rules, and give all my attention and care to this person, so that
       they can feel that coming towards them, why else would they be with
       me?

TH   With the worm that you are?

Session 3

Maggie started the session by discussing her experience of completing the
Relationship Test. This is a dyad repertory grid (see Appendix E) in which a
set of relationships are rated according to how far a set of descriptions
(constructs) are seen to apply; some constructs are supplied and some are
chosen by the person doing the test. The results are presented as a map (see
Figure 4.1, p. 76), and as measures of correlation between the constructs
(see below).

PT   I found it a very useful exercise to do. One thing that came out of the
       notes I had been scribbling down about various people that I had listed
       that came up quite frequently, was *respect*, and I realized that although it
       seemed very important, the only person I had rated positively was
       Diana. I then thought about the list of people I had made. The only
       two females are Helen and Diana, and when I started to think about
       my women friends, I realized that respect was a word I would use for
       my feelings for almost all the women whom I am in any way close to
       or friendly with. Of the men I am close to, I had in the past actually
       thought I respected Stuart for the fact that he was tremendously
       refreshingly straight after Ralph, I mean, absolutely direct about his
       feelings, and in that way, very unmanipulative, absolutely above board
       about what he happened to be feeling at the moment, and I respected
       him for that, and for being able to voice sometimes quite difficult
       things. But this is a fairly limited area, I would say. But otherwise, of
       the men I know well, there weren't any that I would use that word
       about easily. I would sort of have to hunt around [*TH* For reasons?]
       Yes, for reasons, for qualities.

After discussing further some of the other people she had selected for the test, Maggie continued:

PT   In those different categories, there was a lot to forgive, and guilt, and I put down respect, but that was what I wanted to talk about in terms of what it brought out for me, in terms of my feelings about women and men and dependence. There are three major people in my life who are dependent on me, my daughter, my mother and Stuart. I have been trying to do a bit of work on saying what I want, and it has been very hard. I can only give you three examples, but I feel OK about that actually. One of them (I'll tell you about it in a moment) was not really saying 'I want to do this'. The others I found really difficult. The first time I heard myself saying to Stuart, 'I've been asked to go out for a drink with Tom, an old friend of mine, whom I have known since university. He has asked me to go out and I would like to go, I want to go.' And I had to run over and over the script in my head before I could say it to him, because of my natural inclination. I kept on modifying it in my head, I kept on sort of thinking, 'Well, I am terribly sorry about this, and I know its going to be a bit depressing for you this evening, but would you mind if ...' and those sorts of phrases kept on coming, and I had to push them down again, and then remind myself of the script, but, I did do it! The other one was one that came up a bit more spontaneously in a way, although a kind of signal came up when it happened. We were watching *Hotel du Lac*, and Stuart was leaning back on the sofa and saying 'I'm not enjoying this', and 'I'm getting really bored by this, let's turn this off'. For a moment I hesitated and I probably normally would have said 'OK', but I was enjoying it, and a little warning signal came up and said, 'No, I am not going to!', and so I said, 'No, I am enjoying it, and I would like to carry on watching', and I was quite pleased with myself for it.

Maggie continued with a description of an interchange with her mother, in which she had successfully resisted responding compliantly to a request which she resented, and with an account of her difficulty in finding among her acquaintances a couple, whose pattern of relationship she felt she respected as a good model. She ended with an account of a couple who had split up after the infidelity of one, but had later come together again, and who were now married and had a child.

PT   It was something about the way in which he handled that situation; it was being able to come back quite open and dignified, and not ... I mean sometimes when Ralph came back to me, I would find myself absolutely despising him, he was sort of whiney. So I think about the quality of this friend being able to go back and be quite open about it, and try to work it through with her, without, I suppose being a little boy, without turning around and sort of saying, 'Mummy, do you forgive me?'

TH Well, is this about giving care, whilst allowing the person to be strong?

PT Yes, yes, that's right. You don't, when they return after having a fling with someone who sounds pretty foolish, you don't kick them down to the ground and disable them and then say, 'OK, now you can come back'. You don't need to do that.

In response to a question from the therapist, Maggie then spoke of her own father, about how little trace of him there was, and about how her mother had spoken much more about her first husband than about her father. The conversation continued:

PT Really, she was very much of a child in that relationship because of the level at which they lived. She didn't know how to cook, she didn't know how to boil an egg until she had to. Everything was done for her, and she never had anything to do with money, and all this sort of thing. I think that was done more particularly by her first husband, who took the entire responsibility. So yes, I guess she needed to have somebody around like that, really.

TH What has Stuart been like since last week?

PT A little better, I think. Part of that is my feelings that although I don't feel I am getting very far at the moment, nevertheless, I have managed to say a couple of times, 'No, I want to do this' or 'I want to do such and such'. And also feeling that, although I am feeling very blocked about it, I am struggling to try and work out what I want to do about this particular relationship.

TH How directly are you involving Stuart in discussions about the terms of it?

PT About the terms of the relationship? Only on a very practical basis at the moment, not any other way. I find it very difficult making a direct statement. He really does have to get a job, and I would like him to get a job, and he wants to. I want him to pay for Helen's crèche fees, so it was my saying I wanted something from him. I find it difficult to even say something like that. I think that it is easier, though, if it is something practical. No, I haven't really involved him at all.

TH Do you know why you haven't?

PT I think it is the controlling again. I feel that I need to do all this thinking on my own, and when I am clear ... [*TH* You will tell him?] Yes, I think I probably will.

TH It's not that you feel he is in such a terrible state he couldn't face the issues?

PT   I feel I have to be very careful how I handle it.

TH   Would it be outrageous to say 'your going away like that, and now coming back like this, has made me think about whether I want to go on, and if so, on what terms'? I mean, would that speech be absolutely terrifying for him?

PT   For him? It frightens me! I kept feeling my stomach contracting as you said it.

TH   Is it because he is too tender to say those things to, or is it because you want to keep it secret?

PT   Given that he is so deeply depressed at the moment, I feel . . .

TH   What does that mean? What does 'so deeply depressed' mean? I mean he is not so bad that he is unable to move is he?

PT   No, it means that he spends all day at home, and he doesn't want to go out, and he doesn't want to talk to friends, mother, relations, or whatever.

TH   Well, those are all descriptions of his behaviour, not necessarily about his mood.

PT   Well, I suppose his mood is low because he is so quiet, and he talks so little. I can only . . . [*TH* Guess?] guess what his mood is from that, and from what he occasionally says about how awful he feels. He says he feels awful, and he is just quite desperate to feel better, and will try anything to feel better. We had that discussion over the medication he has got.

TH   Do you think he will take medication now?

PT   Yes, but it is all very complicated.

TH   Well, I am pleased about the fact that he has seen a psychiatrist, and about the fact that he has got some pills, because that will get rid of any depressive-illness-type component. But I think you have to be very careful about what the right behaviour is. As I see it, this is a relationship in which the axis has become more polarized, with him more childlike in certain ways. He has this powerful mum, who probably prepared him for you historically. He does this neurotic bound into freedom with this girl from the pub which is a kind of desperate statement, rather than a move. Having done it, and recognizing it was a desperate statement, he then comes bounding back with his tail between his legs. In a sense, by accepting that he is now this child or this person who actually can't be told the truth to, you are reimposing the framework which may be the cause of the depression. He could be very angry with you, perhaps, for being a bully.

PT   Oh, I think that he is.

TH   Perhaps like his mother?

PT   Yes.

TH   So this belief that it is necessarily thoughtful, and anti-depressant of you to be very gentle, and keep your thoughts to yourself, is not

necessarily true. It would be much better, probably, to get the truth
spoken. You are not saying that you hate him, and to go away, you
are saying that you are pretty shaken up about thinking about things,
and want to think about them differently, and maybe he should too. It
doesn't seem to me to be an outrageous thing to say.

PT No, of course not, but it is interesting that I have a very exaggerated
reaction to it.

Session 4

This session opened with Maggie announcing two pregnancies; Her own,
and that of the girl Stuart had left her for. Her very mixed feelings about
this news, which Stuart had kept from her for a very long time, were slightly
assuaged by his very clear statement that he did not intend to resume the
other relationship, even though the girl had decided to keep the pregnancy.
Stuart's family had been involved in talks with the girl, and Maggie again
felt under pressure to take on the managing parental role with him.

TH Well, I suppose you have got to work all this out in the right order,
haven't you? You have got to make some kind of decision about your
pregnancy [*PT* Yes], and you have got to consider what keeping the
pregnancy or a termination would mean in terms of the evolution of
your relationship with Stuart, not just about whether he might agree,
or not agree now, but in terms of knowing what it is sensible to
predict.

PT As regards a termination, we agreed not to talk about it until the dust
settled. We both felt that it was just impossible to talk about it and
make a sensible decision, so that we quite deliberately said, 'Let's
leave it for a week before we talk about it.' But I would guess fairly
strongly that he wouldn't want, at the moment, to have another child.
If I had a termination, it would be easier for him to feel he can settle
back and maintain the present roles within the relationship. What do I
suspect would be his feelings, if I were to say 'I am going to go ahead
and have the child'? I think that, unless he works out on a very
profound level some of the things that would be going on in the next
few months, then he would probably do another runner. This is my
picture at the moment, because I think . . . Oh, the other thing I didn't
tell you is that apparently Stuart's girlfriend is threatening to come and
live nearby, which is great news.

TH Is she a very immature person from your understanding?

PT Oh is she! I think that was . . . [*TH* One of the attractions?] Yes.

TH A reversal of you?

PT Yes, in that he was in the stronger role. It sounded as though she had all sorts of loopy ideas and was very weird and mystical. He found it good that she was fairly strange, and also the fact that she was pretty immature, and was pretty weak, and that he was the stronger one. Yes, a very definite escape from all these powerful women around.

TH So, If you are going to keep the pregnancy, you think that he would probably find the pressure too much. If you got rid of it, what would you feel towards him?

PT I can see myself feeling very angry under those circumstances.

TH It does seem to me that you can't plan a future in which you know he would definitely be around. [*PT* No.] There are so many neurotic patterns at work between you. In reality, I think you had better decide whether to have two children, or one, by yourself. I think you have to look at it as that kind of equation.

PT Yes, I do think you're absolutely right.

At this point, the therapist turned to the reformulation task, something which Maggie had, not surprisingly, somewhat neglected during the past week.

TH Well now, I have made three provisional descriptions which seem to describe the issues which have come up so far. The main one is the one which I have said to you before, to do with relationships. I think you will agree, it applies to relationships with close men only. The choice seems to be 'As if *either* sensitively and controllingly attending to the needs of the other (like yourself to your mother), *or* depending, demanding (like your mother to yourself).' [*PT* Yes.] How one might escape from that dilemma would be to be more able to express your own needs, to be more in control of yourself, and not to have to be in control of the other in the same way. Something like mutuality.

PT Yes, because it feels like a real strait-jacket dilemma.

TH But am I right in thinking this only applies in relation to emotionally important men?

PT I can't pick out any important female friends to whom it would apply, no.

TH I linked one which may be a variant, which I think does apply to women which I put down 'As if *either* independent of and respecting, *or* perceiving weakness and looking down on.' That one really came out of the conversation about respect last time.

PT I am not sure that is the case. I can think of two close women friends in particular, one of whom is a teacher, and the other is Diana, and I think in both cases I am able to respect, if you like, and to talk to them about what I would myself regard as weak.

TH So you feel more mutually dependent rather than independent?

PT   Yes, and I find it a much more satisfactory relationship. Sometimes I have felt about Diana that she is so phenomenally strong and energetic, that I am overwhelmed by that, and I am always immensely relieved when a sort of reciprocal need emerges. It feels that there is a much better balance in our relationship, and it actually endears her to me more.

TH   So, mutually dependent would be all right but not independent of. [*PT* Mmm.] But what about the other half of that? You know that you felt that the application of the word respect was quite difficult, no men for example. [*PT* laughs.] So, it would be true for a lot of people that you don't really bother with them, because they are not really seen as having very much, unless they are enlisting your care. I think I also thought about your fantasy of when your ship came in and you had a million pounds, how would you live then. It turned out that there was nobody worth bothering about, nobody to include in the plan.

PT   Yes, I suppose that is right.

TH   In a way, your own need to be strong is fed by seeing yourself as strong to others who are relatively not so strong, so you might actually feed off the weakness of others to help you maintain your view of yourself. You have been very good at picking up lame ducks. Do you think that is true?

PT   Yes, I think that is fairly accurate, and I think that a good few years ago, after I started my present job, two or three people were trying to persuade me to train as a counsellor, and it was immensely appealing, but something, something in my head rang that warning bell, 'Well, why is it so appealing?'

After further discussion around that dilemma the session continued:

TH   The third one, which I think you have actually partly solved, is the 'domestic drudge versus dazzling sex bomb' [*PT* Yes (laughs).] Will that do?

PT   It's ridiculous isn't it?

TH   Well, a caricature, or shorthand, right? You seem to be half-way through that one anyhow.

PT   Yes, I feel much more sorted on that one, much more at ease on that one; getting there.

TH   Mmm? Well, my description of resolution there would be: a person with a career, a good mother to Helen, enjoying home and being a lover to a reliable partner.

PT   Mmm.

TH   I really think that the dilemma which is most related to your present difficulties is the first one.

PT   Yes, can we go over that one again?

TH   Either sensitively and controllingly (that part not always quite acknowledged perhaps) attending to the perceived needs of the other (and that
is what your mother taught you, that if you are able to anticipate, get
it right, you'll have them, and they will be able to have you) that's the
more powerful pole. What seems to be the opposite stems from your
mother's dependence on you. So you can see her as being childishly
demanding and controlling, and yourself as being caring and actually
controlling, although not always calling it that. The problem is that, to
a degree, you have remained trapped in that dilemma and in a way
which does mean that emotional closeness with men hasn't been possible
on any other terms. [*PT* Yes, yes.] Thanks to the antennae by which
you select the appropriate partners, it had always turned out that those
you chose ended up obligingly to be childish and demanding, and that
didn't entirely satisfy you, and has caused you a great deal of pain as it
has turned out. Now, because Stuart so clearly fits that pattern, and
left you because of it, and came back because of it, I think you do
have quite high percentage doubts about the future. [*PT* Yes, yes.]
Now, in response to this latest bombshell, you haven't been entirely
insensitive of caring I hope? [*PT* No!] He is still allowed in the house?
[*PT* Mmm.] Did you know what you felt this time fairly clearly? [*PT*
Mmm.] I think what I can't know, and what you can't know at this
stage, is how much you are going to be able to stand far enough back
realistically to predict that pattern between the two of you, which you
are both established players in, or whether that pattern can be changed. I
think that his inpenetrability to talk about it is probably a defence
mechanism, and that his anger and so on isn't on the surface, by and
large. It would have been very nice if you could have had six months
to think about it in a less stressed situation, but the fact of the matter
is, your pregnancy cannot be ignored. [*PT* sighs]. It seems to me that
you have got to push it with him, and not be in any way protective;
you are entitled to make it perfectly clear what it means to you, and to
be quite direct and unprotective in saying what you think, and what
you feel about other issues now. [*PT* Yes.] Now whether he can
actually engage at that level I don't know. If he can't, then you have
got to decide 'Do I go into limbo and make a decision about the
pregnancy in a situation of total uncertainty or do I end it now?'

PT   I'm not sure whether perhaps some of this has been working inside me
without me being conscious of it, but I do actually feel that the first
step of telling Stuart what I want, and what I need, is something that I
now feel OK about. I think I would have felt quite frightened about
that a few weeks ago. I suppose I feel less emotionally embroiled and
a bit more self-protective really, whatever decision I make.

Following this, Maggie considered whether she might organize a meeting of Stuart's family to discuss her situation, and then at the end of the session, returned to the reformulations.

PT You don't have a copy of the reformulation do you?
TH I'll type it out for you.
PT Will you? Oh that would be great, because it would be really useful, I mean it has been very helpful to have that to think about and to agree with in some respects, and disagree with in other respects.
TH Well, I'll modify it and I'll bring it in next time.
PT About what you were saying when you got to that last bit, the domestic drudge versus the dazzling sex bomb; I don't know if there is any connection, but I was thinking that I would like to go away and think about the way in which I feel much stronger and more assertive about that one. I'd like to try to think about how that happened, what actually happened, and whether there isn't something that I can use and draw from in terms of the relationship with Stuart.
TH Like having all the parts of you in one place?

Session 5

After briefly explaining that the meeting with Stuart's family had not yet taken place, the issue of the pregnancy was raised.

TH Have you had your pregnancy confirmed?
PT No, but I am quite sure. I'm going to see the doctor this afternoon. We had a talk about it, but as with everything else with Stuart at the moment, it is pretty difficult to get anything coherent out of him. His initial reaction was that it was really overwhelming and confusing and he has been trying not to think about it, although he obviously had been. But, apart from that, it might be nice for Helen. That was as far as we had got with that. I got quite angry with him, about his concealing so much from his therapist, and I told him I thought he was sabotaging those sessions, and he wasn't talking about the things that were really crucial and were happening to him at the moment. So, I asked him to try to concentrate with his therapist on what he felt about my pregnancy so he could have something to bring back from that session which we could discuss between ourselves. I don't know whether anything will come out of that at all. My own feeling about it at the moment is, er, well, panic really! I feel very frightened about having two children reliant on me, and eventually greater restriction on freedom of movement and so on. I mean, if Stuart was more supportive, and didn't

need looking after the way he does, things would be very different. I have been trying to think about it in terms of 'If he does have some positive changes, great, that would be a bonus, but ...' Some steps have happened this week. He applied for a job a couple of weeks ago and he's got an interview for that on Wednesday. I would have predicted that he would have been unable to do that, but he did. He rang up immediately and confirmed the interview.

Maggie continued with her discussion

PT ... I think I feel quite panicky about spending the next few years with him really. What that is going to be in terms of restrictions.

TH Calling it panicky makes it sound rather feeble. Is it as simple as that?

PT [Laughs] Well, I feel a bit feeble.

TH It sounds like when you contemplate not being responsible for anything, it indicates that the only alternative is to be feeble, as if there were no other way of deciding about Stuart and the pregnancy which might be quite sensible and not necessarily feeble at all. It might be properly self-providing or it might be changing the terms. I hear you rattling across one of those dichotomies, as if not coping with everything in the whole world, then ..., which I don't think is how it has to be.

PT Yes.

TH This might be the moment to look at the Relationship Test. It does relate to all that.

PT You sent me your summary through the post. I didn't quite understand it.

TH Well, essentially what we have got here is a kind of map [see Figure 4.1], which is a distillation of the ratings that you made. It leaves some of the differences and connections out, so it is a simplified map of the way things are in your judgement. Being a map, it has territories, and round the edge you can see these descriptions which tell you the nature of the territory; for example, the top right is 'gives in' and 'blaming', and the bottom right is 'cross with' and 'controls'. On the left are all the nice, positive things, and then below is 'looks after', and above 'dependent'.

    Is that right? Now, in the map, each of the relationships you rated is located by two points. One of you-to-the-other, and one of the-other-to-you. The first obvious thing is that the lines are almost parallel, which means that the relative role you play in relation to others always seems to be the same. In your case, this points to somebody who is firmly identified with the same role, namely the need to be looking after, and not to be dependent and giving in to other people. If you look at it in detail, the relationship with your two men and your

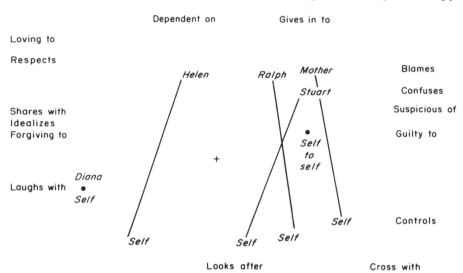

Figure 4.1 Relationship test, two-component graph, pre-therapy: Maggie

mother are very closely parallel. With Stuart, you see yourself as a little bit less controlling and cross than you were with the other two, and you are similar, but still less cross, with your small daughter. So the map does illustrate visually what we have been saying, that your central self-identification is as the one who is managing, controlling and looking after, that is where you feel you have to be, that is where you feel safe, and the alternative is to be submissive and out of control, which is what you are frightened of. So, what I am saying is that this particular pattern is the one with which you solved your particular history, but not one you actually have to stay in forever. There are other ways of dealing with people, not defined by these opposite poles, and not defined by this particular map. For example, it might be possible to look after somebody without their being submissive and dependent. It might be possible for you yourself to be dependent and loving without giving in to the other. The whole system is your own private, arbitrary one. It is quite understandable, but it is not the only one available.

The results of the test do give some other data as well. [The construct correlations.] We can see, for example, how far the different descriptions are used together, and we can compare that with the results of people in general. For you more than for most people, for example, if you see yourself as looking after somebody, you see yourself as controlling them, and giving in to them. It is rather odd that controlling and giving in go together, but it actually happens quite often.

PT Yes, very true.

TH Looking after also implies crossness, and the implications of controlling others is also very strongly to be cross; that is two standard deviations from the average. So, the test does suggest that issues around control are very central, and also that there is a lot of crossness about. When we think about your history with your mother, these particular polarizations are quite explicable, but, as I say, they don't really define the range of the possible in the whole world, and that is why we are trying to open them up.

PT Yes, I understand all that, hopefully!

TH OK, well that is stage one. How do you change? You have got an accelerated situation to deal with because you are pregnant, and making a decision about the pregnancy is related to all that stuff, and doesn't leave time to edge your way into it. A sense of panic seems to me to be an absolute reflection of the fact that if you don't accept him back, soothe his brow, understand him thoroughly, have another baby, earn all the money and upset nobody, which is what your predisposition would be, if you don't do all that, it is very hard for you to visualize how you might be. You see yourself falling into a pit of helplessness, or some quite unknown quantity.

PT Yes, that's right. Its just a big question mark, it is finding those alternative ways of being, and trying to struggle towards them, and trying to work out what they are that I find quite difficult, and I find I can't identify what they are. I can identify a few things, but that is all in my head. It is very hard to relate to them.

TH In a sense, by calling a family conference you are behaving slightly differently. You are not saying, 'I can't manage this person entirely alone', I mean (well, I don't want to put words into your mouth, but I will . . .), in a sense, one can imagine the speech you could make to Stuart, like this: 'Look mate, we fell together by mutual arrangement, on grounds that have turned out to be a bit dodgy, and the axis between us which has emerged is one which neither of us wants. It led you to a foolish infidelity, and another pregnancy, and has driven you now into a depression. In some ways, I stand to you for something which you need as much as a hole in the head, and I feel the same way about you. Whatever else was there has become focused down on this maternal control versus helpless, depressive axis, and is not what either of us need!'

PT I talked to him about this a bit last week, oh, I don't know . . .

TH In a sense, you say, 'I talked to him about that', 'I told him what to say to the therapist today', and so on, but you are still in the role, what you are not saying is 'I can't stand it, you just moon around and never do any work!' Right? Or 'You are irresponsible about the pregnancy without thinking what it means to me.' In a sense, you still can't quite get that out, you still feel that all you can produce for him is a lesson. Isn't that so?

PT   Very much so, I think, yes, very much so. I have done that before with him. I got terribly excited when I thought I had discovered the origins of quite a lot of his difficulties in something which happened to his father, and I started talking to him at great length about this, and a quarter of the way through, he did the classic thing of uncontrollable yawning. I was just imposing an idea on him, teaching what I thought was the right interpretation.

The session continued with a discussion of an episode from the previous week when Maggie had successfully made a small act of self-assertion, and then continued as follows, with the therapist introducing some transference issues:

TH   Do you think there is any problem in this room here, about occupying the chair of intelligent co-therapist with me?

PT   Occupying a co-therapist chair? I'm not quite sure I know what you mean by that.

TH   Well, you chose to come to me because you knew that my way of working appealed to you, you have joined in, have done your homework and have thought a lot about it, and you have in fact worked very hard. I am not saying it isn't genuine, but in a way the conversation can remain very safe, like we both understand this phenomenon and we can operate in a way that saves you having to acknowledge being a needy person, and having to deal with what it means to you to have to depend upon a man. After all, men are not people that you have that much respect for, or remotely intend to depend upon, right?

PT   Well, I think it is very good for me. I think one of the things I am having to learn to do in this relationship is to regard you more as someone I can talk to in that way, in an emotional way, rather than in an intellectual way. I thought about this over the last week or so, and it is actually quite helpful for me to have you as a model, or an alternative if you like. Most of the men I know, I suppose because of the way I selected them, most of them are not like that. Probably only one is, a friend of my mother's in fact, who happens to have kept in touch, but most of my male friends I have chosen, as you say, in my role as universal aunt. I suppose they recognize me as being somebody who is very attentive and good at listening, and good at picking up their needs.

TH Your early history did not in general put much trust in men staying around for you. I mean, you must have been aware of your absent father throughout your childhood.

PT Did I tell you, I think I might have done, did I tell you that, very recently really, I think it was when I was pregnant with Helen, I went for a walk, and I was just walking along by myself, enjoying the sun, it was winter, but nice clear weather, and, I don't know why, but I started to think about my father. I suddenly realized for the first time that I felt really furiously angry with him, it suddenly broke through 'Goddam you for having bumped yourself off, you abandoned me, you never even bothered to stay around to get to know me.' Those feelings had obviously been there all that time, and never got through to me at all. I think the other very strong influence is the way my mother was always rather scornful of my father. She said he was a rat and got himself in such a mess and so on, and was no good at supporting her. The model of a man that she always held up to me was that of her first husband. He was a wonderful person, exciting, wealthy, upper class, which is very important to her, looked after her and provided for her in every way.

TH But he also left her.

PT Well he left her to go to the war. I am not quite sure how that fits in. I am sure it is crucial to my relations with men, that as well, that picture of the first husband, I am not quite sure how.

TH Well, there is that sort of idealized picture of somebody perfect, but with the moral attached that they also can't be relied upon to stay.

PT I am not sure that it is an idealized picture now, but it might well have been an influence when I got married.

TH But the constant seems to me that both sorts of men go. Do you think that affects how you feel, thinking about the present situation, with Stuart being in line to be a father who disappears as well? I know that with your pregnancy with Helen he did stay and he was involved, but with this one now, you are feeling very uncertain about it. Maybe that puts you back in touch with your anger about your father.

Most of the rest of the session consisted of further talking through of Maggie's feelings about the pregnancy, and towards the end some home-work was suggested.

TH Well, in today's session, there have been a few more sentences beginning with 'I want, I feel, I think', and fewer which began with 'you' or 'he'.

PT Yes, I must hang on to that.

TH Would you keep for me next week a little two-column sheet of major conversations you have, and try to give me an estimate of the 'I feels' and 'I wants', and the ratio of these to maternal statements?

PT   Yes, OK, I will do that.

TH   You can call it psycho-bludgeon on the left and feeling statements on the right, OK?

PT   Yes, OK.

TH   I have typed out the list of target issues as we agreed, but we haven't finally discussed the timing. My sense is that another ten sessions would be about right. It won't solve everything, but it will be enough. Does that feel OK to you?

PT   Yes, that feels fine to me.

TH   Well, I'm sorry I can't wave the magic wand about all this ...

PT   [Laughs] It wouldn't be much good even if you could, I mean it is not good enough for a puritanical person like me, I have to do it myself, otherwise it is not valid.

Session 6

This session took place after a two-week gap in which Maggie had been ill. After a brief discussion of the illness, she described how she had decided she would seek a termination of her pregnancy.

PT   When I actually had to sit down and say, 'OK, what do you think it would be like to be very possibly on your own, and have to pay the crèche not only £140 a month for one, but £280 for two of them, and to have yet more of your time taken up. How would that feel?' I don't want to spend the next few years of my life just managing to cope, and having very little time for my own interests and my own friends or whatever, and I think my own quality of life would suffer. Under different circumstances, where I had masses of money, or if I had sufficient money to employ a person to do all the housework, and live in, and so on, it would be different, but I actually think in the present circumstances it would be detrimental to Helen. There would be so many hassles and resentments about it, all these calls on my time. Really recognizing the fact that although I have got this very strong pull to feel I can cope, and to have more and more people relying on me, that is actually quite destructive on other people as well. I mean, Helen is central to that. I think it would be quite destructive to her. I would be feeling very angry for much of the time, so perhaps I feel I have made this decision in quite a ...

TH   Cool and collected way?

PT   Yes.

TH   Did you have to do it more or less on your own?

PT Pretty much. Stuart was able only to say 'If I was feeling differently, I would probably give you a different answer, but at the moment I just don't feel I can really cope. I feel a bit overwhelmed by the feeling of having two children.' That was as far as we were able to go. But I am making him pay for it. I said I felt he ought to pay for it because he has just got a job, and that is quite liberating for me in all sorts of ways. I've talked to him already about when he starts earning, that he should make some contribution, either by taking over Helen's crèche fees or by buying food every week. So from that point of view he will actually be having something to contribute, which I think . . .

TH You seem to think that it is good for his character, but maybe it is quite good for you as well.

PT Yes, I said that at the beginning. It certainly does feel good for me. It feels good for me financially, and it also feels good for me in that it is going to feel much less like this enormous responsibility I return to each evening. It is like a baby bird with its beak open, needing feeding, and I think that will change, partly because of the structure of his hours, which is shift work, so one week in two he is working on a shift from 2 until 10 p.m.

Maggie then explained how the meeting with Stuart's family had not so far taken place, and continued:

PT There was one other thing which I found incredibly difficult to deal with; I was amazed and furious with myself that I found it so difficult to deal with. I spent nights having all sorts of fantasies about the fact that my ex-husband (although he is not quite ex at the moment, formally) was asked to be the witness at the marriage of some old friends, and I felt pretty bad about that, and I then went to the reception and discovered that they had been married in the morning, and they had had a private lunch party before the main reception, to which Ralph and a couple of other people had been invited. I felt so awful about it, so hurt and furious.

Maggie continued to discuss her rivalry with Ralph for their old shared friends, and her anger with him for having been supported by his parents after their separation while she was struggling financially, and also her envy of his glamorous lifestyle at the present time. She then returned to thoughts about the pregnancy and about her relationship with Stuart.

TH How are you actually feeling towards Stuart?

PT Rather distant at the moment really. Quite relieved that I am going to have more time to myself. Better really, I just feel, well, a bit more distant. I feel that I have been able to ask him for things more. The emotional things are the most difficult, and I even find it difficult asking for money, but I have found that I have been able to do that and it hasn't been terribly tricky. I still think it is going to take quite a long time to get the emotional tangles untangled, but I just begin to see it as more of a possibility. When you first sort of modeled for me what I might say to him, I felt total panic, I couldn't imagine myself saying or doing anything like that.

TH   But in some ways you have. [*PT* Mmm.] It seems you have talked quite a bit on particular issues.

PT   Yes, I think just now, from a practical point of view, his having a job helps, I don't feel in some sense that because I am fond of him it makes it absolutely necessary to have him there, even if I felt I didn't want to, because he wouldn't have any money, and he wouldn't have anywhere else to go. Which is what I did feel, justifiably or not.

TH   So he doesn't need care and protection in that way?

PT   No, right. This is one issue which on a practical level has been cleared away, which is useful. In a way, it's probably a bit of a red herring, that it's no longer around so ...

TH   Well, it's not really. It is a part of the whole structuring of the relationship that it seemed quite normal for him to stay there without contributing, and to come back after leaving you and still not contribute. I mean, that is a definition of normal which could be seen as shared deviancy. So the correction of it is something quite important. You haven't had a lot of time to feel how you are with Stuart because you had so much to deal with.

Maggie then returned to the subject of Ralph and her envy of him.

TH   Why do you think that Ralph's particular lifestyle excites your envy?

PT   It is very complicated. It is to do with lots of things actually. It is to do with the dynamics that there have been between us. Since he left, there has been a constant urging on his part for me to consider having him back, and until quite recently, I never quite clearly said, 'No, absolutely not, I will never consider this.' What I tended to say was, 'Well, no, not at this moment, maybe', you know, dangling him on a piece of string.

TH   When was that, and when did it end?

PT   Very recently.

TH   Like last week?

PT   No, it was after Stuart left, and he started coming around again quite often, and we made an arrangement to meet and have a drink and to go out for dinner together the night before I was to go off on holiday.

He just never turned up, and I learned afterwards, when I came back from holiday, that he had just been talking with someone. There was something in that — God knows why that incident in particular — I just suddenly saw that our relationship never changed, and that nothing would ever change, and that he was not any more *the* love. It was an emotional change in me, and I suddenly felt, 'No, not ever, no way.' But I am envious of his ability to star in a group, envious of it, and I hate it when we have been at parties together. I despise his desperate need to have all these people around him, but I am also envious.

TH   You wouldn't mind having the trick? Is there any reason why you shouldn't develop qualities just as appropriate to you?

PT   No, not really.

TH   But does it feel in a sense, that there is only so much to go around.

PT   No, you see I think that is why I feel better about myself. In the last few days, since I have taken the decision myself to have the termination, I am clear in my own head about what I want and what I hope my life is going to be like in the next two years. It feels like I have made a decision to give myself more space to do just that — to develop my writing again, for instance, and to build up work, and just to develop more contact with friends.

TH   So you are chosing to do things for yourself?

PT   I feel sad that I have had to make myself go through this to realize that; because it is not a pleasant experience that I have pushed myself into. I mean, I wish I hadn't had to go through such an extreme experience in order to be emotionally able to realize what I wanted and what I was doing unconsciously. But I am glad that I have very strongly realized it now.

Maggie then went on to describe a consultation with her new GP, by whom she had felt very badly treated when she consulted him about her pregnancy and termination.

PT   You are going and saying 'Please treat me as a human being'. If you are not treated that way it's quite out of proportion, quite shattering and strange.

TH   It is also a difficult role for you, the patient role?

PT   Yes, it is. Very. I couldn't really express at the time, you know, while the awful session was going on, I could not say 'Look at me for goodness sakes, as if I was a human being', or 'I am finding this really upsetting'. Instead I just sat there absolutely dumbstruck, not able to say anything of the kind, and it was only once I had left that all my hurt and anger came out. I think it would help me a lot if I was more able to do that at the time.

TH To fight back?

PT Yes, if I was more able to say to people on the spot, 'You make me very angry!' or whatever it is.

TH I'll give you some practice, I'll start being nasty.

PT [Laughs] The only person I can do that with actually is Helen, I don't know if that is significant. I am totally direct in my relationship with her, which is not always a good thing, but some of it probably is. If she pushes me a little too far, then I will flare up in a way I cannot do with anyone else. I did once have an occasion at work where I was interviewing this man, who was a graduate and stuck in some menial job, and he was making me angry and I was suddenly conscious that I had a smile on my face. I was sitting, and smiling, and nodding, and what I was actually thinking in my head was 'Christ you are making me feel very angry' and this gap between how I was seeming and feeling was really quite extreme. You know I am always in the role of understanding, which is just not always appropriate.

TH Let's just keep a note of that disjunction going for a couple of weeks. Just note the occasions when you have done that number.

PT It is all a kind of insecurity about how people will react. I feel that people will back away from me.

TH Won't love you?

PT Yes, won't love me. And yet I have the model of Diana, who I am very close to, whom I feel fonder of when she makes me feel angry, or when she is angry. I feel very comfortable because she is enormously good about expressing anger, she blows up, and then it is over in five minutes' time. So I know from my own reaction that I don't run away, and I don't stop loving her.

TH You are looking quite sad thinking about that.

PT Yes, I feel quite sad.

TH Why did the sadness come on when you were talking about that?

PT I think with myself really.

TH Do you mean sad that you have been trapped in that way?

PT Yes, I didn't want to be trapped in this mould, yes that is obviously a problem. It does feel like something fairly major. Very important in my relationship with Stuart too. I want to be able to react spontaneously, to react from a feeling inside, not always to have this sort of strait-jacket, to be this smiling, warm, all giving person.

TH You are much nicer when you are not being nice.

PT Yes I think that is right, and I am also aware that other people must feel very puzzled about my lack of angry reactions.

In the above passage, Maggie explored the feelings associated with her habitual role of attending to the needs and concerns of the other, and came to realize very directly the anger and the need denied by that role. The reformulation of her central dilemma had enabled her, or forced her, to see how actively she pursued that role, in a way which acknowledged its historical roots, and which was non-blaming. With her new understanding, she was able to experience and acknowledge her feelings in a new direct way, and with less need for defensive denial. The session ended with a discussion about the wording of the Target Problem Procedures, and when these were agreed, Maggie rated how far she felt she had changed since before therapy.

Session 7

The session opened with Maggie confirming a message which she had sent to the effect that she had had the termination. So far, she was both physically and emotionally undisturbed by that.

PT Yes, the thing I have actually been grappling with ever since I last saw you, is this business of my feelings about anger, and how to express it, or about not expressing it. It just seems that it is something I hadn't really realized at all, and talking it through, it just suddenly seems to have surfaced as something terribly important, in terms of the effect it is having on me. I have been keeping a mental note over the last two weeks about the times when I have had particular difficulty, and there were several, but one sticks out in particular. I also realized that I spend a lot of my time feeling angry, actually; it is just a sort of general, rather diffused feeling. I found that rather horrifying.

Maggie then went on to talk of an episode where Stuart's mother had been somewhat unhelpful in providing some care of Helen, being unwilling to alter her arrangements to suit Maggie's needs.

PT ...I think I am more aware now of needing people to help me, but I am not getting to the point where I can actually say, like to Stuart's mother, 'No, I am afraid I can't bring her out to you halfway through the morning, so you will please help me by coming in to pick her up!' Oh, I feel such a wimp. I think partly that is what my tearfulness is all about, I find it very difficult not to feel bad, both about current incidents, and also when I look back at all those years when I was doing this sort of thing, and I think, 'What a wimp! Why can't you just come out and say to people—"You are bloody annoying", or "Clean the kitchen floor", or, "No, I haven't got the time to bring Helen to you this morning".' I suppose then a lot of the tearfulness is anger against myself.
TII When you imagine making those speeches, what do you experience?

PT   I feel so good, I really want to be able to do that.

The session continued with further exploration of these feelings.

TH   The important shift you are facing is from being Maggie who can
        understand everybody's needs perfectly and will always manage, to a
        Maggie who is in need of some care and protection, and as a result
        feels she is a wretch or a destructive person. I think that is the reason
        it is so difficult for you. It is not just a question of changing your
        tactics, it is like a redefinition of the self, and for you, to put it
        crudely, it feels a bit like becoming your mother, becoming a bad,
        weak person, rather than being the Atlas who can carry everything.
        Do you think that is right?
PT   I am not sure. I mean it is those feelings, those extremes which make
        me react in an exaggerated way to what is in my head; quite a small
        incident can make me feel like it is something very big.

In the rest of the session Maggie described two quite successful situations of
assertion, in the first of which she had confronted and managed to persuade
her garage to remedy a badly done job, and the other in which she reported
with pleasure that Stuart had found the money to pay for her termination
(by selling some of his possessions).

Session 8

Quite early in this session Maggie reported that she had begun to take active
steps to apply for a divorce from her husband, with whom she had postponed a
meeting to the subsequent week.

PT   ... When I rang to put off this meeting, there was an absolutely
        classic reaction, a long silence, and a terribly hurt 'Well I see, yes, all
        right', almost not voiced, but clearly communicating, 'So you are
        putting it off, and putting this other friend above me?' That hurt
        reaction definitely came through ...
TH   What about this very, very long postponement of the divorce. How do
        you understand that?
PT   Well, I'm not sure actually. I understood it recently, or until recently,
        as just that this was a process I didn't need to go through. The
        marriage was irrevocably broken, and therefore I had just erased it
        with all the other painful things, and didn't feel I needed to go through
        the bureaucratic process of ending it. But I also recognize that my
        marriage going wrong was an awful failure in my life, and getting a
        divorce was putting a final seal on that. But now I am not sure,

because I am doing it myself, going about it, and so it feels different.

TH   Does the failure label still apply?

PT   Much less now I think, much less so. He doesn't feel so powerful now. I think I was very much colluding with his fantasy that one day it would be all right, and that one day we would be back together again, and it would be absolutely fantastic, it would be much better than it was before. Not that we get on so extraordinarily well now, but we have had 12 years of shared experience. Well, you know, I think I find that those last few threads are extremely difficult to let go of.

After further extensive exploration of the history of the rather ambiguous relationship with her ex-husband, the topic shifted to her daughter and her mother.

PT   My mother and I had quite an interesting exchange over the weekend. I suppose it was perhaps a typical one. She rang up towards the end of the week to ask whether we were going to see her over the weekend, and I told her that Helen had quite a heavy cold, and she was going on and on about how I should be careful in the way that I dressed Helen, and how I ought not to take her out if the weather is not very nice as she might get pneumonia, and so on, and I suddenly got very angry with her, and said 'Look, you know, I look after her very well, and if I wrap her up warm, it is good to take her out, and I take a lot of care over what she is wearing, and I don't just take her up the garden in a thin shirt, and you know that.' And I also said that it really pisses me off that every time we come to see her, almost without exception, the first thing she says is 'Helen looks really tired, she looks pale and peaky' and that makes me very angry. There was a long hurt silence when I said that, and then she said — well, she got quite angry really — 'You know, I think it is absolutely ridiculous, you are my daughter, and someone I have always felt very close to, and now I can't say what I am thinking. It seems monstrous to me that I can't be honest with you.' So I said that it did matter to me and that it did upset me that she doesn't recognize that we are different people, and while she can be absolutely upfront and spontaneous, and that might be fine with her, it wasn't necessarily fine with me if what I got was mostly negative, and I did find it upsetting, and as it made me angry, I'd rather she didn't do it. Then there was some kind of reference to my father and the fact that she had always been open and honest with people. I knew she hadn't got on well with my father, and she supposed that he was ... well, there was some reference to the fact that he liked to cover things up. Well, so we left it at that, with her being very hurt and huffy. I tried during the last bit of the phone call to get her back on a more friendly basis, but it didn't work, and then she rang on Sunday morning, when we were supposed to be dropping in to see her, to say that she was feeling very tired and shaky, and a bit weepy and a bit depressed, and she didn't think we had better come around, she said that she didn't want Helen to see her like that.

In the rest of the session, Maggie reported how she had managed to let Stuart do something for himself, and he had managed very well, and then went back to some discussion of her mixed feelings about rethinking her relationship with her husband, and generally ended quite stirred up, but feeling that there was some progress being made.

Session 9

The session opened with an account of Maggie's mother's continuing sulk, and then of her birthday, in which Stuart had actually taken the initiative to get his mother to look after Helen, so they could go out together.

PT Something about that seems quite trivial, but I think it is all an expression of the same sort of thing. On my birthday we were just setting off in the car, with Helen going to stay the night with Stuart's mother and Stuart had arranged all this, and as we were getting into the car I started to say, 'Now, have you got Helen's bottle, have you got this etc.' and he got quite cross with me and he said 'Yes of course I have', and I suddenly thought to myself, 'God! I am just like a bossy mother.' So, we made an agreement there and then, that if I did that again, and he was aware of my doing it, and I didn't seem to be, he should say 'Call a halt'; and that was nice. And he had taken responsibility for the day, and had organized our evening.

During the next bit of the session, there was a lot of discussion about Stuart, some cautious optimism about his more direct and less depressed way of interacting, and some continuing doubt about their long-term prospects, and what would emerge once that neurotic interaction was resolved. The conversation then moved on to what was happening between Stuart and Helen.

PT Yes, she is very angry with him at the moment, a lot of punishing. I mean, we talked about that and I told him what I thought was going on. When he first came back, she was a wonderful Daddy's girl. I think she was frightened he would go away again, and I think now she is getting her own back in some way. I hope it won't continue, I think it is probably quite good for her that she can express this feeling of anger rather than having to repress it and be on her best behaviour all the time to get what she wants from him. He is engaging with her a bit more. An awful lot of it is the control I have over the relationship, because I have almost total power, given these conditions, of how she relates to him, and how he relates to her.

TH So, do you mean you are using Helen against him?

PT No, but I think that I could have been. I don't think I am now. I think that that was one of the reasons he was very angry (which was coming out as physical violence before he left me). I think that I may have been doing just that before he left. I was using Helen as a kind of buffer, and closing up her relationship with me, threading it round more and more, so he didn't really fit in, neither getting in touch with me nor with Helen. I have become much more aware of that. Well, for example, it had become automatic that I always gave Helen her bath. Why should that be? There is no reason why that should be. It is a good thing for Stuart to bath her as often as possible, and for them to be together as much as possible, so I have been trying much more to ensure that that sort of thing happens. You know, a few weeks ago he would have said when bedtime came round, 'Oh, I am so tired and I am so depressed, I don't feel like it', but there is much less of that kind of reaction now. It has been a much better week really. I don't know whether it is a fluke or not.

Maggie went on to discuss her own relationship with Helen, and ways in which she was less forced to be totally involved while she was awake but could actually do other things at the same time. A transference link was suggested.

PT Yes, it was good to be able to recognize that and to feel OK about it. It makes me feel very much OK, because I am releasing a lot of myself, and I can now give quality attention, but not all the time, and to recognize that not giving it all the time is fine, so now I am giving attention in a way that I was not able to before, and that is good.

TH How has it felt to be receiving that kind of attention?

PT Receiving?

TH That kind of attention from me.

PT Oh, from you! Yes, that is very good. I was thinking about it the other week. I feel very safe. I think in the first few sessions I felt taken aback and a bit angry when the session ended, and I wanted to go on and on talking. More recently when I was thinking about it, I decided that was actually fine, and I can now come away not feeling aggrieved. That is the contract that has been set up, and I can accept that I have your full attention for the time. I am able to be an adult much more I suppose, I am able to go away feeling 'OK, thanks, I have had my hour, and now I can go away, and I can't be a child who just sits there, and says, you can't give up and make me go away.' In some ways you have made me feel more responsible for myself, and it has made me feel what Helen feels, actually, it has made me feel that I *can* get confident attention from somebody. It doesn't mean that because that attention has to be limited it suffers, or the relationship suffers. It is actually better that way. So yes, it does very much link in with what I talked about earlier. I guess, at the moment, I have got quite a long way to go on negotiating with Stuart and myself, although I don't feel like the princess and the pea anymore. The pea has disappeared, and there are lots of mattresses to fall back on to. I feel I have got much more equipment to work with now, though there needs to be more yet. There is more clarity, in terms of what Stuart and I have said to each other. I think the significant moment actually came when we were talking about my anger and about my not being able to express it, and I suddenly felt quite completely overwhelmed, and I can't remember if I ever had a male friend who I felt I could cry in front of ... I think that was a big breakthrough. I guess at the time that the emotion was fairly overwhelming, but I didn't feel, 'Oh my God, how embarrassing, how humiliating!' I didn't feel I was crawling out into reception at all. I think that has been very valuable. I suppose it is a classic thing, in a way, that it has given me a model of something as a relationship which is confined to the hour, but has shown me that it might actually be OK if I am feeling sad, or also very angry about something, to express that immediately and not to feel that I have to try to suppress it. I feel good about that.

Session 10

The session opened with Maggie giving an account of a meeting with her ex-husband which had been resolving.

PT   ... and then he got to the point where he said 'Do you want to get involved again?' I remembered what my previous response would have been, I would always have hedged around that, I would have said 'Well, I don't think there is much point for the time being.' There would always be a qualifying phrase, and an image of the phrase went through my mind, but I came up saying 'No!' and that was it. We just left the pub together, I shook his hand and that was it. I felt very pleased with myself about that.

After more discussion about her husband, Maggie went on describe how she and her mother were on equable terms again, and that things felt clearer, and also that change was still happening in the relationship with Stuart.

PT At the moment I feel much more tuned to the awareness of how to tackle situations and to get what I want in a straightforward way from people in relationships.

TH What do you feel about having a break for a few weeks or so?

PT Yes, I think I would have much more to bring to a session in six-weeks' time than I would to a session in a week's time.

In reviewing things thereafter, conversation turned to Maggie's relationship with her mother.

TH So it turns out that even mothers in their eighties can adjust to the terms being changed a bit?

PT Yes, yes, it was nice that I was able to do just that and not feel terribly guilty and just be straightforwardly angry, and the anger came from what I felt was something wrong on her part, rather than me feeling, Oh God!, guilt, which in turn produced more guilt. It was just more direct and spontaneous, and it probably made me feel much more spontaneously affectionate towards her on Christmas Day.

TH So things are nice when one is able to be nasty?

PT Yes, I think the more practising I do, the more able I will be to do that to people I care about. As regards my ex-husband, I did feel quite high when I came away, it felt like real relief. Part of my programme is to go to court tomorrow to set things in motion for the divorce. I don't feel at all like I felt after previous meetings, in terms of guilt and anger, guilt about being disloyal to Stuart because I haven't absolutely kicked my husband out, and guilt because he has made me feel an absolute swine. It is just so much cleaner, so much nicer, life is much easier without all these underground complications from the past. OK, I do still feel angry in many ways, but that is all right, I feel OK about feeling angry too, not that I am a terribly nasty person.

TH Just out of interest, what do you think were the most important things in your therapy which brought about the change?

PT I think the therapy sessions were absolutely essential, they made clearer to me things that I had almost worked out for myself really, but it is important to have someone reflecting them to you. But that was on a rather intellectual level, I think. The turning point for me was actually the session when we talked about my not being able to be angry, and my surprise at breaking down, as I hadn't realized, it was just an amazing emotion, feeling all that inside me, and being able to break down in front of you without any worries, I mean women are always crying and are uncertain, and that is fine with other women, but I don't ever think I have broken down with a male friend. Those things are actually very ... [*TH* Surprising?] Yes, it seemed to be connected with my feeling bad about myself, that business about not being able to express feelings of anger with other people. I suddenly realized what I was really feeling inside myself, what a wimp I was, surprising myself not being able to do that, but none of that actually coming properly to the surface. So, in my head, that particular session feels like something very significant.

Sessions 11 and 12

At the meeting five weeks later, Maggie reported that things had gone well, and that she was happy. She was still uncertain about the relationship with Stuart, and this was the area she felt least fully resolved. However, she felt more able to be angry, more able to think about leaving, and for that reason more able to stay. The last session took place a month later. Here she discussed how she felt a great improvement in her relationship with both her mother, and with Helen. Talking with Stuart continued to be more open, and she was having to recognize the persistent powerful tendency to take over, which she was still trying to control. She was planning to apply for a job which would involve a move; she felt that if she were to get it, Stuart would be invited to come on revised terms, including a shared mortgage. Generally speaking, she felt ready to end therapy.

Additional Material

Figure 4.2 reproduces the rating chart used by Maggie throughout the therapy. Three ratings were done, one Target Problem, and two Target Problem Procedures. (The third possible TPP discussed in Session 4 was not used.)

1. *Target Problem.* Upset in response to end of relationship. Aim: to understand better the pattern of relationships with men.
2. *Target Problem Procedure 1.* Acting as if in relation to men, having to be *either* sensitively and controllingly attending to the perceived needs of the other (as self to mother), *or* being demandingly dependent (as mother to self), chosing the former.
   Exit: being able to express own needs, to be in control of oneself, but not of the other, to establish mutual relationships.
3. *Target Problem Procedure 2.* As if having to chose between being *either* a domestic drudge, *or* a dazzling sex bomb.
   Exit: to be a person with a work life, to be a good mother, to enjoy home and, hopefully, to be a good lover to a reliable partner.

Maggie's Relationship Tests (Before and After Therapy)

Before therapy. Maggie completed the Relationship Test between the second and third sessions; the rest was analysed with the 'Ingrid' program (Slater,

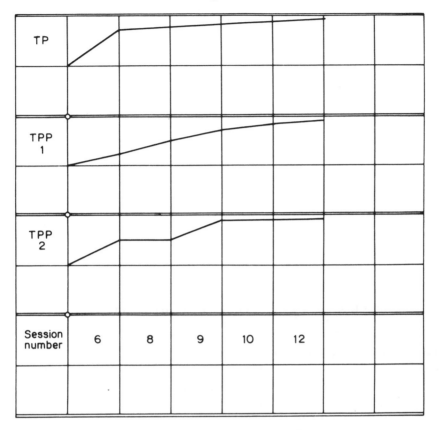

Figure 4.2 Rating chart: Maggie

1972). Her reactions to the task are reported at the start of the third session. She added six of her own constructs and chose, as her elements, relationships with Stuart, Ralph, Helen, Diana, her mother and three male friends (one an ex-lover). The 'map' derived from the first completion was given in Figure 4.1; to simplify, only the relationships with the main 'actors' are plotted. It is at once apparent that there is essentially a single model for relationships (which was repeated for the omitted relationships), in which the self is seen as relatively controlling, cross and looking after others, who are seen as relatively loving, dependent and giving in to. Stuart, mother and Ralph occupy scarcely distinguishable roles, similar to, but less positive than, the role of Helen. Only with Diana is there a really positive and mutual relationship.

A study of the construct relationships identified a number in which Maggie differed (by more than one standard deviation) from population norms. For her, more than for most people, to look after implied giving in, controlling and being cross; controlling implied crossness; depending implied crossness

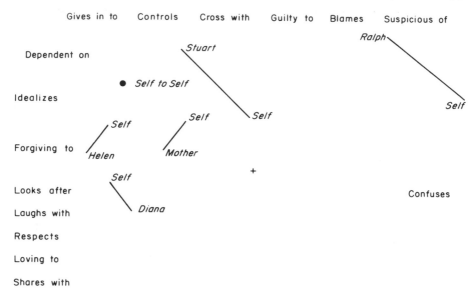

Figure 4.3 Relationship test, two-component graph, post-therapy: Maggie

and giving in. Controlling and giving in are associated. This last finding (implying that these seemingly opposite attributes are found in the same relationships) indicates serious problems in the area of control in close relationships. The link between these findings (based on a grid of self-to-other elements only) and the clinical reformulation, and topics covered in therapy will be clear to the reader.

After therapy. It was predicted that these correlations would fall as a result of therapy, in the direction of the mean, and this prediction was tested by post-therapy administration of the same test. In the event, in most cases only small differences were revealed and the majority of the associations remained in the range of over one standard deviation from the mean. The biggest changes were: (1) in the relation of *looking after* and *depending upon* — here, the correlation was in the normal range at the initial testing (but the two constructs defined opposite ends of the second principle component, as Figure 4.1 shows), but on retesting it had become strongly positive; (2) the relation of *dependent on* and *controls* moved from the normal range to the unusually associated range; (3) the same was true of the association between *dependent on* and *looking after*. In summary, Maggie's assumptions about relating are characterized by a clustering together of looking after, dependency, control, giving in and crossness. However, looking after (the role with which she was most closely identified) had become more compatible with depending on and less associated with crossness and control.

Inspection of the map (Figure 4.3) shows that, within this system, the dyadic relationships have been rearranged, in particular the relationship with Ralph is now contrasted negatively with the others and the relationship with mother has been revised and is less polarized. Overall, there is more variety in the reciprocal roles recorded.

One other grid measure may also be reported, namely the construing of the relationship of self-to-self. Many positive changes have occurred. The following changes in the angular distances between the element self-to-self and the constructs lie in the range 49–26 degrees; they are ranked from the largest difference to the least: self-to-self after therapy was more forgiving, more sharing, less blaming, more controlling, less anxious about, more looking after, more giving in to, more laughing with and less guilty.

CHAPTER 5

Complex Reformulation and Object Relations Theory

So far, the reformulation process has been described as a descriptive one, the essential task being the recognition of recurrent underlying patterns in, and the fitting of accurate descriptions to, the rich, unorganized information gathered from the patient. This approach serves well enough when one is dealing with the restrictions on choice and characteristic distortions of role seen in the neurotic patient. But as one considers progressively more seriously disturbed patients, the need for a more complex basis for understanding and describing the patient's procedures becomes increasingly apparent. In the present chapter this elaboration will be discussed and illustrated. The treatment of such patients, reformulated in this way, will be considered in Chapter 6.

To understand the difference between reformulating neurotic problems and those of personality integration an analogy may be helpful. It is as if we are born into the world with a blank map of it and with an empty book in which to inscribe the rules and instructions needed to guide us. We construct our maps and accumulate our instructions on the basis of our actual experience, but this experience is shaped, both deliberately and unconsciously, by those who look after us. The features which we record in the map and the rules that we accumulate are partly drawn from our direct experience, and this experience is heavily influenced by our parents and other adults. But our need to preserve a sense of our selves and a sense of being recognized as of value to others, which is an inevitable result of our dependency and relative powerlessness, means that our maps and rule-books inextricably combine records of fact with instructions about meaning. Moreover, embedded in our values are judgements about how far to trust our own capacities as map-makers and also instructions on how to resolve discrepancies between our own maps and those of others.

By the time we are adults, we have usually acquired a fairly stable map of reality and a relatively consistent set of rules; however, none of us has fully

96

mapped out the possible extent of our world, due both to the inevitably partial nature of our own particular experience and to the acquisition of some restrictive rules. The neurotic person differs from the normal in having a quantitatively greater amount of such restriction; large areas of the map are labelled as deserted or dangerous or forbidden, and the routes he follows are often dead-ends or circuitous or are arbitrarily and narrowly selected from the variety of possibilities. Moreover his trust in himself as map-maker is to some degree shaken and he remains more bound by rules concerned with safety than inspired by the wish to explore. These patterns of self-reinforcing limitation, of falsely narrowed options and of the extensive closing off of the world of the possible are described in the prose reformulation of neurotic dilemmas, traps and snags. Such reformulations challenge the arbitrary restrictive rules and empower the individual to explore reality anew, revising his maps and altering the rules he has hitherto relied upon.

In the poorly integrated personality, however, the problem is more complex. The same neurotic features may be recognized in it, but in addition there is a discontinuity between states. It is as if there are now a number of fragmentary maps rather than one defective one. Within the territory defined by each fragment, the procedural rules may be more or less effective or they may show more or less marked restrictions or distortions of the kind found in the neurotic map; but there will be numerous occasions when the map fails and will be replaced by an alternative, often contrasting, fragmentary version. When this happens the terrain suddenly appears unfamiliar or very different and the guide-book describes quite different dangers, requirements and possibilities. Reformulation of the poorly integrated personality requires some mode of describing these partial or fragmentary maps and some way of uniting the guides to the various versions of the self and of reality. Only in this way is there some chance of forming a new construction whereby the individual can be guided by an integrated map and a coherent set of rules. In the present chapter methods of achieving this will be considered.

Object Relations Theory and Reciprocal Role Procedures

One main source of this discussion is object relations theory. This development in psychoanalysis is particularly concerned with the impact of the infant's earliest years on personality structure and patterns of relationship. The language of this theory, and the theoretical disputes between protagonists of different versions of it, have made this a somewhat inaccessible field. An account of the main issues covered by the theory in terms of the procedural model will now be presented. Good accounts of the theory and its developments and divergencies will be found in the following psychoanalytic texts: Fairbairn (1952), Guntrip (1961), Sutherland (1963), Edgecumbe and Burgner (1973), Friedman (1975), Ogden (1983). A more theoretical discussion of object relations, restated in terms of the procedural sequence model, will be found in Ryle (1982). The aim here is to provide an accessible account and to relate this to the reformulation process; after this some practical ways of applying the model will be suggested.

The basic procedural sequence whereby intentional or aim-directed action is organized, is maintained by a repeated, circular sequence which goes through the internal (mental) and external (behavioural) stages discussed in earlier chapters. To rehearse these, the sequence is as follows:

1. Aim definition (maybe in response to an external event).
2. Evaluating the situation and one's capacity to act in relation to it.
3. Relating the aim and the situation to systems of memory and meaning.
4. Anticipating the consequences or pursuing the aim or role and its compatability with other aims and values.
5. Choosing the means for pursuing the aim from a range of available sub-procedures.
6. Action or role-performance.
7. Perceiving the effectiveness and consequences of the action.
8. Confirming or revising the procedure and pursuing or abandoning the aim.

When we consider interpersonal behaviour, this process has particular characteristics in that *to anticipate the consequences of our own role behaviour we must predict the reciprocal role behaviour of the other, and in perceiving the consequences of our role behaviour we must evaluate the responding role of the other.* Hence it follows that to pursue a relationship satisfactorily we need to understand *two* role procedures and be able to match them correctly. Procedures for organizing relationships are therefore called *reciprocal role procedures*, or RRPs for short.

Object relations theory is concerned with these procedures. It is clinically particularly valuable in understanding couple interaction and the transference–counter-transference between patient and therapist. The particular power of object relations theory is that this understanding is linked with a model of development and of personality structure. Both individual personality and the patterning of interpersonal behaviour and experience are seen to be formed from the same early infantile experience. As with most of psychoanalytic theory, this model is based on a retrospective reconstruction of infancy, elaborated to make sense of material produced in the analytic treatment of older individuals, but the account can be framed in ways which do not contradict parallel understandings from other sources, such as attachment theory (Bowlby, 1969), the work of Mahler and her associates (Mahler, Pine and Bergman, 1975) and current cognitive and developmental psychology.

The Infantile Roots of Reciprocal Role Procedures and the Structure of the Self

The infant's earliest post-natal experience is under the control of an immature central nervous system 'programmed' to organize attachment behaviours that elicit and mesh into the mother's care-taking behaviours. Over the early years, on the basis of this earliest self–other relationship, increasingly complex reciprocal role procedures are elaborated, but these inevitably bear some of the traces of the form and limits of the infant's particular experience, notably his extreme dependency, and his immature but developing capacity to shape and make sense of it.

The first discriminations necessary to conduct a life as an individual are built upon the basis of bodily experiences. The earliest cognitive tasks are to tell inside from outside and body from not body; even these discriminations may be lost in adults in psychosis. The discrimination of self and other follows, but this development involves a *satisfactory integration of what is originally a range of separate discrete experiences of the other*. The earliest experience of the mother will not be of a whole person; a small infant first develops a range of RRPs in which he plays, for example, the needy or satisfied child to the providing mother, the excited child to the stimulating mother, the compliant or protesting child to the controlling mother, the deprived child to the abandoning mother, and so on. These discrete RRPs are the foundation upon which later integrated RRPs for relating to whole others will be elaborated. The acquisition of these partial RRPs already requires the understanding of *two* roles, one played by the self and one by the parent. Hence, a version of the parental roles must be 'internalized' and in due course the individual can play not only his own but also this other role, being able to enact either child-derived or parent-derived roles in subsequent relationships.

The building up of reciprocal role procedures at this stage is accompanied by the development of a sense of the self, and of a relationship with the self. In due course, we can recognize in the individual a parentally-derived 'I' (often verbalized by toddlers in self-instructions), which variously cares for and controls a child-derived 'me'. Hence the child forms procedural models (1) for relating to others and (2) for self-care and control on the basis of the same parent–child interactions. In his relationship with himself he may identify either with the parent's or the child's 'voice', and in relation to others he may enact either the parent- or the child-derived role, seeking to elicit the reciprocal role from the other. In the subsequent experiences of childhood and later the degree to which these primitive RRPs are flexibly integrated, and the extent to which a more independent, more widely derived sense of self and other is elaborated, will vary, but none of us lose entirely the stamp of our earliest patterning, or fully integrate its conflicting elements.

How Dilemmas in Neurotic and Personality Disordered Individuals Differ

To oversimplify, dilemmas of the neurotic patient usually show signs of his being restricted to a limited model of parent–child interaction, where certain of the original range of discrete RRPs have been emphasized, undeveloped, distorted or repressed. An example of this would be the case of Maggie, described in Chapter 4, in whom anger and the direct expression of need had been largely inhibited. In other cases particular interactions may have become the dominant pattern; for example, an individual who has learned harsh controlling parental procedures may crush spontaneity in himself and be a critical bully of others. Typical neurotic dilemmas, therefore, will be: (a) between parent- and child-derived roles, as in *either* controlling caregiving *or* submissive dependence; (b) between crudely polarized responses to perceived parental roles, as in *either* defiant *or* compliant; or (c) between crudely polarized parental roles, as in *either* ideally caring *or* abusive. The neurotic individual is characterized by deficient or costly patterns of self-care and control, and by failures of mutuality in relation to others.

Borderline Personality Organization

The dilemmas of patients with poorly integrated personalities, however, are different, representing failures to integrate the full range of discrete RRPs into a whole sense of self and others, with the persistence of separate sub-systems of procedures or sub-personalities through each of which the world is differently experienced and action is differently organized. 'Patients with poorly integrated personalities' refers to patients who display those forms of personality organization characterized as borderline according to the structural criteria proposed by Kernberg (1975). Holzman (1978) described borderline states as heterogeneous, characterized variously by affect storms, infantile clinging, histrionics, extravagant acting out, sexually perverse behaviour, scary feelings of disintegration, unreality feelings, paralysing obsessive states and waves of projective thinking leading to temporary paranoid states. He places these states on the continuum proposed by Menninger (1977), of which *level two* contains the neuroses in which life is curtailed by costly compensatory devices, *level three* is the borderline level marked by regression, *dys*-organization, disequilibrium and the escape of dangerous impulses, and *level four* is marked by the abandonment of reality of psychosis. The exact definitions and limits of these categorizations of neurosis and personality disorder are a matter of controversy; in reality we are dealing with a continuum between integrated and unintegrated personality structures. Within the borderline group are included the descriptively derived categories of histrionic, sociopathic and narcissistic personality disorders (Pope *et al.* 1983). The latter is characterized by grandiosity covering self-contempt, often expressed (projected) in contempt for others.

Patients with serious personality disorders experience their lives as discontinuous and fragmented, and they are also experienced as such by others. They suffer not just from an instability of mood and behaviour but may switch from one state of mind and one sense of the world and the self to another. In object relations theory this is the result of splitting, which is conceived of as a defensive intrapsychic process whereby the destructive and valued aspects of the inner world are more or less stably separated and are invested in different aspects of the self, of reality and of others. Such people will operate with polarized judgements, their angels have the habit of falling to join the predominant demons populating their world and they know no middle ground. The uneasy co-existence of such opposed senses of self and other is associated with the pattern of relationships described as *projective identification*. This is a process whereby, in a given relationship, the conscious pattern of reciprocal role relating is accompanied by an alternative, less consciously operating system. The equivalent reciprocal roles may be elicited from the other in respect of both the conscious and alternative, possibly unconscious, procedures. Relationships based on matching at the two levels and marked by mutual projective identification are likely to be unstable due to the emergence of the alternative pattern; both individuals will contribute to and share the experience of discontinuity and switching.

I would argue that a relationship characterized by projective identification does not differ essentially from any other relationship, in that it is based upon the successful matching of reciprocal role procedures. By projective identification, however, is usually implied the operation of the reciprocal role procedures derived from a split-off, incompletely acknowledged or denied alternative version of the self. To relate on this basis requires that the other offers, or can be induced into providing, the appropriate reciprocal split-off partial version.

The roles sought for, or elicited from, the other may represent (a) aspects of the self that are discounted, devalued or denied (for example, childish, needy or weak) or (b) aspects that are mistrusted and destructive (for example, persecutory or controlling). In both these cases, the other person is being induced to carry negatively valued attributes. However, precisely the same process can occur with positive attributes, as when (c) idealized forms of power and care are projected into the other. These positive roles may represent a defence against destructive feelings or a compensatory fantasy, elaborated out of what little care was actually received by the individual in his earlier experience.

According to object relations theorists the defensive function of projective identification is that it reduces conflict within the self. However, the projection of need into the other, with the self playing the reciprocal caretaking role, may deprive the person of any ability to have his own needs satisfied. The projection of persecutory or controlling aspects of the self into the other leads to guilty submission and the acceptance of the other's destructive behaviours. The projection of ideal caring qualities into the other leaves the self depleted and prone to extreme possessiveness and to massive disillusion. The extent to which these procedures are defensive, that is to say the extent to which they reduce anxiety or preserve a continuing sense of self, seems doubtful. More fundamentally, projective identification can be understood as a loss of discrimination between self–self and self–other procedures, and as the enactment of unintegrated, sometimes unacknowledged, partial procedures.

In all of us, but most markedly in those with poorly integrated personalities, the parentally derived RRPs tend to be caricatural, being invested with more absolute power than was present in the parents in reality. This is so even when adolescent separation has been satisfactorily achieved and when the contemporary relationship with parents is more or less realistic. This caricatural internal parental pattern is matched by the persistence of child-derived RRPs which reflect the weakness and dependence, or the omnipotence, of the child rather than the reality of the adult. These primitive, child-like procedures or intentions can in turn provoke, within the self, retaliation from the caricaturally harsh parental internal procedures and can lead to the establishment of patterns of self-limitation, guilt and self-destruction. It is a sad fact that the child victims of abusive parental behaviour are prone to repeat abuse in their self-care and often in relation to others. But it is also a sad fact that some children, out of their childhood omnipotence and incomplete understanding, respond to adverse life events or to quite modest degrees of parental overcontrol or rejection with exaggerated self-blame.

Most individuals with poorly integrated personalities have developed a dominant pattern of interaction which may seem relatively normal and effective. It is useful to conceptualize this as the *survival strategy* or *coping mode*; it usually represents a role of limited emotional force which worked well enough in the individual's original family context or which gained recognition at school. In most cases, however, the narrowness or cost of this survival strategy is apparent, for example, in patterns of extreme competitiveness or over-compliance, in emotional blunting or in the distancing of a schizoid personality, in the need for grandiose self-inflation and for contempt for others in the narcissistic personality, or in the persistence of self-denying care-giving, characteristic of the deprived 'parental' child. The RRPs characteristic of the split-off, less conscious and less acknowledged sub-personality systems are likely to be more obviously primitive. The parent-derived roles will often be split between extremes of persecutory harshness and abuse on the one hand and powerful care-giving on the other, the child-derived roles being correspondingly rebellious, crushed or punishment-seeking on the one hand or seeking of idealized care and fusion on the other. These more primitive destructive RRPs become the dominant patterns in people showing sado-masochistic and perverse behaviours, in addiction and other forms of self-harm and in the antisocial personality.

An Aid to Complex Reformulation: Reciprocal Role Analyses

In order to recognize phenomena we require a conceptual framework. Applying the ideas discussed above to the understanding of patients can be aided by the use of a simple form designed to record individual patterns of self-care and control, and of relationships. The reciprocal role analysis sheet (see Figure 5.1) lists parental roles on the left, and more-or-less reciprocal child roles on the right. To use this sheet to think about an individual, lines are drawn across to indicate the reciprocal roles described by the individual in his past and present emotionally significant relationships. Dominant self-to-self patterns of relationship are also included. For relationships which are described in split ways (or for which split-off aspects are hypothesized), two such lines can be drawn. From the accumulated pattern of the lines of the significant relationships, the individual's dominant RRP structure can be identified. In cases of splitting, the reciprocal roles will tend to cluster at the top and the bottom of the diagram, with the 'good enough' area being empty.

Case Example: Maureen

Maureen, a woman aged 32, presented with a complaint of sexual frigidity, depression and numerous psychosomatic symptoms of some years' duration. From childhood onwards she had been supportive of her mother whom she still idealized. She had also looked after her younger siblings and still gave much practical and emotional support to them and to her friends. Her mother, however, had failed to protect her from childhood sexual abuse which she had suffered from a neighbour and a cousin. The patient had married a man from a different culture in her late teens; she and her husband had separated repeatedly and they were currently apart. During one of these separations she had had another relationship; she had sex with this boyfriend but experienced it as being raped. There were two children, the son, aged five, was described as a caretaker, getting her tea and asprins for her headaches; the daughter, aged 18 months, was described as a tyrant.

Figure 5.1 Reciprocal role analysis sheet

These relationships are summarized in Figure 5.2. One can see in this a pattern which can be described verbally as a split dilemma between the idealized relationships at the top and the conflicted ones at the bottom. (*Either* idealized fusion *or* conflict and abuse.) In the lower, conflicted, half two neurotic dilemmas can be identified, both between parent- and child-derived roles. The first could be described in summary as: it is as if in a relationship the choice lies between *either* rejecting dependency, *or* submissive care giving. The second one could be described as *either* abusive, *or* a victim.

The way that the roles are dispersed in the reciprocal role analysis sheet provide a simple reminder of the varieties of adverse childhood experience and of the resulting structure of the individual's internal reciprocal roles. The idealized fusion fantasy at the top may combine elements of compensatory fantasy based on care received with a defensive fantasy covering up

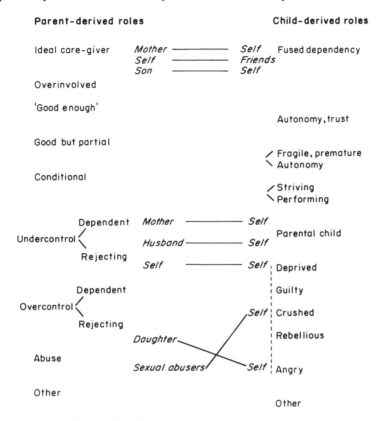

Parent-derived roles   **Child-derived roles**

Ideal care-giver   *Mother* ——————— *Self*   Fused dependency
                     Self ——————— *Friends*
                     Son ——————— *Self*

Overinvolved

'Good enough'
                                              Autonomy, trust

Good but partial
                                              ╱ Fragile, premature
                                              ╲ Autonomy
Conditional
                                              ╱ Striving
                                              ╲ Performing

        Dependent   *Mother* ——————— *Self*
Undercontrol ╱   Parental child
        ╲   *Husband* ——————— *Self*
        Rejecting
                    Self ——————— *Self* ┊ Deprived

        Dependent   ┊ Guilty
Overcontrol ╱
        ╲   *Self* ┊ Crushed
        Rejecting
                    Daughter   ┊ Rebellious

Abuse
                    Sexual abusers *Self* ┊ Angry

Other
                                              Other

Figure 5.2 Reciprocal role analysis: Maureen

hostility. Below this are located the (intrusive, indirectly hostile) parental behaviours which deny the child separateness. In this sense the top and bottom of the list can be seen to be close and a circular model could be envisaged. The next region represents the Winnicottian concept of 'good enough' parenting, and this is followed by the common, relatively minor distortions of parenting that lead to everyday neurotic difficulties. These merge into more extreme varieties of parental hostility and neglect, and thence into frank sexual and physical abuse. In patients of borderline structure it is usual to find the reciprocal role procedures located at the top and bottom of this chart; this represents the common pattern of splitting into the dominant sub-personalities, one idealized and one violently conflicted, each potentially or actually manifest both in patterns of self-care and control and in relationship patterns. Simple structural diagrams of borderline and narcissistic personality structures ('broken egg' diagrams), are given in

Figures 5.3 and 5.4. While narcissistic personality structure is essentially similar to other borderline states, the weak and destructive aspects of the self are defended against by (a) grandiosity and the seeking of admiration from idealized others and (b) by projective identification whereby others are dismissed as weak and the self is contemptuous of them. In borderline personality disorder the defence is less successful. Idealized relationships are based upon fantasies of perfect care and fusion rather than admiration, and the roles enacted in conflicted relationships are those of abusing and abused (which may include elements of contempt). In both conditions, abuse or contempt of the self may take place. In borderline personality organization the breakthrough of unintegrated extreme feeling states may occur, but the narcissistic individual is characteristically out of touch with deep feeling. These diagrams serve to emphasize that the task of therapy is integration.

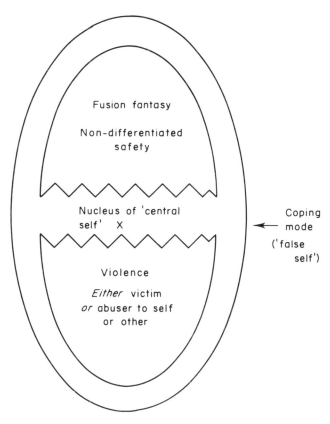

Figure 5.3 Diagrammatic reformulation: borderline personality

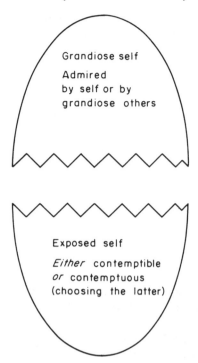

Figure 5.4 Diagrammatic reformulation: narcissistic personality.

Sequential Diagrammatic Reformulation (SDR)

The different states described in the verbal reformulations, reciprocal role analysis sheets and diagrams serve to characterize both self-to-self and self-to-other relationships. Relationships or relationship episodes in patients with poorly integrated personalities need to be understood in these terms. The therapist working with a patient of this sort will often experience bewildering switches between the different states, expressed through the patient's speech, demeanour and behaviour and, more subtly, experienced by changes in the therapist's own feelings. These counter-transference feelings represent the therapist's 'reverberations' to the attempt being made by the patient to elicit reciprocation to a particular role. The therapeutic response, of course, is to recognize but not to reciprocate. The power and subtlety of these invitations can be considerable, which is why therapists need to be unusually self-aware and self-observing. The task of resisting collusion is, however, much simplified if a satisfactory model of the different states is available.

Verbal descriptions and structural diagrams are only partially helpful here. If, however, each of the patient's different states can be identified in terms of the relation to self and to others (reciprocal roles), of the access to feeling, and of the dominant mood or symptoms in it, then the therapist can build up an accurate account of the patient's discrete states and can identify the transitions between them. In this process patients can play a part both in careful description and analysis of their different states and in learning to recognize and record state transitions. This kind of data can be represented by a diagram which, as well as being of value to the therapist, provides a basis for the patient to develop a self-observing and self-integrating capacity. This fuller form of reformulation, therefore, describes both the states and the transitions between the states, identifies the state sequences and permits monitoring of factors which trigger state changes. Such reformulation represents an analysis of structure and change similar to, and in part derived from, the retrospective 'configurational analysis' developed by Horowitz (1979) in his study of transcripts of psychotherapy sessions. A sequential diagrammatic reformulation (SDR) developed at the start of therapy represents a precise and powerful tool guiding the therapist in his interventions and offering to the patient a basis for a fuller control and integration of the self.

In patients for whom SDR is most appropriate it is usually the case that one can identify a *core state* which represents the unresolved residue of early experience which has been neither integrated nor fully repressed. This core state commonly includes elements of unmet needs, sadness and destructive feelings which relate to deprivations or adversities experienced at the time of life when the child was unable to control the situation and unable to deal with the feelings aroused by it and also by parentally derived critical or abusive elements. In the adult, the procedures adopted can often be seen as attempts to remedy this state but also as a means of avoiding fully experiencing it. These individuals' experiences of life are constricted by this avoidance, whether by means of schizoid distancing, by symptoms representing false solutions, or through impoverished or conflicted patterns of relationships to others.

In constructing the SDR diagram it is usually helpful to start with this core state, naming the more prominent feelings attached to it if these have been defined. Unacknowledged, possibly repressed feelings may be hypothesized and written in brackets. The internal relation of parent- and child-derived aspects may be indicated within the core state. Initially, however, it may be enough to write 'unmanageable feelings', and these can be differentiated as therapy proceeds. In most cases the individual will have developed one more-or-less satisfactory method of coping in the world which can be labelled the *survival* or the *coping mode*; commonly this represents a competitive striving for success or an interpersonal pattern of compliance. These procedures usually go back to childhoold and were originally a means of surviving situations confronting the individual. In addition there may be other interpersonal procedures which are often best described in terms of the traps and dilemmas enumerated in the Psychotherapy File, and finally there may be symptomatic procedures. In addition to these procedures one may identify snags whereby any pleasurable or successful procedure tends to be stopped or undone. Snags seem to represent the action of a split-off, destructive, self-sabotaging element derived from the core state. These diagrams depict how the individual seeks to escape from his core state through these various procedures. The procedures in question, however, do not achieve the aim and plotting the subsequent experience of the individual following such procedures demonstrates how they end up by confirming or reinforcing the negative core state.

These diagrams have three main functions in therapy. For patients they represent a new and often startling understanding of the recurrent pains and distresses which they are suffering. The effect of this can be profoundly stabilizing on patients who have been quite markedly disturbed and it very often makes treatment enter a far more constructive phase. Moreover, the diagrams, once elaborated, provide a very satisfactory basis for the patient's self-monitoring. The diagram can be used by patients between sessions and by therapists in sessions, being used to make sense of the experience during the week since the last session and of the events of the session itself. The third function is to aid the therapist in his use of the transference and counter-transference. For this purpose it may be helpful to construct a corresponding counter-transference map so that the responses evoked by the different states the patient is prone to go into can be quickly recognized. The rest of this chapter consists of examples of the impact and use of sequential diagrammatic reformulation; further examples of their use in treatment are given in subsequent chapters.

Case Example: Beatrice

Beatrice, a 24-year-old nurse from another hospital, was referred from the Accident and Emergency department after a Paracetamol overdose. She gave a history of frequent self-poisoning with increasing doses of Paracetamol, and also of some episodes of self-cutting. She had been a binge eater for some years, but had not resorted to purging or vomiting, and she had also had 'binges' of overspending and was currently markedly in debt.

Two Target Problem Procedures were agreed in this case. The first:

> If you are involved emotionally you quickly feel out of control, both doubting yourself and also getting in touch with your early feelings of sadness and anger, so you tend to withdraw. The choice

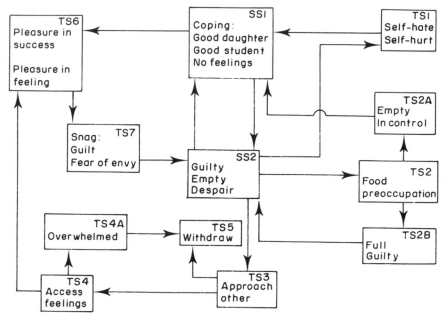

SS – Stable State; TS – Transient State

State	Mood	Self	Other	Description
SS1	Shallow	Painless coping	Role defined Manageable	Survival strategy
SS2	Despair	Self-blame Bad	Out of reach	Inner state
TS1	Hate/Hurt -relief	Bad-blank	No other	Guilt + relief
TS2a	Empty/Control	-SS1	No other	Bulimic dilemma
TS2b	Full/Guilty	-SS2	No other	Bulimic dilemma
TS3	Anxious	Boring	Critical	Social anxiety
	Self-critical	Unattractive	Rejecting	Social anxiety
TS4	Intense	Alive	Intense	Access to deep
	Confused	Confused	Mixed	feeling
TS5	Relief	Self-critical or blank	Safely distant	Retreat
TS6	Pleasure	Happy	Accepting	Taste of
	Delight	Alive	Respecting	life
TS7	Crushed	Disallowed	Critical + envious	The snag

Figure 5.5 Sequential diagrammatic reformulation: Beatrice

has become polarized, as if you have to choose between being *either* involved, and out of control and upset, *or* distant and lonely. To overcome this we will try to deal both with your unreasonable guilt and self-blame and your difficulty with sticking up for yourself and help you get through facing the feelings that come from the past.

The second TPP:

> You act as if you were so bad that any pleasure or success that is acknowledged has to be discarded or paid for; for example, the way you walk out of the room when music you really like comes on the radio, or the depression you felt when you were promoted. While this stops you feeling irrationally guilty it leaves you feeling hopeless and empty. We will need to learn to recognize these self-sabotaging and self-destroying tendencies and challenge them.

The understanding conveyed in this reformulation was extended over the next sessions and finally a sequential diagram was produced (Figure 5.5). This clarified how the different states were maintained and connected and indicated which points therapy must address if more positive states were to be achieved and sustained. The diagram describes two more-or-less stable and fundamental states, the defensive, coping one and the underlying bereft one, and a series of transient states. For each of these stable and transient states, descriptions were worked out jointly; these are summarized in the figure.

This example illustrates the use of SDR to work out a complex pattern of behaviour which presented considerable problems for the therapist, in so far as any kind of closeness caused withdrawal and any kind of success was dismantled.

The following case history emphasizes the containing effect of SDR on a very disturbed individual.

Case Example: Steven

Steven, a 34-year-old man, was referred from a local advice centre. He was seen in a research project where he was allocated to eight sessions only. He was suffering from anxiety and anger linked with the fact that he had recently fully remembered his history of childhood sexual abuse by his father, which seems to have commenced during his third year, or possibly earlier. This had been accompanied by physical abuse. He had run away from home in his early teens and had ended up as a male prostitute, a life from which he had escaped some five or six years before his referral.

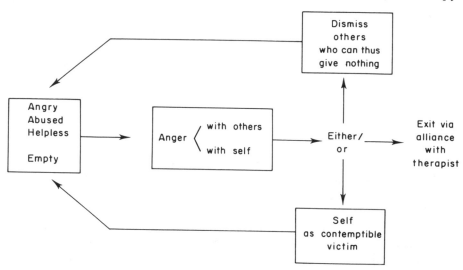

Figure 5.6 Sequential diagrammatic reformulation: Steven

During the first five sessions of his therapy Steven failed to complete any of the tasks set (these included monitoring his physical symptoms and reading the Psychotherapy File) and he spent the greater part of the sessions being either overtly angry or scornful of his male therapist. He was given the verbal reformulation: 'it is as if I *either* abuse people, *or* I get abused'. This did not have any impact upon him, and by the end of the fourth session the therapist was feeling fairly ragged. At the fifth session the provisional SDR (Figure 5.6) was presented to him; this produced a change that astonished both the patient and the therapist. Rather than expressing contempt and anger he began to work at understanding his history, and for the first time felt he had some control over the very disturbing experiences. This was reflected in his managing a difficult negotiation concerned with his attempts to get retrained. At follow-up after a two-month interval this new attitude was still evident, and further sessions were agreed.

The next case example describes the use of SDR in a patient with a narcissistic personality structure.

Case Example: Sheila

Sheila, a 32-year-old junior executive in an expanding company, consulted because of an awareness that her life was not satisfying. At the end of four sessions the following prose reformulation was agreed:

Dear Sheila

Over the past weeks of therapy you have gained some awareness of your need to intellectualize your daily problems at home and at work in order to avoid the much deeper pain of feeling unloved and rejected, which you experienced as a child. At this stage of therapy we need to address this core pain of rejection in order for you to understand how the strategies you used then to cope with rejection have become your day-to-day problems.

The experience of rejection makes you feel unloved, worthless and humiliated. Your mother, domineering and harsh, humiliated you by making you kneel in front of her whenever you challenged her authority. Your father was lazy and uninterested in you, and although affectionate was liable to have episodes of violence; he also ignored your academic achievements and called you stupid. You were, in particular, humiliated in comparison to your older sister whom your father always favoured and said you ought to imitate.

Your early experience of humiliation now makes it feel as if the chairman of your firm undermines your authority and as if those under you are determined to make you feel that you are not the boss. The lecturers at the college where you are going make you feel scared and insecure. You chose your last boyfriend for being upper class but then you felt stupid in relation to him. The humiliations and rejections often make you perform: to faint, to exaggerate, to feign illness, to hold dinner parties to impress people, all in a vain attempt to gain love and affection; however, you then become contemptuous of your need to conform, you see that you are attempting to make up for what you see as your inadequacies. So, trying to deal with past rejection, you now think and act in ways that confirm your perception that you are bad and therefore unloveable and deserve to be humiliated and rejected. Often you act as if you have to reject and humiliate others before they reject and humiliate you, so you often become contemptuous of other people by seeing in them all the bad things you see in yourself. Everybody you talk about is liable to be dismissed as weak, lazy and stupid. As a result of this behaviour you become isolated, which further confirms the feeling that you are bad and contemptible, so bad, for example, that you can even imagine that you might contaminate other people just by using their lipstick.

The problems we need to work at can be summarized as follows: I act as If I am *either* a punishing contemptuous performer, *or* I am punished and treated with contempt for being weak, lazy and

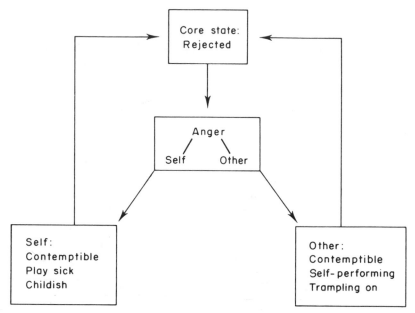

Figure 5.7 Sequential diagrammatic reformulation: Sheila

stupid. Aim: To become less hard on myself and other people in order that I might experience giving and receiving love.

Related to this, in relationships I act as if I must *either* trample upon people, *or* be trampled on by them. Here I need to explore the kinder, unhumiliating, uncontaminating, unrejecting world so as to get in touch with the kind, unhumiliated, uncontaminated and rejected world inside.

This prose reformulation was supplemented with the SDR (Figure 5.7). The patient continued both in and out of the sessions to alternate between the different states described in the SDR but became progressively less concerned to perform and more able to feel. It will be noted that this SDR is similar to that of the previous case, Steven, and seems to represent the basic structure of many borderline patients.

The next example describes how a patient's development of her own diagram was the means of finally mobilizing her treatment co-operation.

Case Example: Gabrielle

Gabrielle was 32 years old when seen, by which time she had a long history of bizarre behaviour and symptoms. Currently, her symptoms included extensive obsessive rituals and a residual eating disorder, which had been more severe in the past. She had spent three years as a vagrant but was now living in a hostel and was about to start a new job, which was causing considerable anxiety. Her background is well summarized in the prose reformulation:

Dear Gabrielle

The purpose of the therapy so far has been to assess the areas of difficulty in your life and to discover in what way you would like them to change. You describe an existence that is barren of all emotion other than fear and sadness. You suffer these emotions whenever you participate in activities in the real world and you imagine that the only solution is to isolate yourself, avoid all contact and, in effect, become a non-person. Fortunately there is still a part of you that wants to be a part of the world and feels that it deserves a chance to exist. It is this part of you that keeps trying and risks the anxiety and sadness. Further problems arise from the patterns of behaviour which you developed in response to your family situation.

In your childhood you were isolated from normal relationships. After the death of your father you lived in the household of three generations of lonely and embittered women. They appear to have employed a system of scapegoating, attacking the youngest in the group. It seems that whilst you were a child your mother was the scapegoat and suffered all the bitter and twisted remarks and attentions. Once you reached puberty it seems that you were unable to escape this fate yourself, and even your mother, with whom you had previously been allied against the others, turned against you. Your family seems to have expressed only anger and envy: anger at the position in which they found themselves and envy that the young might possibly escape their fate. Sadly your mother could not resist this system and turned her anger on you. Your description of being beaten by her after a tantrum when you were only seven years old, and your acknowledgement of the fear you felt in that situation, helped explain why you eventually determined that the only safe way to exist was to withdraw and become a non-person. Yet even that was not to be allowed. Your withdrawal provoked even more anger in the family, because they felt more justified in their attacks and berated you with your wicked ways. Your increased anxiety from which there was no escape led you to develop your rituals of absolute control in your daily life, which were a means of proving to yourself that at least there was something that you could achieve yourself. Your abnormal eating patterns also started around

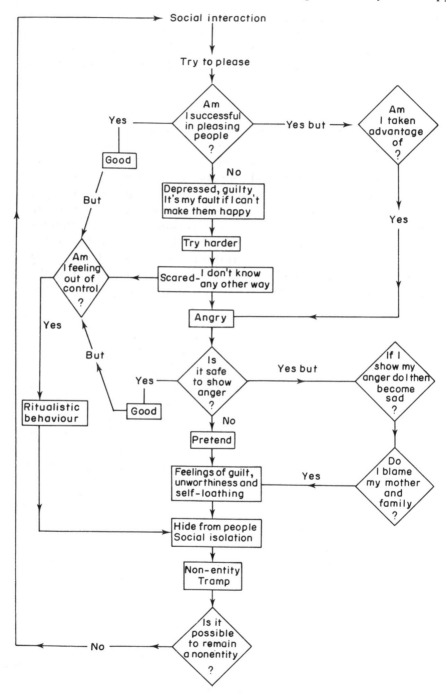

Figure 5.8 Sequential diagrammatic reformulation: Gabrielle

that time. Ten years ago, once you had completed your studies, you ran away from home and forsook all the controls that had been placed upon you. By being a tramp you were at last able to lose control away from the anger of your family, but it also meant that only by being a nobody could you escape from, and make up for, the hate you felt for your mother.

The anger that you feel towards your family is very frightening to you. You have witnessed and experienced uncontrolled anger and stuggle always to dam this in yourself. Any situation that allows you to feel justified in your anger has to be accompanied by a session of self-punishment in case the anger should emerge. Perhaps this can only be solved when you can acknowledge that the deserving you is strong enough to overcome and control your rage. If you once believe that, you might even feel safe to visit your family once more.

This patient had entered therapy with a good deal of scepticism and an understandable reluctance to commit herself to it, given her history. Following the prose reformulation, the therapist spent a session with her elaborating the beginning of a sequential diagram, although the sequences at that stage were not clearly worked out. The patient returned to the next session having re-ordered this and placed at the centre of it a state called 'is it safe to show anger'. It is of interest that when the therapist's first draft was discussed in supervision the seminar had suggested the need for more emphasis on the problem of anger. The patient's own map consisted of the vertical axis of Figure 5.8; the elaboration of this diagram in the sessions consisted of completing the loops which demonstrated to the patient how her attempts to get away from her anger led only to its reinforcement (see Figure 5.8). In later sessions, discussion of this diagram and of the prose reformulation revealed the necessity of identifying different 'lenses' through which her experiences could be construed. These were (a) her mother's, (b) those of the child her mother wanted her to be, and (c) those of her precarious adult self, which therapy aimed to strengthen.

SDR can be of value in the termination of treatment as the following case demonstrates.

Case Example: Angela

In this eight-session therapy the sequential diagram was of value in mobilizing appropriate termination feelings. Angela, aged 24, had consulted with depression and a morbid preoccupation with an abdominal scar. The scar was a focus for her negative self-image and her own difficulties in accepting sexual intimacy. The relation of these symptoms to her neurotic procedures

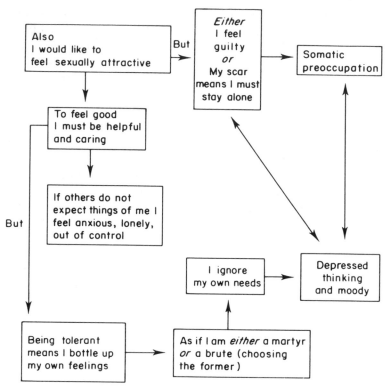

Figure 5.9 Sequential diagrammatic reformulation: Angela

is demonstrated in the SDR (Figure 5.9). She came to the sixth session having for the first time failed to carry out her self-monitoring. She did not accept that this was linked with the impending end of therapy, assuring the therapist that she had no bad feelings. When the SDR was referred to, she could see how she was once more bottling up her feelings to protect the other. She was reminded of her earlier painful losses, especially her father's mental breakdown when she was 13 and her mother's frequently demonstrated propensity to forget her, something which started on the occasion when she was left in the garden in her pram for many hours 'being a quiet baby'. The SDR was again used to show how this early bottling up of feelings always led on to depression, and she was able to remain more emotionally engaged during the remaining sessions.

In the following chapters further examples will be given of the use of SDR in the treatment of a number of different kinds of patients.

CHAPTER 6

Treating Patients with Personality Disorders

The classification of individuals as normal or neurotic, or as neurotic or personality disordered, depends upon somewhat arbitrary distinctions being made along what is essentially a continuum. In simple terms, a neurotic is a relatively coherent individual whose sense of self and safety is maintained at the cost of diminution; the spectrum of possible action and experience is dimmed in certain segments. The personality disordered individual, while also having diminutions, shows in addition a greater degree of extremity, inconsistency and discontinuity in his behaviour and experience, often with areas of a more massive defensive blocking out of aspects of his nature.

Classification and Features of Personality Disorders

The DSM-III classification suggests three groups of personality disorders. The first (paranoid, schizoid and schizotypal) may be seen in mild forms by psychotherapists, but are relatively rare. The third (avoidant, dependent, obsessive-compulsive and passive-aggressive) are quite common, but blend indistinguishably into the neuroses where their characteristics are common enough features. Patients in the middle group, however (the borderline histrionic, antisocial and narcissistic personality disorders), are encountered in many settings.

According to most psychoanalytic writers (e.g. Kernberg, 1975) a basically borderline structure is common to all the patients classified in this last group. Psychoanalytic understandings of personality structure are based more upon patterns manifest in therapy, particularly in the transference, than they are on descriptions of observable behaviours, but the descriptive features and the analytical constructions show a reasonable match. Many schizoid patients, behind their withdrawn defences, show similarly organized patterns. Most of the patients to be discussed later in this chapter demonstrate features of borderline personality organization.

This underlying structural similarity can be understood in terms of the object relations developmental theory discussed in the last chapter. The early discriminations made by the child are fragilely established and the process of integrating the disparate role procedures governing early inter-actions with care-givers is incompletely achieved. This is manifest in splitting (polarization of judgements and role behaviours) and in projective identifi-cation (a pattern of reciprocal role relating based on the mutual elicitation of unconscious or disavowed aspects of the self).

As indicated by the examples of sequential diagrammatic reformulation presented in the previous chapter, this picture can be understood structur-ally in terms of the following: (a) a core of primitive feeling variably accessible to consciousness which the individual attempts to contain or avoid by a range of procedures; (b) by an underlying division in this core between an idealized fusion-seeking or grandiose part and a violent abusing/abused part; (c) by self-referent behaviours reflecting this division — for example, omnipotent fantasies, the seeking of fusion experiences through drugs, or by attacking the self with drugs, alcohol or self-cutting, or manifest in snags whereby success or pleasure is sabotaged; (d) by interpersonal modes reflecting the central divisions — for example, primitive idealizations, grandiose admir-ations, seeking ideal fusion versus violent or contemptuous interactions, or by divisions in each part — for example, *either* ideal care-giver, *or* perfectly cared for, *either* victim, *or* aggressor — or in costly procedures in which care is sought through self-diminishing procedures (e.g. placation); (e) the con-fusion engendered by emotional exposure may be avoided by various degrees of schizoid withdrawal. This is compatible with successful (coping or survival mode) performance in role-defined work situations. It may be accompanied by the elaboration of symptomatic transformations or evasions of emotions as in obsessive compulsive states, eating disorders, atypical pain or other sickness behaviours; (f) the experience of discontinuity (state shifts), a frag-mentation of the self which occurs in borderline disorders, and frequently leads to depersonalization and derealization, symptoms indicating a loss of a coherent grasp on reality and on the self. Accompanying symptoms in some states may include the full range of neurotic disorders especially diffuse anxiety, phobias, fugues and amnesias. Uncontrolled outbursts of anger or weeping and temporary paranoid states may occur. Other personal procedures may be manifest in perverse forms of sexual behaviour and in antisocial behaviour.

In psychoanalytic writing, splitting and projection are seen as having a defensive function. The term 'object relations' refers to interactions between autonomous or semi-autonomous agencies in the mind, some of which are ego-derived and some are object-derived. These agencies are seen as being capable, in some sense, of interaction — caring, attacking, envy, etc. — and splitting and projection are seen to be the means whereby the destruction of positive elements is prevented. In the restated terms proposed within the PSM, the reciprocal role procedures for self-care and control and for relating to others are seen to have evolved in parallel and both bear traces of the original division of roles into those that are parent-derived and those that are child-derived. The complementarity between parent and child roles and the contrast between split, polarized versions of possible parent–child patterns occurring in poorly integrated personalities, can be expressed as dilemmas, as considered earlier. An individual will, at any one time, be identified with one or other pole of the perceived polarized roles available in the terms of his dilemmas. The capacity to feel coherently in oneself will be aided if the polar alternative is denied or if another can be elected to play it, and in that sense splitting and projective identification are stabilizing and reduce uncertainty and anxiety. However, equally, or more importantly, they represent serious restrictions and confusions in the perception of the self and others, and failures to discriminate between self and others, the result of which is considerable anxiety as the individual is confronted with discontinuities, and loses the sense of self as being in control and in a predictable relationship with the world. Many of the symptomatic features of borderline states (e.g. depersonalization, diffuse anxiety, amnesias) reflect this discomforting experience.

The battling internal objects of Kleinian theory ['innumerable independent micro-organisms that are also micro-dynamisms' as Schafer (1968) wrote] are, I believe, a confusing and unnecessary theoretical construct, representing the characteristic psychoanalytic vice of reifying processes, of making theoretical constructs out of fantasies, and of focusing attention on primitive mental functions while neglecting higher-order integrative processes. It is, moreover, hard to see within this theory how the infant is defended by his projecting dangerous persecutory aspects of himself into the care-giver on whom he most depends. However, while unsatisfactory as theory, these ideas relate to real observations; in dreams and fantasy the split, disorganized roles of the poorly integrated individual are often personified and may do battle with each other. In the course of therapy, a home must be found for all of them, that is to say, the higher integrative capacities of the individual must be strengthened so that adequately flexible and coherent role procedures may be developed.

Causes of Personality Disorder

In the majority of cases of severely personality-disordered patients there is a clear history of major and prolonged childhood adversity, often including gross physical and sexual abuse, and associated with alcoholism, sociopathy and other severe disturbances on the part of the parent. In other cases, less severely pathological parenting can be seen to pay a part, the child's self-definition having been curtailed by parental needs. For example, separation may be delayed by parental hostile over-protection or dependency, or the child may have been seen as an extension of the parent, required to perform in order to gratify the parent's narcissistic needs. In some patients who have not suffered gross adversity one may postulate other causes for early failures of integration; sometimes a history of disruption of care through illness on the part of the child or the parent, or through the early arrival of siblings, suggests that the child developed early on a 'survival mode' (false self) involving emotional distancing, which prevented the normal subsequent integration of feelings. The contribution of innate genetic factors is hard to assess, but clearly variations in the intensity of emotion are recognizable from birth. The concept of 'ego weakness' represents little more than the recognition that integrative functions have failed, for whatever reason; it seems less likely that this capacity would be genetically determined.

Treatment of Patients with Personality Disorders

The majority of personality-disordered patients do not receive any effective treatment, and in many cases, treatment agencies compound rather than cure their difficulties. This is a direct result of the nature of the disorder; the inconstancy, self-destructiveness and extremity of feeling displayed by these patients confuses and exasperates most professionals. Some workers may respond, for a time, with deeply felt concern to the evident neediness and suffering of these patients only to be confronted before long by extremely dependent behaviour or by angry disappointment. Others, from the start, are wary or explicitly rejecting, doubting the sincerity of the suffering, appalled by the emotional indifference or cruelty evident in the patient's treatment of themselves or others, or frightened by the extremity of the need expressed. Only a very small minority of these patients reach psycho-therapists, and those that do are considered to need prolonged and skilful therapy. Initially, according to most recent writers, this should be supportive therapy rather than classical psychoanalysis. Such treatment is only rarely available in the public service.

Personality-disordered individuals are seen in many different contexts, depending on the dominant expression of their difficulties. Much of the statutory and other work of social workers is concerned with supporting these patients, or with defending vulnerable others from them. Courts, prisons and the forensic services will receive those whose dominant expression is in antisocial behaviour. Those who are primarily self-destructive may end up seeing mental-health professionals in drug or alcohol dependency settings, or after admission to Accident and Emergency Departments following self-cutting or self-poisoning. Some, often as a result of the relatively common accompanying depressive illness, end up in psychiatric care. In none of these contexts are they very likely to receive any consistent, long-term care directed towards the underlying personality problems, although some may receive valuable containment. Often, as suggested above, they are likely to evoke collusive and ultimately rejecting and hostile counter-transference responses.

Whether or not long-term psychoanalytic treatment is appropriate or effective for such patients remains, to my mind, uncertain. However, our understanding of these patients owes a great deal to psychoanalysis. In any case, such treatment is for the most part impracticable and this fact has contributed to the general air of hopelessness about any kind of therapeutic intervention. It is here, I believe, that CAT has a contribution to make.

In essence, the therapeutic approach to borderline type patients with CAT follows the same general rules as those observed in treating less severely ill patients, being based on the early establishment of an explicitly collaborative working alliance and upon the achievement of an effective reformulation. The time limit represents a safety-net for both patient and therapist, guarding against the emergence of malignant destructive transference−counter-transference relationships, so easy to set up by inexperienced therapists with these powerful patients. What, however, is surprising to therapists from psychoanalytic backgrounds is the possibility of rapidly establishing an effective working alliance. Even these severely damaged individuals usually have the capacity to observe and reflect upon themselves, given the opportunity and the tools. (Therapists from non-psychoanalytic backgrounds seem largely unaware of the pitfalls and difficulties of treating these patients, and general psychiatrists often underestimate the difficulty and assign them to junior staff for 'a bit of support'.)

The main tool in the CAT treatment is reformulation, and particularly for these patients sequential diagrammatic reformulation. This has three functions. First, it turns out to have a powerfully containing effect on many patients, sometimes to a dramatic degree. The diagram, worked out over the first few sessions, gives visible evidence of being understood. Even the usual form of these diagrams for these patients, in which all arrows out from the central primitive and painful core state end up by returning to it, is strangely comforting, offering an empathic understanding of how it is that the patient has not been able to change. Second, the SDR represents a firm basis for the therapist's understanding of the patient's structures and state shifts and for his accompanying counter-transference. For the trainee this is an excellent educational experience, and for all therapists it offers a prepared awareness of the likely shifts, which is of great value, enabling recognition and containment to be offered reliably and quickly. Third, the SDR, even more than the verbal reformulation used with the majority of patients, provides a basis for explicit learning in the post-reformulation stages of therapy. Work may need to be done on specific neurotic procedures, especially if they influence the therapy, such as may occur with the placation trap or the 'if I must then I can't/won't' dilemma. But the main aim of the work with these patients is to aid integration, to build up an observing eye, that can contribute to the formation of an integrated 'I'. This is best done by diary-keeping, aiming to record the different states and the shifts between them and (especially where the patient is not able to do this, as is not infrequent) by the *meticulous and repeated use of the SDR* in the sessions. The diagram should be on the floor or table between the patient and therapist, and as external events are described or as shifts occur in the room their location on the diagram should be indicated. This needs to be done on every possible occasion, which may mean referring to the map two or three times during a session. Only in this way can the patient begin to take on board the new superordinant view of himself upon which integration depends.

We will now look at some examples of CAT applied to personality-disordered patients.

Case Example: Terry

[Evidence of personality disorder included compulsive gambling, alcohol abuse, a history of promiscuity, a submissive abuse-accepting relationship, social withdrawal and phobias.]

Terry, a 29-year-old man, presented with a number of problems. In particular he described very frequent panic attacks, with tremulousness, sweating and tachycardia and difficulty in breathing. The panic attacks came on in relation to closed spaces, especially in tubes and buses, and they started with the precipitating thought that he was about to have a blackout. He also reported a problem concerning choking, usually occurring in social situations, also initiated by thoughts of choking. He complained of general tension, anxiety and depressed mood, difficulty with concentration and pessimistic thoughts about the future. Terry had a long-standing gambling problem, spending up to £100 a week on fruit machines and being in debt to the tune of £1500. He was also a heavy drinker.

Terry was currently employed as an administrative clerk but he was finding the job boring. This was a recurrent problem for him; he had frequently changed jobs and had rarely found any job satisfactory.

He was in an unhappy, unstable, at times violent, homosexual relationship which he was finding difficult to terminate. His lover also had many psychological problems. This was Terry's second non-casual homosexual relationship.

He had had a very difficult and painful childhood. He was the second youngest of a family with many problems. Three of his siblings had psychological problems; a brother had a 'nervous breakdown' with depression, a sister had panic attacks and depression, another brother was dependent on drugs. His father was a chronically unemployed alcohol drinker who was violent towards Terry's mother and Terry himself. He recalled many quarrels and scenes of violence during his childhood and described how he waited every evening with fear for the impending arrival of his father and the following fights. He had tried to oppose his father but had failed. At school he recalled having been a very anxious, shy, withdrawn child who was looked down on by his schoolmates, mainly because he was a late developer. He had never had any sexual relationships with girls.

Terry was treated for 16 sessions. These sessions are summarized by his male therapist as follows:

Session 1

Having described his problems (depression, panic attacks, drinking, etc.) he started talking about his difficulties in relating to others. He agreed that perhaps the difficulty with other people was the origin of the symptoms. He said that he felt that he could not cope alone with life; he needed someone on whom to depend. His difficulty in terminating his unhappy relationship with his lover was linked to this. Asked what he expected from the therapy he answered, 'A friendly, relieving chat, nothing more.' He was sceptical about the future because his problems were numerous and unsolved.

Session 2

There was a discussion about drinking and gambling. He said that the drinking helped him to relax and to feel self-confident. The gambling gave him the hope that he 'will win', that he 'will succeed'. However, afterwards, he felt more anxious, blamed himself and was more depressed. The relation of drinking and gambling to his lack of confidence was pointed out and he agreed that lack of self-confidence and feelings of inferiority were the main long-standing problems, which he tried to solve with drinking and gambling. Whilst speaking about panic attacks and choking he recollected a scene from his childhood when he woke up and saw his father gripping his mother around the neck; she was choking and having difficulty in breathing.

Session 3

He came having failed to do the self-monitoring which we had agreed in the first session. He said that he had thought of cancelling the appointment because he didn't know what my reaction would be, saying he felt like a student who had not completed his homework and was afraid of the teacher's reaction. He could not confront this possible situation and he thought that it would be better to withdraw. It was pointed out that this was not a teacher–student relationship and that he had shown his characteristic wish to withdraw instead of to confront and take responsibility. Thereafter he completed his self-monitoring to the end of the therapy.

Terry went on to describe close similarities between his lover and his father. Just as he had felt scared every night waiting for his father's return, unable to escape or intervene to change the situation, so in the same way he waited anxiously for his lover's return. He felt that someone else determined his way of living and not himself, feeling that if he took responsibility for himself, he would end up alone. Being alone made him initially calm and relaxed but that lasted a short time, after which he again became anxious and depressed. It was pointed out how he equated responsibility with loneliness; To be with others meant to be at their mercy, out of control, while to be in control and take responsibility meant to be alone.

Session 4

From his monitoring it was apparent that on one particular day of the week he had a lot of anxiety. At first he said that he could not remember anything, but soon he started to describe an event at his office; there was a discussion in which he did not participate, dominated by a man who was very popular, extroverted and very confident. When asked how he had felt during the discussion he said that he had felt a little angry towards this man because he was very noisy and also because at other times he made jokes about homosexuals, but he also felt a little jealousy, wishing he could be like him and able to express and support his opinions. However, he was too afraid of the reaction of others. Asked what would be their reaction he could not say at first, but then he said that perhaps the others would find his remarks stupid and then they would laugh at him and he would feel humiliated or perhaps they would answer with violence as his lover used to do. At this stage his Psychotherapy File was looked at and the reformulation and map presented. With this it was traced out how his past (schoolmates who looked down on him and laughed at him) had left him unconfident and how as a result he didn't participate in the discussion at work, didn't support his opinions or express his anger. He then felt isolated and anxious, which in turn led to more under-confidence and then again to more anxiety.

Reformulation.

> Undoubtedly you went through very difficult and painful experiences from your early childhood. From early on, through your family life you assumed that relationships with others meant to be at their mercy. Your father's drunken and violent behaviour created fright-

ening scenes which left you waiting with fear every night for his return home. Neither yourself nor any other member of your family could intervene to change or control this situation. So you learnt that relationships and involvement with others entailed violence, abuse, giving in to others and not being in control of your own life. The behaviour of your schoolmates who looked down on you and laughed at you reinforced this position.

The sensation of being out of control and at the mercy of others made you feel very angry towards them but they were powerful and frightening. You also became self-blaming, under-confident and inferior. It also created a sense of tension which led to panic attacks, feeling depressed and non-assertive, which in turn augmented the feelings of under-confidence and inferiority. Another result was that you avoided responsibilities and would not finish things that you had started (remember our discussion about changing jobs); everything appeared to depend upon chance, as though your life was a gamble.

Drinking and gambling ('I believe that I will win, based on chance') give you short-term relief but finally create more tension, anxiety, self-blame, under-confidence and inferiority.

The other pole of the control dilemma, trying somehow to be in control, is to keep away from people and not be involved with them, because as you told me to be in control and to take responsibility is synonymous with non-involvement. This, however, isn't helpful or relieving, making you feel alone and unloved, rejected, under-confident, inferior and then tense, depressed and more under-confident. These patterns have repeated constantly throughout your life, as you have told me, and you are experiencing them at the present time in your relationship with Michael.

It seems to me that the main dilemma of your life is: *either* involved with others and abused, giving in, looked down on, out of control and at their mercy, *or* uninvolved and in control but alone, unloved and rejected. You use up most of your internal 'energy' struggling hard and painfully with this dilemma. However, as you have already begun to realize, there are other ways of going about life than this entrapped one. You can be the master of your own life and assertive (as you have found in the discussion with Michael and your friend) and equal in your relationships; you are the captain of your ship and need not be at the mercy of the wind.

Session 5

He came saying that this week, after the discussion of the previous session, he had felt more comfortable and was more sociable at work. He had participated in some discussions and generally felt less isolated. That satisfied him.

Session 6

He started by saying that this week had been a bad one. The first four days he had felt very well but then he had gambled (losing £30) and also drank, and on the next day had had a panic attack on the tube. Asked why he had gambled he said that he was going to buy a pair of shoes and could not find the shoes that he wanted in the shop. Next door was a shop with fruit machines. He thought that he would only put in £1 but (as was obvious) went on to lose all his money. The evening before the gambling Terry had quarrelled with his lover who had insisted on cooking for and feeding him, as a result making him eat more than he wanted. He had felt angry, but had said nothing, and then had felt guilty because both of them had gone on to drink too much. The events of the two days were then related to the SDR (Figure 6.1). He saw how, through giving in (eating more than he wanted), he felt inferior and unconfident and then angry. This had led on to self-blaming and to further feelings of inferiority, which led him once more to give in (he had not bought the shoes because his lover said they were too expensive). Giving in also made him feel angry but not expressing his anger made him feel tense, which he sought to relieve by gambling and drinking, but this only gave short-term relief, being followed by self-blame which led once more to feelings of inferiority and non-assertiveness, followed by depression, tension and the panic attacks which he had experienced the following day.

He said that he realized that he was repeating a circle but that he felt that it was difficult to break the circle especially given his difficult relationship. He felt that he had taken a step backwards and was angry with himself and disappointed. He was encouraged to see how he could learn from his errors. In the remaining part of the session Terry described a quarrel with his mother of a very similar pattern, and talked about how his father had always preferred his brother and denigrated him, especially after he had confronted him about his drinking. That experience had made him feel that to be assertive was bound to lead to rejection.

Session 7

This week had been better despite some 'bad' days. On Monday afternoon he had felt depressed, finding his work boring. He thought that he was 29 years old doing this boring job while all his schoolmates were more successful than him. During the lunch break he gambled (losing £30) and did not return to work. However, the next day he decided to manage the situation differently; he went to work and had a discussion with the manager, asking

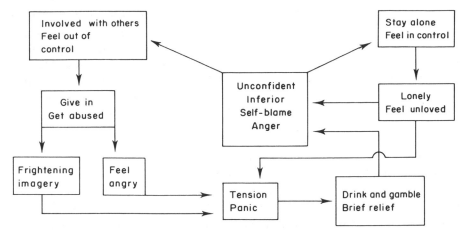

Figure 6.1 Sequential diagrammatic reformulation: Terry

for a transfer. The manager said that this could be done in the future. Terry had felt more relaxed and satisfied. This sequence was discussed, with reference to the Psychotherapy File, looking at the depressive trap, and how from a depressive thought (feeling that he couldn't succeed in comparison with his schoolmates) he had decided to gamble and after that to abandon his job. The reformulation and the SDR were considered, demonstrating how, through feelings of inferiority and depression, he had been led to gambling which offered him a temporary relief but which finally led to self-blame, further feelings of inferiority and to the decision to abandon his job. This sequence was a repetitive pattern in his life, manifest in his frequent changes of jobs, his not finishing things that he had started, and his avoidance of responsibilities. Now, instead of following this vicious circle he had been more assertive and had achieved a better practical result and a better sense of himself. He went on to describe how he had angrily responded to being teased by a girl at work, but how he had later felt guilty; the importance of not returning to the old pattern of suppressing feelings was underlined. At the end of the session, Terry said that he realized that he had changed because he felt more relaxed and had much less urge to gamble or to drink. However, he felt a strange feeling; even when relaxed, the tension was there, as if it were not possible to live without tension. He felt as if he was forbidden to change, or as if a divine power was observing him and was not satisfied with his change.

Session 8

He said that despite some stressful events it was quite a good week. He had an intense quarrel with his lover who had decided to visit his parents and had wanted Terry to go with him although he knew that Terry hated these visits. Terry refused to go and they quarrelled but he stuck to his guns. He was pleased but he felt a little tense and then went out alone and gambled. He then felt trapped, guilty and anxious as in the past, but these feelings were not so intense because he had managed not to spend all of the money he had on him. It seemed that he had been afraid of a possible violent reaction when his lover returned, which had made him feel angry but also nervous and tense. These events were related to the reformulation and the SDR: this time he had not given in, but in response to the frightening idea of his lover's possible reaction he had felt tense and had then gambled, an act which offered him a temporary relief but led him again to self-blaming and feelings of inferiority and then back again to tension. However, at work he had felt comfortable, he had not found it so boring and had been more talkative, and he was very pleased with that. He attributed this change to his behaviour of the previous week when he had decided, instead of abandoning this boring work, to discuss the possibility of a move to another position with the manager. Instead of being isolated and afraid to express his opinions he had found the alternative (to be assertive) and had gained both emotionally and perhaps practically, as the manager promised to arrange a transfer.

Session 9

He said that this week had been horrible. He decided to leave his lover, and told him so, but surprisingly the response was fair, not violent or angry. Then his lover proposed that they went out for a drink to a pub as friends. There, everyone completely ignored Terry and he had spent the evening completely alone. He felt that he had no friends and would remain alone and felt that he would not be able to tolerate the loneliness. For the next two days he had felt terrible (depression, tension, panic attacks) and had not gone to work; he had decided to stay with his lover. He spent his time drinking and gambling. He felt guilty because of that and angry with himself because he had failed. All the improvements of the previous weeks had disappeared and he thought it was not worth continuing the therapy because after ten weeks he was still the same. It was pointed out that this was only a question of some 'bad' days and that it was depressive thinking to overgeneralize from only a few days to the whole of his life and to ignore all the 'good' previous weeks. He accepted that and said that for a couple of days he had in fact been better, but today, when the time of his appointment was approaching, he had started to feel anxious. His feelings about the therapy and the therapist were further explored. At first he said that he felt that he had failed and was worrying about the therapist's reaction. Asked if there was something more, he said that he thought that the therapy didn't help him and that he felt a little angry. Expressing these feelings was helpful but he was worried about the therapist's reaction. He was told that therapy is part of life and that it would be unrealistic to have only positive feelings in the therapy with all the negative feelings remaining in life outside of therapy. Some earlier memories came up at this point, about how his father had turned his affection on to his younger brother after Terry had confronted him about his drinking, and how he had felt abandoned. From this, the end of therapy was discussed. He felt depressed, anxious and pessimistic about how he would manage his life without the therapy. Referring to the re-formulation, a link was made between his decision to leave his lover, his experience of loneliness in the pub and the experience of the therapist's recent holiday. These had all combined to make him feel unloved and rejected, then unconfident and inferior, and then depressed and anxious with panic attacks. However, the choice of drinking and gambling as a relieving solution had once more proved unhelpful, and had in fact reinforced the problems as had been seen in the past. Terry said that he realized that therapy could not be endless but interrupted the therapist saying 'I understand I will have the ideas of the therapy with me.'

Session 10

He said that at the weekend he had been alone again but the way he had felt had been completely different. He was not terrified by the loneliness and had tried to think of how he could have a good time. He thought of visiting a friend and did so, and had had a really good time. Going through the SDR he saw that he had not tried to relieve the loneliness at any cost but had found an alternative, whereas the previous weekend, being scared of the loneliness and feeling 'unloved' had led to the perpetuation of the vicious circle.

Sessions 11–16

He reported a discussion with his lover who had accused him, saying 'Now you're OK and have solved all your problems you don't care for me.' Terry had explained 'I have not solved all my problems but the difference is that now I am aware of them and I realize the real causes and have learned to handle situations differently in alternative ways. It is possible that I will make mistakes but I've learned to try to think and explore why I felt or behaved like I did.'

In the remaining five sessions Terry reported how he had coped with some return of the feelings of inferiority in the context of a new evening job and how he had survived some stormy scenes with his lover, despite being trapped by the need to pay off some debts before finding new accommodation for himself. He was apprehensive about living alone for the first time in his life, and wished he could have the support of therapy during that time; he knew, however, that he was less scared and more confident than in the past.

Follow-up

At follow-up, three months after therapy, Terry showed a remarkable improvement. He had retained the things that he had achieved during therapy and had improved further. He had stopped drinking and gambling altogether and reported that this was the first Christmas that he had saved money. His anxiety and general tension had also disappeared. His panic attacks occurred considerably less frequently and were of diminished intensity. They still occurred on the tube but he was able to cope with them.

He now felt much more sociable and pointed out how the attitudes of others had changed towards him as a result. He now received invitations to social gatherings at which he felt quite comfortable. He felt this to be satisfying but also explained that he now realized that he wasn't in fact an extrovert, that was not his character, but even so he was very pleased with the change.

He had renegotiated his relationship with his flatmate and they were now living together as friends, peacefully and more equably. He was feeling more confident in expressing and supporting his opinions (especially at work) compared with the past, and he had made some plans for the future, thinking about training at college. He remembered a lot of things from the therapy in detail.

Case Example: Linda

[Evidence of personality disorder included severe personal restriction and the repeated acceptance of being the victim of abuse; she could be seen as an example of dependent personality disorder.]

Linda, a 28-year-old woman, presented with several psychological problems. She complained of lifelong depression, manifest in a loss of interest and energy. She found it very difficult to cope with her daily duties as housewife and mother. She had thoughts of unworthiness and inferiority, and she suffered from poor sleep and physical tiredness. She reported that she felt uncomfortable in social gatherings, either avoiding them or staying withdrawn when she participated in them. She felt unable to show affection to other people including her husband and her daughter. Partly for this reason her husband had left home some weeks previously, although they still had contact.

Linda was the third of four children (two brothers, one sister). Her mother left home when she was four years old because she had met another man, and Linda had few memories of her, although she remembered vividly the day she left home after an intense quarrel with her father. Her father became alcoholic and violent, unable to care for his children, so Linda was brought up by her uncles and aunts. She has terrible memories from this period and cannot recall any good ones. One of her uncles abused her sexually (fondling her breasts and her genitalia) from the age of six until the age of nine. She did not mention this to anyone because she was afraid of his reaction as he also used to beat her without any substantial reason. She was abused physically by other relatives as well. She remembers with bitterness that she did not receive any physical affection or any presents during her childhood. She also had largely bad memories of her time at school, where she had no friends and where her schoolmates looked down on her and laughed at her because she was skinny and wore dirty and old clothes.

She left home when she was 17 years old and soon after became pregnant during a casual relationship. Then she met another man with whom she cohabited for two years. This was a terrible relationship with enormous violence and humiliation. He was a criminal who spent much time in prison. During a period when he was in prison she met her present husband and they started to co-habit. For a short period they had a good relationship but soon after he too became violent and on many occasions left home for other women. They have a son who is aged eight years. Two years ago, during a quarrel, he beat her very badly, fracturing her jaw. Since that time he had stopped the physical violence but she described him as very domineering, treating her as a child and wanting her to follow all his rules and desires. She tries very hard to please him putting aside her own needs and desires.

Linda was treated for eight sessions. These sessions are summarized by her male therapist as follows:

Session 1

She talked about her avoidant behaviour concerning social gatherings. In some instances she goes to social gatherings but feels uncomfortable and does not participate in the conversation, remaining withdrawn. She feels that if she were to say something the others would find it irrelevant or stupid and then they would think her ridiculous. Sometimes she is ready to say something but she hesitates and tries to think carefully whether it is worth saying. Then she feels anxious and usually her second thought is that it is not worth saying. At the end of the gathering she is usually in a bad mood and jealous of the others who are talkative and confident. The similarities of this situation to that at school when her schoolmates looked down on her and laughed at her was pointed out.

Session 2

She reported that she had remembered something relevant to the discussion we had last time concerning social gatherings. She has a friend who is very self-confident, sociable and assertive. Everyone likes her. She wants to be like her but feels herself to be the opposite. She sees her frequently, which she doesn't really like but feels unable to refuse to see her, because if she did her friend would reject her and she does not want that. She feels inferior in comparison to her and sees that the problem is the same as that which occurs in social gatherings, her sense of inferiority. It is the same with her husband. She has always felt inferior, as if she is down and other people are up and that they push her down (she made a gesture to demonstrate this). I said that she always seems to put aside her own needs and desires and follows the desires of others, and how this is unhelpful because it leads to depression and also confirms her sense of inferiority. She agreed with that. I asked her how she felt at that moment and she said that she felt tense, but that that was normal as she always felt tense. I suggested that we could find alternative ways of coping with her life.

Session 3

This session was cancelled twice, the second time without leaving any message. She refused to see any connection between the cancellations and her feelings towards me, and said that she had not written anything in her diary because she felt lazy. She then spoke about something she had written in her diary the previous week: 'I need someone to hold me.' She said that she felt like that because she did not believe that she could cope with life on her own, she felt so under-confident. This was the reason that she tried to please others, as was discussed in the last session. Then I asked her about the expression of her feelings. She said that she doesn't express her feelings; for instance, if she is in a bad mood and has some visitors she will give the impression that things are all right. When asked about her anger she said she never expressed it because she is afraid how others might react. Asked to define what that reaction might be, it emerged that she feared rejection or violence; she reported feeling terrible when recalling scenes with her father and her husband; they were vivid and unforgettable. I reminded her that during the first session she had told me that she also felt very angry towards her mother because her mother had abandoned her. She said that she still felt angry even now, but did not express it directly, only indirectly, when meeting her mother very rarely (her mother had only reappeared in her life when she was sixteen). When asked about expressing her anger directly, she explained that it's terrible to behave angrily towards your own mother because she might be hurt, she might get angry and you would be the cause of her anger. It seemed that she was avoiding expressing her anger because of fear of violence or rejection, but also because of the belief that her anger would be the cause of something terrible happening to others. However, not expressing her feelings meant that she did not feel OK and she was obliged to give in. She agreed, and said that she had recalled something relevant. Whenever she has an argument with her husband she knows that she is right but cannot prove it, she cannot find the right words to convince him. She then feels so anxious that she cannot hear what he says, only hearing a buzzing noise, and feeling depressed, defeated and inferior. When asked what she thought before engaging in such a battle whether she would succeed in convincing him, she felt 99 per cent sure that she would lose. The results of this negative belief were discussed and in addition I pointed out that others who saw her as a vulnerable person would only try to exploit her more. Then I asked her how she was feeling. She did not answer for some time, then she said that she realized that she had to change. However, this was a difficult task because she would have to change so many things in her life.

Session 4

After the third session the reformulation and SDR (Figure 6.2) were prepared and these were given to her at the start of the fourth session:

Reformulation.

> You went through very traumatic and painful experiences in your early childhood. Your mother left home (you vividly remember the day although you were only four years old). Your father was unable to act as a satisfactory care-giver. So you were deprived of the affection and love which were indispensable to you during this period of your life. The relationships with uncles and aunts proved to be dangerous and painful because not only did they fail to provide what you wanted (you still remember with bitterness that you did not receive any cuddling or birthday or Christmas presents) but they also used and abused you physically and/or sexually. So, from very early on you learned that involvement with other people entails lack of affection, violence, exploitation and abuse. The behaviour of your schoolmates, who looked down on you and laughed at you (even those who seemed, at first, to be real friends) reinforced this view. All these experiences created an uncertain and insecure image of yourself. You tried to escape from these horrible situations by leaving home at 17, but your relationships with the two men you ended up with confirmed your earlier beliefs.

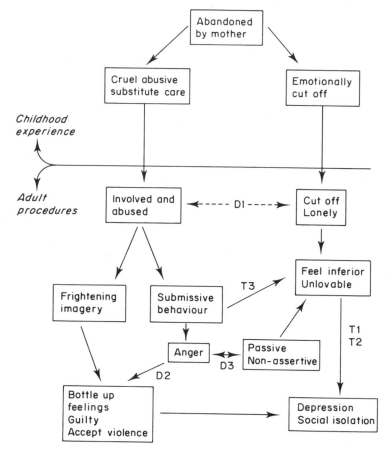

D1 – *Either* cut off, lonely *or* involved, abused
D2 – *Either* destructively angry *or* show no feelings
D3 – *Either* destructively angry *or* submit
T1 – Depressed thinking trap
T2 – Social isolation trap
T3 – Placation trap

Figure 6.2 Sequential diagrammatic reformulation: Linda

The feeling of uncertainty and insecurity made you feel under-
confident, inferior (I remember how you described this with a
gesture) and this led you to give in, to try to please others, putting
aside your own needs and desires. This pattern of behaviour made
you feel depressed and tense; your uncomfortable feelings led you
to avoid social gatherings, as we discussed, which in turn increased
the feelings of under-confidence, inferiority and insecurity. Further-

more, all these traumatic experiences made you feel angry towards others, but you did not express your anger because of the risk of a violent answer or rejection by them, or the fear of hurting them. So, finally, you learned to bottle up your feelings and to feel emotionally distant from others, unable to show affection to them, a fact which made you feel guilty and self-blaming, which led you again to depression and tension. The other solution is to be away from others, not involved with them. However, this solution is rarely helpful or relieving because it makes you feel alone, needy and unloved, which leads again to tension.

Therefore it seems that you were caught in a basic dilemma concerning your relationships with others: *either* involved and used, abused, giving in, looked down on, bottling up feelings, *or* not involved and alone, rejected, unloved and needy.

Undoubtedly you struggled very hard to survive through the difficult and painful situations in your life, but you used up much of your internal energy trying to find solutions and ways which have not led to the happiness you want, as you wrote in your diary. However, as we have discussed, you have started to realize that there are some alternative ways which it is worth trying. You can be the master of your own life, more assertive about your own needs, trying to please yourself first and then others, being involved with them on the basis of equality, respect and mutuality in order to achieve a satisfactory sense of internal certainty and security.

She found this reformulation very helpful, in particular the SDR; on seeing it she said 'This is the vicious circle of my life. I have to break it.' She went on to describe an event of the previous week. Two friends of her husband had come to her home. They did not know that she and her husband were currently living separately and they were looking for him. She decided to take them to his house. However, she felt very anxious, thinking that her husband would be dissatisfied with that; she found herself anticipating and fearing his verbal violence. She felt scared and humiliated because she was not able to handle the situation. In the event, her husband did not react like that but she still felt depressed as she realized that it was still the result of his behaviour and not of hers. When asked how else she might have coped with that, she said that, if he had spoken angrily, she could have said, 'Shut up. They are your friends. Why are you shouting?' Then we looked at the SDR and saw how if she bottled up her feelings, being afraid of a possible violent answer, she would not be able to behave as an assertive adult and how this leads to feelings of inferiority, depression, worthlessness and anxiety. It was explained how feeling unable to confront her husband was an example of the depressive thinking trap which leads to anxiety and depression and reinforces lack of confidence. She said that she realized that, and went on to remember how scared she was as a child when her father used to return home every night drunk and angry. I said that that was in the past when she was a little girl. Now that she is a woman it was unfair to herself to behave and feel like a child.

Session 5

She reported that she had felt depressed and tense every day. She thought that the future was hopeless. She had many problems; for instance, how she was going to cope all alone with two children. She felt that she had failed in her marriage and that the whole of her life was a failure. Then I asked how she felt about therapy and her therapist. She did not answer immediately. Then she said that in the beginning she did not feel that therapy could be helpful. I asked her if she felt that she could trust me, given that she had had very bad experiences with people in the past. When she asked if I meant that everyone who approached her had tried to hurt her, I replied yes. She then said that in the beginning, she had not felt comfortable with me, but now she was uncertain how she felt. She believed that she trusted me a bit. Referring to her SDR, I pointed out that due to her past experiences she had believed that involvement with others meant being abused and used, giving in and getting hurt, so she could not trust me. I suggested that this had perhaps been the cause of the cancellation of the third session. In addition, as she had revealed her 'inside world' to me, perhaps she thought that I would look down on her, as her schoolmates had in the past. I suspected that, after the reformulation, she might feel more ambivalent; she now had the choice — to follow the old way or the new one — and perhaps this conflicting choice had led to the bad mood during this week. She was a little surprised at this and immediately said that she now remembered a dream she had two days earlier. In this she was in her father's house. She felt very anxious, distressed and scared because she was waiting for her father's return. She was trying to run away but she could not move her feet. I said that this sounded as if she would like to escape from the past, which was painful, but that something was holding her still attached to it. However, the desire to escape represented the new knowledge that she had. She said that she understood that, and saw that it was as if she had grown up physically but not emotionally. I said that this realization was important, but that perhaps it was not absolute. Some bonds still held her connected to the past and use up much of her internal energy; perhaps now this could be spent in more useful and pleasurable ways. During the remaining weeks of therapy, she manifested considerable improvements and rated greater position changes on her TPs and TPPs.

Session 6

She described a very good week, the first after many months without depression and tension. She had been much more sociable and was participating in discussions comfortably for the first time in her life. She described some issues concerning her relationship with her husband which she had dealt with differently from in the past. They had had an argument and he had tried to devalue her, to treat her as a child and to impose his opinion. She was not afraid of him and she felt able to confront him; when they did not come to an agreement she told him, 'You have your opinion, I have mine.' On another day, he noticed that she was not wearing her wedding ring; he commented angrily but she was not frightened, nor did she try to make excuses, saying that now they were separated there was no reason to wear the ring. We passed through the reformulation and the SDR and she saw how, when she did not give in and bottle up her feelings, she felt confident, and had been free of anxiety and depression. Also she had been able to join in at social gatherings with comfort. She said that she felt that she had broken the vicious circle.

Session 7

She again reported a good week with several important events. First she had been able to express her opinion in a discussion with her sister and her brother-in-law, helping them with some problems that they had. Her brother-in-law was amazed to see her, for the first time, supporting her views and offering important and constructive opinions. She was pleased that he had noticed that and had written in her diary, 'I felt happy that I was appreciated.' We discussed that in relation to her depressive thinking trap, noting how if she felt self-confident she was able to give a better performance and was also able to present a completely different image of herself to others. The other event was that she had decided to go to a dance where her husband would be present. Some weeks ago there had been another dance, but the fact that her husband would be there had prevented her from going, and she had felt depressed. Through the SDR she saw that she had given in and then, through this placating behaviour, had felt under-confident, inferior, angry and then depressed. She said that she now realized that it was important to please herself first and then others, so she had decided to go to the dance.

Session 8

Speaking about the dance, she said that she was surprised because for the first time her husband did not try to devalue her; he had actually been complimentary. This was a completely new style of behaviour. I said that this was an example of how her style of behaving, feeling and thinking could influence the way in which others behaved towards her. She realized that and she said that she would have to retain this new style. She felt uncertain, now, about whether or not to live with her husband again, although some weeks ago she had been scared when he left her and had felt that she would accept him back without any conditions as she had done several times in the past. Now, she felt sure that she would not go back to an unequal relationship.

The following is Linda's 'goodbye letter'

> When I first started my therapy, I had a very negative feeling towards it. I kept thinking it wouldn't work! I suppose I felt like this because however much I spoke to people about my problems nothing ever changed the way I felt. Anyway, after a few weeks went past, I began to notice slight changes in my attitude. I also began to realize how important as an individual person I was. During my therapy, my therapist has opened my eyes to certain situations, i.e. equality, assertiveness and satisfying myself first. I always thought things were normal in my life (although I was very unhappy) but now I see myself as a person with my own thoughts and feelings (something I didn't think was important). Sometimes I feel it is going to be hard to try to change my way of thinking. But I am happy the way I feel now, so I know this feeling will give me the strength to carry on. I once thought of myself as a failure and useless and I am glad to say I no longer feel like this.

Follow-up

At follow-up, three months after therapy, Linda was very well, having kept all the good things that she had gained in therapy. Her depression and anxiety (her two target problems) had disappeared. She felt cheerful and energetic. She was able now to deal with the everyday activities in her house and to look after her two children. She also felt more able to show affection to her daughter (this TPP had not improved during therapy). She had re-negotiated her relationship with her husband very assertively and clearly. In the past their relationship had been very confused as her husband lived separately but came to her home whenever he liked. As a result he was not pleased with her change and he accused her of using therapy to break up the marriage rather than to mend it. Now he says he has a need for therapy. She felt more sociable and confident and quite optimistic about the future. Clearly she had gained and retained a lot from her therapy. She did not feel the need for further sessions and this was my opinion as well.

Case Example: Joy

This account is given by her female therapist.

In the initial session we came to an agreement that the first three sessions would be spent getting a picture of the problems Joy was facing, looking at what was currently going on for her and getting a perspective by taking her history; and then by the third session we would plan a set amount of sessions (12) to face and work on the established problem areas before reviewing.

Over the first three sessions Joy was frequently defensive, unsure and untrusting of the help being offered (and would sometimes refer back to attempts of help from friends, relatives and other professionals that had only compounded problems or 'added to the hurt').

Joy would often become hostile and angry, raising her voice and swearing, critical that I and the sessions in general would be of little help to her. Despite this, however, Joy continued to attend, giving her history and monitoring carefully. Those areas looked at in her monitoring were:

1. The frustration at her inability to help herself returning to those people she felt used by, the alternative, she felt, being left feeling lonely and abandoned.
2. When interacting with people she felt either like a 'doormat' or would become aggressive (on the inside she would be feeling miserable, angry and frustrated).
3. Her anger at her inability to sustain 'good things', she feared they would bring disappointment and that it was better to stay with the 'devil you know'.

Her history portrayed a chaotic lifestyle in which people rarely put her needs high on the list. Joy was brought up with her elder brother and younger sister. She got on well with her father when he was around, but his life was spent almost exclusively at work or at the pub. Her mother was the one that was there for Joy, but she was intermittently alcoholic and used large amounts of prescribed drugs, with lucid periods in between. She was jealous of any attention Joy got from her father and would verbalize this.

At the age of 8 Joy stayed with her aunt for a year but returned home following quarrelling with her cousin. When she was 11 her parents split up, the mother blaming Joy, saying that she has slept with her father.

The children then lived with the mother. At this time Joy remembered her as sober and friendly but lonely too. At the age of 12 Joy was thrown out because the mother became jealous of her and her relationship with the mother's live-in boyfriend.

Between the ages of 12 and 13 Joy returned to stay with her aunt; however, this did not work out because of problems with the cousin again.

At around this time Joy's brother was kicked out of home by the mother's boyfriend and went to live with the father.

At 13 Joy returned to live with the mother and sister; however, mother had to go to hospital for treatment of her alcoholism, so the girls went to live with the father and brother.

Joy stayed at her father's from the age of 13 to 15, until his death, doing the shopping and cooking for him, her brother and her sister after school. She was the first to discover her father after he had fallen in the house, knocking his head. She helped him to bed because she thought rest might help but he was dead by the morning.

The mother did not attend the funeral and accused Joy of killing her father. Following the death Joy went with her sister to live with the aunt again, but she only stayed a couple of days, then moved back to the flat where they had lived with the father and stayed there for three to four months with her brother until discovered by the Social Services.

Joy was moved temporarily to a bedsit by the Social Services, where she experienced an attempted rape. She was then sent to a home for adolescent girls for four months till it closed down. She was then fostered for a couple of months until she was beaten up by the foster mother. She returned to live with her brother in her father's flat and moved with him when he got his own council flat when she was 17, where she still lives.

Currently, her longest relationship with a boyfriend is coming to an end. She had not a lot of feeling left for him as he had beaten her quite badly, but she feels she would be lonely if things did decidedly end. Most of her female friends are single parents who, she feels, have little time for her.

Previous psychiatric history. At the age of 8 she remembers attending five to six sessions of family therapy, which she described as 'useless'. At the age of 13 she spent two days in a children's hospital, followed by weekly appointments for the next two months. She had accidently overdosed while with friends, using her mother's tranquillizers.

Education. She has been to four secondary schools and also attended a support unit, due to her being constantly on the move and to some trouble she got into in the class. She then went to college where she started five O-levels but ended up taking only two.

Employment. She has had various jobs and is at present unemployed.

The final reformulation reads as follows:

> Throughout your life you have had to cope with continual changes, moving from place to place and so forming and reforming relation-

ships with different people. For the most part it seems these changes were brought about by circumstances out of your control such as your mother's jealousy, your parent's split and your father's death. However, you have been able to survive these changes relying on your own resources and reserves of strength when no one seemed to put your needs high on the list.

In relationships you have experienced rejection, for example your mother's feelings of jealousy towards you, and to a lesser extent your cousin's. Your mother's jealousy also ended what relationship you had with your father. You have experienced loss in relationships, in particular your father's death, for which you still feel guilt. You have experienced feeling used in relationships, like when your mother needed your company after the break-up with your father, and you have also experienced abuse, being beaten up by your brother and boyfriend.

You are able to describe sadness, anger and confusion in being unable to help yourself returning to those hurtful relationships which result in your feeling used, abused and rejected. When help is offered you become untrusting as to motives, and appear either defensive and reluctant to engage, or angry and accusing. Help in the past appears to have been offered by those who have brought you pain, or have been seemingly unaware of your pain when you were experiencing it, like your mother and your friends.

Having read the file you were able to identify with quite a few of the procedures, some of which overlapped and which can perhaps be identified as follows:

Traps.

1. Depressed thinking. Being depressed, it is quite likely that one is less effective than usual in judging how one manages one's depression. This often leads one to accentuate the negative, eliminating the positive in the memory of the event.
2. Placation, trying to do what people want to please them, you end up feeling taken advantage of, resulting in either withdrawing emotionally or becoming aggressive, but still unable to be assertive.

Dilemma. It is as if relationships involve *either* getting close to someone and giving in to them/submitting, *or* remaining safely/coldly apart, lonely/miserable/sad.

Your relationship with self parallels your relationship with others, but you are not able to be nice to yourself, but persecute yourself.

Snag. Feeling that you are a 'Bad' person, you can't allow good things to happen to you.

At the end of the third session I brought a rough copy of the prose reformulation including procedures that Joy had identified with from the file. This initial draft was left open for correction and change by her, which she did, focusing more often on details of wording than content. Her manner continued to be critical and abrupt.

During the following weeks Joy continued to monitor, on the basis of the procedures, focusing particularly upon the placation trap. We looked at her difficulty in sustaining and asserting herself in various friendships, for fear that she may lose the person involved and be left alone. This led to placatory behaviour with occasional outbursts of anger, which would leave her feeling alone inside.

In these sessions Joy would fluctuate between either being hostile and critical, or less defensive and trusting enough to voice her own needs and feelings. On such occasions she was frequently tearful and would share hopes (good job, understanding partner), disappointments (relationships past and present), and fears (being 'open' would leave her vulnerable). A pattern emerged whereby, following a session in which Joy had become hostile, she was sure to return the following week, whereas following a session in which she had shared her vulnerability, she was likely to miss the next week.

She felt she was going round in painful cirles, painful because she was frequently aware of what she was doing, but was unable to sustain change, saying 'better the devil you know', and that she had survived using the old coping techniques although now they frequently left her feeling depressed and alone.

The eighth time we met I produced a rough draft of the diagrammatic reformulation, the final copy of which is given in Figure 6.3, reconstructed after she had taken it away with her and made her own additions. I have also written my responses to the different states as experienced in the sessions, which I verbally made known and which occasionally made sense to her as illustrating the way people interacted with her outside the sessions.

Joy's hostility became less frequent over the ensuing two to three sessions, and she was in fact sharing more, and seemed to be involving herself more in life outside of the session, making arrangements to meet friends to go swimming and going to the Job Centre.

However, while often painfully aware of herself as she slipped back into her usual self-harming ways of coping, she avoided working on these issues in any greater depth. I suggested that she should number the difficult states as depicted in the diagrammatic reformulation so she could monitor how she

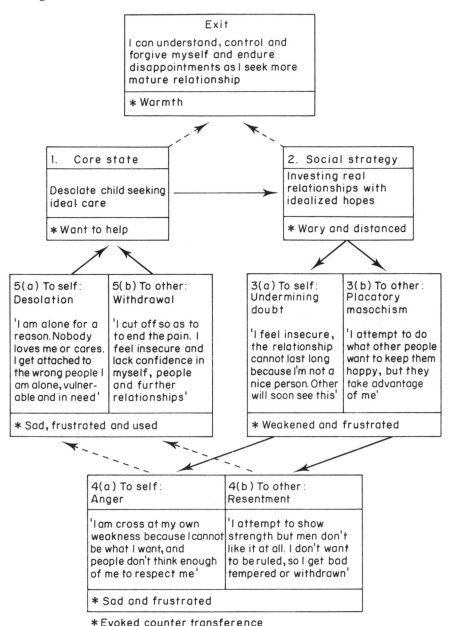

Figure 6.3 Sequential diagrammatic reformulation: Joy

moved from one into another, and note her mood, how she felt about herself and about others in each state, but this never materialized.

She ceased attending with only three sessions remaining before the time set for reviewing what further input would be necessary. My feelings at that time were that I would probably offer her further support on a fortnightly basis, since important issues were still being addressed. The last time we met Joy was warm and communicative throughout, but was confused about her ex-boyfriend who was contacting her again. He was bringing back painful memories but at the same time she was inevitably becoming involved with him again.

Case Example: Nelly

Sequential diagrams can be used as a basis for behavioural interventions. One very disturbed day hospital patient was prone to disruptive behaviours when distressed, such as dialling 999 for the police or letting off fire hoses. On one occasion, frustrated by a delay in seeing her therapist, she stole a goldfish from the aquarium and went into the street with its tail protruding from her mouth. She was brought back by the police (to whom she showed her diagram) and the goldfish was restored to the tank. The tank was removed from the day room (the fish being reported to become agitated when people approached) and its return was made conditional on the patient earning 'goldfish points' by successfully replacing disruptive acts with more appropriate requests for help, or other coping mechanisms.

Discussion

The above case histories provide some indication of the possible effectiveness of CAT in more severely disturbed patients. It appears that for many such patients crucial changes can be achieved in terms of breaking self-destructive patterns and acquiring a more integrated and stable sense of self. Reformulation, especially SDR, has an immediate containing effect on many patients, and allows some therapeutic work to be done in a brief intervention. It is likely that many will need further help. Some of these, at follow-up or later, might be offered further CAT intervention, some might be referred on to group therapy and a few might go on to longer-term individual therapy. At the very least, these brief interventions test the individual's capacity to use psychological help; in a surprisingly large majority of cases the result of brief CAT is to reveal their capacity to do so. This experience casts some doubt on the widely held assumption that therapy is inevitably very prolonged and of uncertain value in these patients. However, systematic study and follow-up of patients in this group treated with CAT is only now beginning, and formal conclusions must await further research.

There are other possible applications of CAT techniques to more severely disturbed patients; some will be discussed in the next chapter when longer-term individual treatments are considered. The use of reformulation, especially SDR, in the management of in-patient or day hospital patients could well be valuable as in the case of Nelly, described above. The therapeutic input in community treatment settings is often relatively unfocused, consisting at best of a supportive environment, the encouragement within limits of the expression of feeling and perhaps some 'off the cuff' interpretations of particular interactions. The capacity of disturbed patients to extract conflicting, collusive counter-transference responses from staff members and other patients within these settings, described in Main's (1957) classic paper, is well known. To achieve a therapeutic effect it is important to prevent this and also important to avoid the alternative danger of evoking in patients their compliant coping but emotionally null role behaviours. These goals would, I believe, be better achieved if the main procedures for each patient were reformulated and the SDRs for all patients were available to both staff and patients as a basis for understanding and controlling negative interactions.

CHAPTER 7

CAT Techniques with Long-term Patients

Psychotherapists working in the public sector, as I do, have to chose between either providing long-term therapy for those few patients who fight or wait their way to the head of the queue, knowing that their long waiting lists for assessment and therapy will in due course reduce the apparent pressure of demand, or they must facilitate access and provide efficient, minimally sufficient therapy for as many people as possible.

Many dynamic therapists believe that time-limited work is a poor second best, merely scratching at the surface rather than producing real therapeutic effects. As a result they often justify their choice of the first alternative, on the grounds that it at least does real good to the few. This conviction is often strengthened by the fact that their own experience of therapy and their own first supervised therapeutic work were commonly prolonged for two years or longer, often at a frequency of two or more times per week. Many therapists have very little experience of brief therapy, except for the not uncommon patients who drop out after a few sessions, a phenomenon seen to be the result of resistance or of a 'flight into health'.

My own definition of my role is that of a consultant psychotherapist to a community, in my case to an inner-city community of some 165,000 people, of which population I assess myself about one per 1000 each year, clearly only a fraction of those potentially in need. In this situation, I offer time-limited therapy to almost all the patients I see, some 10%, perhaps, being distributed between longer-term treatment, pure behavioural treatment, psychiatric treatment, or being deemed not suitable for therapy or not in need of it. Had my resources been richer, I would have felt inclined to make longer offers of therapy to a larger proportion of these patients, but having no choice, I have been able to observe how much use people can make of brief CAT, and have become increasingly confident in making this my main offer.

It is still, in my experience, difficult to know in advance which patients are likely to require longer treatment. Certainly a simple measure of severity of disturbance is not an absolute indication of the length of work needed; indeed, it sometimes seems that the more severely disturbed and deprived patients work that much more effectively in therapy. In other cases the fear of dependency is such that only time-limited offers would be acceptable to the patient. Even in individuals who have a major difficulty in accessing their underlying feelings and memories (for example, schizoid personalities, patients with marked childhood amnesias), or in those with highly developed resistant symptomatic behaviours (such as anorexia, and bulimia), an initial brief intervention can achieve significant change, although further therapy will be required in most cases. For this reason it seems to me that the initial offer of psychotherapy in virtually all cases could well be one of 8–16 sessions, with a follow-up. This intervention is enough to meet the needs of the majority of patients, and provides for the rest a trial of therapy on which to base a decision about further needs. This pattern saves patients from the dangers of unnecessary long-term involvement, with the implication of serious need and with the imposition of dependency, and serves to remind therapists of the resources available even in quite damaged people. Therapists who have no experience of, or faith in, brief intervention, who work solely in the classical psychodynamic mode, will generate in their patients familiar patterns of therapy with which they feel at home, but they are often, I believe, depriving their patients of a more immediate and effective form of help. I believe that many long-term therapies, called dynamic, are actually rather static, marked by a certain vagueness of aim or resembling infinite games of chess. An initial time-limited contract serves to show the patient very clearly what is on offer and tests his capacity to work.

In the present chapter, the application of CAT techniques to patients receiving long-term intervention will be described. Clearly the basic form of CAT, as described in this book, is designed for the time-limited context, but the time can be longer than the conventional 8–16 weeks, or therapy can be organized in a series of intermittent brief therapies. Some CAT techniques, especially reformulation, can be useful in long-term work. In the rest of this chapter examples will be given of patients treated in longer-term therapy in these ways.

Intermittent CAT

Many of the potential dangers of long-term therapy with disturbed patients, such as malignant, desperately regressed transferences and dangerous acting out, are less likely to occur if therapy is broken up into a series of time-limited interventions with gaps of some months between them. In general, patients work within the time provided and termination is not usually a problem. Different therapists may be involved in successive interventions depending upon the way in which the therapy has developed and on the transience or permanence of the therapeutic staff, a factor of importance in training institutions.

In the case presented below, three interventions took place over two years with the same male therapist in each case. This pattern had not been planned in advance but was imposed by problems around the termination of the second therapy with incomplete resolution of a powerful transference which had been quite confusing throughout the therapy. This might have been managed more quickly had SDR been available before the third therapy, but the technique had not at that time been developed.

Case Example: Elaine

[This patient had a borderline personality structure with some narcissistic features and an associated eating disorder.]

Elaine was referred for CAT at the age of 31. During the preceding four years she had had six months in-patient cognitive psychotherapy for anxiety and panic and somatic symptoms, depersonalization and social withdrawal. This was followed by one failed four-session dynamic therapy with a male therapist and then 18 months with a female therapist, which she had terminated herself when the issue of ending was raised. Her referral now was prompted by a return of anxiety, a pattern of alternate bingeing and self-starvation and by emotional confusion occurring especially in her relationships with men.

Elaine had been brought up by strict parents and she had always felt that her sickly younger brother was the preferred child. She had found her mother critical and punitive and never directly expressive of affection. Her descriptions of her father alternated between seeing him as weak and un-available or as intrusive and over-demanding; the latter, for example, in his coaching of Elaine in athletics. As an adolescent she had suffered intense anxiety about her facial acne. She had a briefly rebellious phase at school but had completed a number of O-levels and then left home, and in the following decade had completed various training courses and worked in a variety of jobs. She was currently working as a personnel officer, largely with young school leavers, and found the work interesting and challenging.

Elaine's sexual history was a painful one. Her first relationship at age 19 with a quiet introverted man was quite satisfactory, but she had felt very angry when they had drifted apart and he had taken up with someone else. All her subsequent relationships were with men who were seen as strong and exciting, whom she would feel drawn to and whom she would often tease and provoke into physically assaulting her, following which she would either become depressed or seek revenge, often provoking a repetition of abuse from the men. Nice men were seen as weak and dull. This dichotomy was evident in the pattern of the transference during the first therapy. By the end of this first therapy Elaine had control over her bulimic tendency and had avoided any further involvement in damaging sexual relationships. At follow-up, however, she reported continuing anxiety and depression and a second 16-session CAT was offered. During the second therapy the main theme to emerge was to do with her relationship with her brother, now seen as the embodiment of all she wanted in a relationship and all she wanted to be ('I want to eat him, be him and sleep with him'). Towards the end of the therapy it became apparent that her feelings towards the therapist had many of these intense features. Termination was experienced by Elaine as an unmanageable abandonment, and during the ensuing three months she became incapacitated and depressed, lost over a stone in weight and was unable to work. Her third therapy, also 16 sessions, was devoted to completing the understanding of her idealization of her brother as being a defence against her earlier extreme envy, and towards completing the termination of her intense relationship with her therapist. During this therapy the SDR (Figure 7.1) played an important role as it encapsulated all that had been learnt or experienced through the work of therapy. In the relatively complicated diagram, the conflicted core state is seen to generate:

1. Illness behaviour, possibly linked to her early experience of her mother's giving care to her brother, in return for illness.
2. Her eating disorder, the dilemma *either* binge and feel guilty, *or* starve and feel in control.
3. Placatory behaviour evident both with friends and work colleagues.
4. The envy—idealization—disappointment cycle manifest with her brother and in the transference.
5. Her (narcissistic) dilemma enacted with men and in the transference whereby she identifies with *either* her angry envious self and devalues the other, *or* with her weak, needy and guilty self, for whom she seeks punishment from the other.

The goodbye letter written to Elaine after her third therapy reads as follows:

Dear Elaine
This letter is a way of saying goodbye after the three periods of therapy.
    The central issue throughout therapy has been a core feeling of almost overwhelming neediness, deriving from childhood feelings of not being loved, combined with anger and resentment that others, particularly your brother, seemed more favoured with affection. All of us have to express neediness and anger from time to time (otherwise we wouldn't be human), but your feelings have seemed so overwhelming that you have used procedures that, ultimately, reinforce the central feelings.

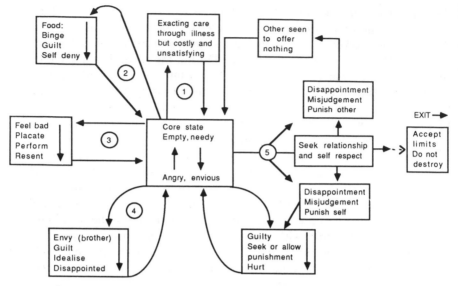

Sequential Diagrammatic Reformulation: Elaine

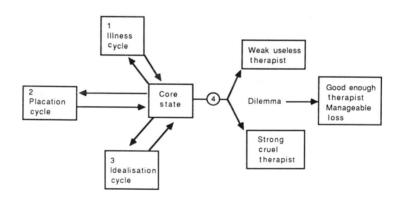

**Schematic sequential diagram (Elaine) indicating Therapy
behavours and transference issues.**

We have examined these procedures including the sickness role,
the binge/self-denying cycle, the placation/rebellion cycles, the use
of abusing men, your controlling and devaluing other men, and the
idealization of your brother as a defence against destructive anger
towards him. The trouble is that, ultimately, these procedures

leave you more needy or angry than before. Each procedure is often associated with being in a state of mind where it is sometimes difficult to recognize other parts of yourself.

You do seek fulfilling relationships which don't involve abuse, devaluing control or the sick role, but you have difficulty accepting their inevitable limits because they remind you of the painful limits in the relationships of childhood. You are able to accept relationships with most women friends in a fulfilling way. But with men, the possibility of a closer sexual relationship stirs up stronger feelings of neediness and it becomes far more difficult to accept inevitable human limitations, so that you end up either devaluing the relationship or getting abused.

In a very strong sense therapy is a limited and potentially fulfilling experience, but its intimacy evokes neediness, so that you have found it hard to accept its limitations. As a result the therapist becomes, in fantasy, *either* the abuser, *or* the devalued other. You have also expressed a fantasy of the therapist as ideal partner like the fantasy of your brother, one who has no limits and where there is no boundary between yourself and the other.

Therapy uncovered the procedures you have used and the central issues from which they derive. I think we have managed to get these in perspective so that it is easier to recognize the employment of these procedures, and I think the diagram was useful in this regard. Of course you have not completely abandoned the unfulfilling procedures, but I feel you are recognizing them and using them with decreasing frequency. This means that you have allowed yourself to go into situations where fulfilling relationships with men are possible. You have been careful so far not to get too involved for you recognize the tendency to devalue or be abused. However, I feel you are getting stronger and that for the first time a real and satisfying relationship is on the cards.

Hand in hand with this is the realization that you have lost your brother as an ideal fantasy object. The feelings of loss associated with this are natural and not to be denied, but hopefully the relationship will be far more fulfilling and real than before.

A key issue over the past few sessions is the end of our therapeutic relationship. You have struggled with feelings of anger and desperation, but I can see that the natural feelings of loss, which attend the end of a relationship, are coming through. You are accepting these healthy feelings of loss in a way that you found difficult before. I feel this is a real gain because you are experiencing that loss does not entail your destruction or the destruction of the other. The end of this therapy does not mean the end of you or me and hopefully we will remain in each other's memories in a positive way.

Following this third therapy, Elaine, who was now back at work and functioning effectively, requested long-term therapy. While there was clearly further work to be done, her wish for therapy seemed also to represent a way of continuing with a safe, intimate relationship. The alternative of group therapy was proposed, and after much debate with herself, and with a good deal of regret, Elaine accepted referral to a group and was able to establish herself as an active, concerned and self-revealing member of it. She made considerable progress in revising her relationships with her family, and in particular was now able for the first time in her life to go out with her brother, and to feel like 'pals' and to experience interest in other men in his company. Elaine reported to the group that her diagram was 'burnt into her brain'. Having read through the above account, Elaine wrote about the SDR as follows:

> The diagram is something that myself and the therapist have worked through together. Initially I had rejected it and refused to value its content, however, after a while I began to appreciate its worth, which meant I was able to relate to the diagram and to accept that it was 'about me'. I now view the diagram as my bible and I can refer to it whenever I want to. Furthermore, I feel that it has given me a sense of identity and has helped me to develop awareness about the procedures I have adopted in the past. The most positive aspect of the diagram is that it offers me an exit route, which means that I feel that I can break free from the cycle and choose an alternative route, a route which I know will ultimately offer me self-respect and fulfilment.

CAT Techniques in Long-term Therapy

As has already been argued, the decision to offer long-term open-ended therapy is best made on the evidence of previous brief therapy. With increasing confidence in brief therapy and with the possible use of intermittent brief therapy or of a combination of additional CAT followed by group therapy, I find myself suggesting long-term therapy as a first choice relatively rarely. However, there are undoubtedly indications for it, which might be interpreted more generously if resources were less constrained. In this section examples of the use of CAT methods in long-term once-a-week therapy will be presented.

Long-term therapy will always involve a central focus on transference issues. Such a focus is required when core issues of trust and primitive destructiveness are concealed behind elaborate symptom complexes or schizoid withdrawal, or where the integration of opposed split-off aspects of the self has not been adequately achieved in shorter-term or intermittent CAT. Despite the belief amongst most psychoanalysts that the brief or once-a-week therapy must of necessity be aim restricted, I believe effective transference work aimed at fundamental issues can often be achieved, and that in achieving it aspects of CAT, especially reformulation and some kinds of homework, can play a part. This is particularly the case where therapy runs the risk of becoming a stalemate (see Olds, 1981).

The next two cases were treated by the author.

Case Example: Ellen

Ellen was referred urgently following the breakdown of a three-year-long counselling relationship in which her demanding and intrusive behaviour (expressed through increasingly frequent sessions and numerous phone calls and the production of masses of written material), and her marked suicidal preoccupations had overwhelmed her counsellor. She was a 36-year-old professional woman, currently working part-time and irregularly in freelance work, whose voice and appearance were childlike and disarming. In contrast to this, however, she produced a knife at the first session, and at subsequent sessions for over a year, and reported through this time a vivid stream of fantasies of violent dismemberment and evisceration. In early sessions I had taken the knife from her but it became clear that it represented a necessary symbolic safety and thereafter the rule was made that it was to be placed on the table and not handled during the session. Ellen gave a history of physical abuse from her parents and of sexual abuse between the ages of 5 and 12 from an older brother. She had then been sent to a boarding school and from there on to university. Two years later at the age of 20 she had her first love affair, and following the start of a sexual relationship had a breakdown during which she made a number of suicidal attempts by overdosing and was hospitalized for some months. Some years later, after one or two further relationships, she married a man considerably older than herself. This relationship was companionable and protective, but it was evident, from a joint meeting, that there was a strong parent–child axis at work. Ellen had been sexually unresponsive in all her relationships including this one.

The reformulation. offered, early on in the therapy, was based on the Hans Christian Andersen story. 'The Snow Queen', in which the gentle Gerda's search for her stolen-away childhood sweetheart Kay, frozen in the Snow Queen's palace, only achieves success with the aid of the fierce knife-wielding little robber girl and her reindeer. The Gerda (childlike, inoffensive) versus robber girl dilemma was to be resolved by the acceptance and integration of the angry and destructive parts of her nature manifest in the bringing of the knife and in her dreams.

This therapy lasted a little over three years, during which Ellen was seen weekly and was allowed to deliver three pages of writing the day before each session. After some weeks she brought a gift of some 250 pills of various sorts which she had collected, and in the second year she was able to stop bringing the knife to the sessions. She continued to present herself as a harmless child and expressed directly only idealizing positive feelings, but in her dreams and writing her violent side was continually manifested. Much of the content of therapy was the slow reconstruction by way of vivid and at times hallucinatory recollections of her early childhood, which included parental beatings, the dismissal of her loved nurse (for intervening when her father was beating her sister) and the secret sexual play with her brother, experienced as both gratifying and frightening but ultimately, when he forced intercourse, terrifying.

Her responses to holiday absences or therapeutic failures were catastrophic; for the first two years she would always become ill and take to her bed and suffer a range of physical symptoms and a sense of unbearable despair. By the third year of therapy this pattern became less intense. Ellen at this stage began to construct diagrams herself to try to trace the sequence of her states. She summarized the experience of separation as follows:

> My child's inability to contain different levels of emotion and to balance good and bad components of the other is linked with the fantasy need for perfection. Any kind of separation leads to exaggeration of its meaning, and reality becomes limited to that which refers directly to the self. The other, by venturing outside the field of the self, is felt now as nothing but disappointment and loss and the abandonment is now felt to be deliberate. This leads on to a belief that the abandonment is due to my own badness, and this serves to reinforce my own magical belief in my capacity to cause death and destruction to others.

An overall summary of the main structure manifested in therapy is given in the SDR (Figure 7.2).

During the three years of therapy a number of external changes took place. Professionally, her work expanded and she took on organizational responsibility for an innovative programme. She and her husband, however, became increasingly alienated. She reported that her new capacity for self-assertion was seen by him as little more than badness, and that her attempts to explain something of the nature of her difficulty and her history always met with impatience or incomprehension. His comments on media reports about child sexual abuse were such that she felt quite unable to discuss her history in that respect with him. During the third year of therapy she started a relationship with a man of about her own age and experienced full sexual

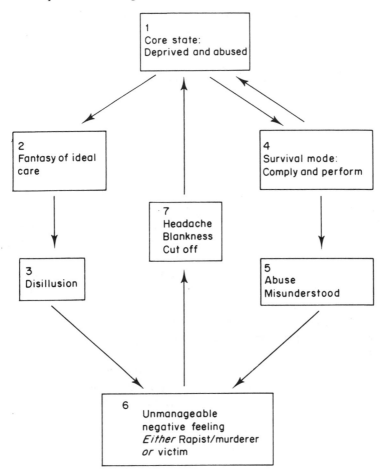

Figure 7.2 Sequential diagrammatic reformulation: Ellen

responsiveness for the first time. She dealt with hesitations and ambiguities on his part with dignity and directness, and the relationship became firmly established.

The reformulation at the start of therapy set out the task of the therapy, which was the integration of a very split personality. The insistence on incorporating rather than removing the destructive aspects and the insistence on working within the clear limits of access which were laid down at the beginning were also important. The use of writing helped Ellen develop a highly intelligent, critical, self-observing stance and was also a vehicle for expressing feelings not always voiced in the sessions. Reformulation in the third year helped her to cope with the disruptions in her sense of self

experienced in separation. It is possible that earlier use of sequential diagrammatic reformulation (not developed at that time) might have accelerated
that process.

The next case is of a patient who ended a 3½-year individual therapy
considerably worse off than she was when she started it. A second therapy,
in this case conjoint therapy with her husband, was conducted, in which
SDR played a significant role.

Case Example: Susan

Susan was first seen at the age of 37. She had had many years of physical
investigation and much psychological medication for her rich constellation of
often disabling physical symptoms. These dated back to her early teens, and
although she usually pushed herself to ignore them, they represented a
major restriction on her life. Susan was the only child of a weak father and
an angry, restrictive, punitive mother for whom she had to learn early on in
life to cope and perform and to smile. This mode of coping had enabled her
to achieve well at school and to go on to graduate. She had reared two
children, now teenagers, and worked at a responsible job, but had increasingly
realized that she had little or no contact with deep feelings, whether negative
or positive.

The early impact of therapy was magical. She experienced phases of full
energy and loss of symptoms and intense psychological awareness, but these
phases were always transient. In time it became very clear that her symptom
exacerbations occurred in situations where anger or sadness would have
been appropriate, and that symptom relief often followed the direct experience
of feeling. At this stage a rhythm of good days following the therapy session,
followed by increasingly bad days became established. The content of the
sessions included a slow recovery and reconstruction of detailed painful
early memories, but the effects of sessions for Susan were largely characterized
by whether or not she felt she had been heard and she had taken something
away. She would often report little recollection of the previous session,
being concerned only with my voice tone, or, later the image of my face.
She was quite unaware of any angry feelings towards me. In retrospect, she
had a very powerful experience of feeling in these sessions, but virtually no
capacity to use her understanding or to observe herself. This process of
therapy was accompanied by increasing social disability; she was forced to
leave her job, had to give up driving her car, found social contact increasingly
painful and was able to do less and less around the house. Towards the end
of three years, faced with this deterioration and with an unmitigated idealization of the therapist, linked with a derogation of most of the world except
for her children, it seemed best to try to mobilize and hopefully resolve her

split-off, destructive feelings by naming and working towards a termination date. However, neither at termination nor at three-month follow-up was anger apparent, and her disability and depression increased. A second follow-up appointment, requested by her husband, led, regrettably, to an acrimonious exchange, her long-awaited anger taking a form which was poorly contained by me. This session was followed by a response of persistent anger and catastrophic despair.

After reflection, and with the benefit of the advice of a colleague with whom a consultation was arranged for Susan, a second therapy was offered, this time to see Susan with her husband. With hindsight, it had become clear that my major experience of the first therapy had been that, as well as being idealized, I had been unheard and rendered of absolutely no value, and I now saw more clearly how this had represented something of her own childhood experience in relation to her mother. Seeing the couple together at this stage I now saw how Susan's persistent undermining of her husband, who was a patient, long-suffering and highly responsible man, had put him also into the position of somebody whose best efforts were of no avail. Working in this way enabled me to resist renewed attempts to keep me, or restore me, as an idealized person, split off in contrast to her husband, and it freed her husband to be less dominated and undermined by her expressions of need and by her derogations of him. By this stage, Susan was abusing alcohol and medication and was threatening suicide. At this point a sequential diagrammatic reformulation was constructed (Figure 7.3) which highlighted these processes and emphasized the controlling element in Susan's behaviour. Monitoring by both of them of interactions in the light of the understanding of the diagram was proposed. Within quite a short time, Susan slipped into a state of utter hopelessness and angry despair with strong suicidal feelings which lasted, in all, some six weeks. At the end of that period, for the first time for over a year and for the first time with any real conviction since the early magical phases of therapy, she began to experience the return of curiosity in the world and of energy. She began to be able to read and to take over household tasks and experienced the beginning of a sense of being in control of her life and of being able to think about her future. Somatic symptoms, feeling blocked emotionally and feeling hopeless about the future and envious of successful contemporaries continued but were increasingly interspersed with periods of energy and with the capacity to take in experiences and to express feeling.

It seemed to me that the understanding that was encapsulated in the SDR was of value to both her husband and to me in resisting collusion in her powerful, negative indirect control. This had faced her in turn with the final loss of her magical idealized hope which had dominated her therapy and had allowed or forced her to give up her powerful negative control, a control which had dominated her therapy and, in many ways, her marriage. No longer

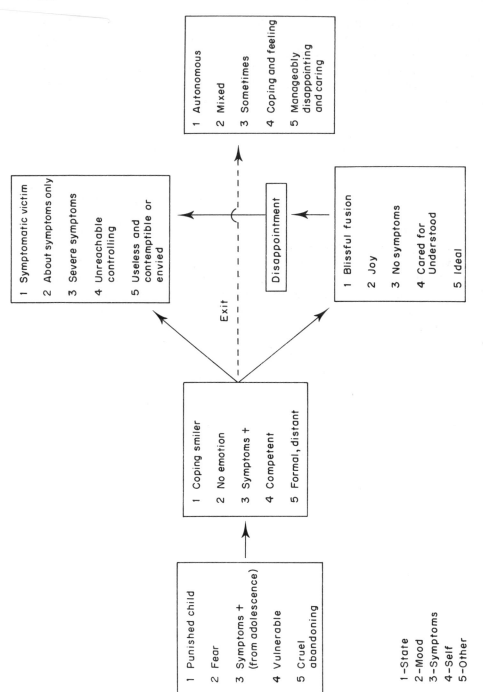

Figure 7.3 Sequential diagrammatic reformulation: Susan

1 – State
2 – Mood
3 – Symptoms
4 – Self
5 – Other

Punished child box:
1 Punished child
2 Fear
3 Symptoms + (from adolescence)
4 Vulnerable
5 Cruel abandoning

Coping smiler box:
1 Coping smiler
2 No emotion
3 Symptoms +
4 Competent
5 Formal, distant

Symptomatic victim box:
1 Symptomatic victim
2 About symptoms only
3 Severe symptoms
4 Unreachable controlling
5 Useless and contemptible or envied

Autonomous box:
1 Autonomous
2 Mixed
3 Sometimes
4 Coping and feeling
5 Manageably disappointing and caring

Blissful fusion box:
1 Blissful fusion
2 Joy
3 No symptoms
4 Cared for Understood
5 Ideal

Disappointment

Exit

needing to be unhelpable and unreachable, she experienced being hopeless and helpless, but was able to go beyond that to a return to an active, if precarious, involvement in her life.

It is possible in this case that the earlier use of SDR and perhaps the earlier involvement of her husband might have diminished the length and the disabling effect of this difficult therapy.

Case Example: Carole

[This is a description by a female therapist of long-term work in a forensic setting with a patient with a severe borderline personality disorder.]

Carole was first seen by her female therapist at the age of 27, having been referred by her GP, the main complaint being fears of harming people. She had at that time assaulted strangers on two occasions, having been overcome by jealousy on seeing couples being affectionate together. She had sexual fantasies of harming others and was frightened of implementing them. In two previous therapies she had become infatuated with her therapist, had sought physical comfort from them and had hit them on occasions. Over the past ten years she had been treated with minor tranquilizers and one course of monoamine oxidase inhibitors. The drug treatment had not had any effect. Her main complaints were chronic depression and anxiety with some suicidal ideation, poor control of anger, alcohol abuse, lack of social confidence, lack of any close relationships, chronic sexual frustration, frequent derealization and depersonalization, the need to reassure herself of her boundaries by touching walls or hitting herself and the belief that she was transsexual and in need of gender reassignment surgery.

Carole had had a normal birth but had been separated for much of the first year of her life due to her mother's illness, and thus it seems likely that bonding of mother to her had never been very satisfactory. Her elder sister was much closer to her mother, particularly after she had had surgery for a cerebral tumour. Her recollections of her early life were extremely bleak, but she was fond of her father, sharing his hobbies and interests and being extremely upset by his death which occurred when she was 20 years old. This death occurred during an argument between her and him and he died in her arms. Carole was educated in normal schools and had gone on to attain two A-levels and gone to college. She had felt different from other girls from the age of 9, always being attracted to female teachers and she began to feel she was a boy in the wrong body. At 13 she had been assaulted by a man and threatened with a knife; she blamed her mother for not being prepared to leave her sister to escort her back from school. Over the past seven years, on some four occasions, her mother had sought close physical contact with her and had become sexually aroused. Carole had avoided those situations for the past two or three years, having found them extremely upsetting. Her work record was very irregular as she often had to leave for fear of what she might say or do. She had also in recent years suffered from a recurrent bowel complaint.

The early sessions of Carole's therapy were mostly spent exploring her fears about therapy, not surprisingly given the problems she had encountered in the past. She talked readily and was also freely hostile and angry. She read the Psychotherapy File and marked it carefully, and Target Problems and goals were drawn up. The main problem was defined as follows:

> It seems as if I can only be *either* defenceless, powerless and dependent like a little female child, *or* a destructive, unlikeable and at times even murderous woman [later revised to man]. This leads me to *either* placate everybody to keep the peace at my own expense, feeling angry, frustrated and guilty, *or* to my feeling destructive and hurting myself rather than hurting somebody else. My sexual feelings as an adult get muddled up in all this hurt and anger.

Early in therapy she would arrive at different sessions with quite different appearances, depending upon her mental state. If she was depressed and anxious she would appear childlike and would be needy and distressed in the sessions, while on other occasions she would appear dressed as a man and be very assertive and hostile, sometimes threatening physical assault. However, she was diligent in her diary-keeping, did much thinking between sessions and always discussed the issues of the previous session when she next attended. There was a period when she became more depressed or more angry and at times drank heavily, but over the first month of therapy her level of depression decreased, her alcohol intake decreased and her derealization feelings ceased. After about a year of therapy she investigated the possibility of gender reassignment by contacting agencies run by trans-sexuals and meeting people who had undergone it. She realized that she was not going to go through with the operation because she felt that she would always be a sham if she did and coming to terms with that plunged her once more into depression because she realized she was never going to have the kind of close relationship she craved. During this period she again drank heavily and threatened suicide, but slowly emerged with alternative goals for her life. Following that she worked systematically on learning to be reasonably assertive rather than placatory and there were no more episodes of self-harm. She also developed her voluntary work concerned with animals, which she planned, in due course, to make her career. She was seen weekly for the first year and fortnightly thereafter, and remains in follow-up contact. She no longer wears childish or highly stylized men's clothes. Her eye contact is moderately good, she gives no evidence of clinical depression and her level of anxiety is manageable. In relation to the therapist she is assertive and appropriate—no longer a needy child or a hostile male—and interruptions or separations in therapy, which early on were accompanied by fantasies of the therapist's death, or extreme anger, were no longer disturbing.

Within the CAT framework a number of techniques were incorporated in this therapy. Carole frequently used writing, including a good deal of poetry, to convey what was happening between the sessions but not said in them. An early problem with the end of each session was slowly solved by strict attention to timing and explicit preparation for the end of each occasion. Her problems in finding appropriate forms of assertion were dealt with by role rehearsal during the sessions, these being linked with the life history and target procedure.

Conclusion

These case histories demonstrate some of the indications for longer-term therapy.

Elaine (48 sessions), in recovering from the severe depression which followed her second CAT, in working through the issues identified in her SDR in the third therapy and in managing the termination of this last therapy, ended up demonstrably freer from her long-standing, self-damaging interpersonal procedures and her damaging patterns of self-punishment and self-care. As well as bringing her SDR and its value to the group, as reported above, she also commented that the resistance given to her request for further individual therapy had in fact been reassuring. None the less, after eight months in the group she left with the intention of seeking further individual therapy.

Ellen (about 160 sessions) worked very hard in her therapy and it is doubtful whether the good result could have been achieved more speedily. There was an enormous problem of mistrust to overcome and (see the SDR) frequent blocking off of memory and feeling.

Susan (over 200 sessions) had a painful and unsatisfactory therapy and I believe the use of SDR earlier on might well have helped me understand more clearly the interaction between us. In the second conjoint therapy her anger and sadness were more present and the introduction of the SDR was helpful to both her husband and me in blocking her derogation and helping her understand her identification with her powerful unreachable mother. I believe her therapy might have been quicker and kinder had it been possible to admit Susan for a few weeks to remove her from the domestic obligations which she could not meet but could not let go of, and to offer non-intrusive care of a sort described in Ryle (1982, Chapter 11) where patients are enabled to enter a regressed vulnerable state, but such provision is unfortunately not available.

Carole (about 100 sessions) was the most profoundly disturbed of these patients. Her treatment over 2½ years (weekly, fortnightly and then monthly) must be seen as something of a triumph. The successful containment of her very disordered and frightening behaviour in a therapy of this intensity contrasts with her two previous therapies in which she had enacted her feared anger and childish need. There seems little doubt that this success reflected the clarity of understanding and the firmness of control exercised by her therapist and by the mobilization of her own capacity to write and think about herself.

All these patients found their way to enough safety to face long-avoided, painful and destructive core feelings. In understanding this process I find Winnicott's (1974) paper on the fear of breakdown is valuable, suggesting that these patients are now able to experience what they had originally gone through at an age at which it was not possible to cope with the powerful feelings. These patients could also be described as having moved, in Kleinian terms, from the paranoid-schizoid to the depressive position, although I would see this shift not in terms of universal fantasies from the first years of life but as the facing and healing of the effects of unmanageable traumas in childhood. The patients described in this chapter needed extended or repeated periods in therapy. There are other patients who do get enough, even from time-limited CAT, to contact, cope with and integrate such core feelings, which is why an initial time-limited contract seems desirable.

Going through such changes always implies a period of vulnerability and uncertainty, and it may be helpful to support such transitions with revised reformulations. As the old dilemmas based upon splitting are resolved (for example, *either* fusion, *or* furious disappointment; *either* contemptible, *or* contemptuous), and as some symptomatic procedures (for example, alcohol abuse or food preoccupations) fade, the patient will face a sense of weakness and need, and will experience a new sense of responsibility and guilt. Their anger, no longer externalized, may also be internally disorganizing and may continue to undo (snag) their gains and achievements. Understanding and trusting the self and others during this transition can be enhanced by a new mapping of this new, unfamiliar world.

CHAPTER 8

CAT and Couple Therapy

Most individuals who seek psychotherapy have difficulties in relating to others, and in some cases these difficulties are primarily manifested in a given relationship, usually marriage or an equivalently emotionally committed arrangement. In such cases patient and therapist need to make a choice between work with the couple or work with the individual. Work with the couple will require, of course, agreement on the part of the other, and this will not always be forthcoming, especially where there is a pressure for the consulting patient to be regarded as the sick one. Couple and individual work are not, of course, mutually exclusive, and it is common for one to be followed by the other. Individuals enmeshed neurotically with their partners may sometimes be unable to work on their own problems unless freed to a degree through couple therapy, others may need personal therapy before they can reconsider the terms of their relationship. In this chapter the application of CAT to work with couples will be discussed and illustrated.

Couple Matching and Mismatching

To sustain their relationship a couple must maintain a satisfactory meshing of their reciprocal role procedures. Similar social and cultural backgrounds make such a satisfactory meshing more probable in so far as the definitions of appropriate mutual roles are more likely to be agreed between them, but, as is well known, even in a socially homogeneous street the actual experiences of a child are very different in each house. The personalities of the parents, their relationship and child-rearing practices, the size of the family, the presence or absence of extended family members and many other factors all play an important part, and in subsequent close emotional relationships the effect of these intimate factors on personality structure plays the dominant part.

The partner chosen by the individual may be expected to match, to complement, and to extend the individual's personality and life concerns, the importance given to these different elements varying. These expectations may be quite explicit and conscious or largely implicit. In satisfactory re-lationships they are sufficiently grounded in reality and sufficiently flexible to allow mutual adjustment and the growth of each as life proceeds. In unsatisfactory relationships, on the other hand, the original reciprocal roles prove in time to be restrictive and harmful to one or both. One example would be when the powerful care-giving partner comes to recognize the need to have his or her needs met, or when the submissive or dependent partner comes to recognize his or her capacity for independence. In such cases the original relationship was based upon a dispersion of the reciprocal roles, in which one filled predominantly parent-derived roles and the other predominantly child-derived roles.

In more severe marital conflict the disruptions represent the emergence of mutually set up, split-off, initially unconscious alternative patterns of reciprocal relating. A common story would be an initial relationship based upon a degree of idealization, with a denial of conflict or with fantasies of perfect fusion, which are disrupted by frightening outbursts of violent de-structive interaction, in which one plays the part of the abusing or abandoning parent and the other the part of the rebellious, revengeful or crushed child. In such cases, the 'sub-personalities' characterized by split-off, defended-against, negative reciprocal role patterns are activated, and within that system each elicits the disavowed role from the other. Conflict in couples therefore represents the interlocking of matching dilemmas, either of the neurotic or of the more profound split dilemmas described in Chapter 5. These are the processes understood in object relations theory in terms of projective identification.

Couple Reformulation

The reformulation of the conflicts between couples requires that the basic reciprocal role pattern of each partner be identified and preferably related to their early experience, and that on the basis of this, the pattern of interaction between the couple, and especially the sequences leading to the emergence of the destructive aspects of their relationships, be clearly de-scribed. Such descriptions, as in individual therapy, need to be elaborated with the help of the couple. Once worked out, they can be used by the couple themselves to monitor and hopefully control their own interactions and to prevent the repeated enactment of the negative spiral, and they can be used by the therapist to plan effective intervention. Three examples will now be given of reformulations of marital conflict.

Case Example: Couple 1 — Roger and Maria

Roger was seen urgently at the request of his brother, a GP, after he had broken down and wept in the ministry where he worked as a relatively senior civil servant. At the first interview he spoke largely about his wife Maria, whose frightful anger and persistent negative mood had provoked this distress. He was a 39-year-old economist who came from a naval family and who had himself served in the navy for seven years before going to university. He described his father, who had died two years previously, as a remote man whom he regretted not having known better. He wept at this point in the interview. His mother seems to have been a more involved parent, but in a somewhat hovering and critical way. He had been at boarding school since the age of 8. There and in the navy he felt himself to have been slightly the odd man out, because of his artistic interests (painting and the theatre). At university he had met Maria; this was his first sustained relationship with a woman. He described her as 'typically Mediterranean' in temperament, she being Greek (she left her country after leaving school). At that time she was pursuing a degree at university; she had not yet completed that when the couple were seen because the process had been interrupted by the birth of their child, now aged 3.

After the first meeting a joint session was proposed but Maria did not accept it. Roger consulted again some weeks later and after this occasion Maria agreed to come. She was seen individually before the joint session. She was an emotional, unhappy woman but appeared less ill than had been anticipated from the way she had been described by her husband. She discussed her frustration at his pernicketiness and controlling obsessionality, which she saw as inhibiting the pleasure they had in each other and in their child. She admitted that her outbursts of temper were often extreme but felt that the eruptions were frequently provoked by Roger's withholdingness. She also felt that cultural differences made him exaggerate and be intolerant of her behaviour. She was currently feeling so depressed that she went to bed in the early evening, and there had been no sexual relations between the couple for many months.

She was one of the youngest in a large family. Her father, a remote, busy, successful, self-made man had been around very little in her childhood, but she had an older brother who had been very supportive, particularly of her academic pursuits. Her mother seemed to have been an unreliable source of love, and, along with her older sister, seemed to have been actively envious to the extent that Maria had felt guilty and unable to accept love through most of her adolescence. At 17 she had had a period of some seven months during which she was anorexic. Her only previous serious love affair was at 19 and this was with a man who had been seriously depressed, and who had killed himself soon after the end of their relationship. In this relationship she seemed to have taken on a kind of expiatory role which was an exaggeration of the role she had had in the family, where she had been busy trying to resolve conflicts and improve communication without very much success. When she met Roger, she had responded positively both to his reliability and also to his artistic side, but over the past two years she had found his obsessionality and controllingness increasingly irksome.

Reformulation was made using the reciprocal role pattern charts (Figures 8.1 and 8.2) and, after discussion with the couple, was finalized in the following form:

> The attached charts offer a way of summarizing your past family relationship patterns and are a way of showing how the roles played by the self, and the pattern of relationships learned at that time, are affecting you now. The first thing you may notice is the degree of similarity in the basic patterns between the two of you, despite your very different backgrounds. This is something that would prepare the way for the re-emergence of old child—parent patterns in the relationship between you. For Maria, childhood was

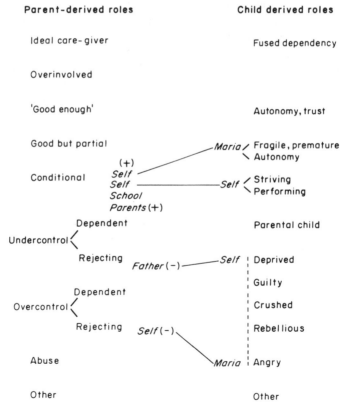

Figure 8.1 Reciprocal role analysis: Roger

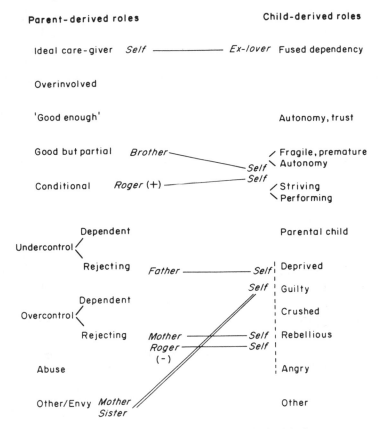

Figure 8.2 Reciprocal role analysis: Maria

insecure with an envious unreliable mother and a remote father, but with care and encouragement from her elder brother. The envy of mother and sister, however, made it hard to hold on to good things. Academic achievement has been an important self-maintained source. Emotional dependence is fragile, however; rejection is easily felt and good things are easily destroyed.

For Roger, childhood was secure in a conventional sense, but his mother was quite critical and controlling and his father was remote. The care of schools and of the navy is likely to have reinforced unemotional control, despite which some precarious, maybe rebellious, interest in the arts was maintained. In general, there is some underlying anxiety which leads to excessive critical control of self and others.

The original mutual attraction would seem to have been based upon Maria finding a man offering security and encouragement, somewhat like her brother, but also apparently sharing and valuing a more expressive side. For Roger, there was Maria's response to, and enlargement of, his expressive side which contrasted with his sense of the family he came from, whereas for himself he had initially enjoyed the role of benign care-taker. The downward spiral was based upon Maria responding to criticism and rejection, real or perceived, by switching into her old child role of angry rebellion, or by feeling crushed and hopeless. These responses evoke in Roger either critical rejection or a heightening of his benign 'parental care-taking', thus further amplifying the cycle. Originally, Roger had sought in Maria the opposite of his mother, and Maria had sought in Roger the opposite of her mother. In conflict, however, Roger becomes like her mother and his mother, and treats Maria like he treats his own despised, criticized, childhood self, and she experiences and treats him like she felt towards her own negative childhood mother. The underlying dilemmas in self-control and care are similar and can be summarized as follows:

For Maria: It is as if she is only able to chose between *either* precariously accepting her lively self, *or* blaming and crushing her bad self (depression).

For Roger: It is a question of *either* precariously permitting a lively self, *or* sternly controlling a 'bad, weak' self (obsessionality).

The above reformulation, along with the two charts, were discussed at the second meeting and revised at the third. The couple attended in all only six sessions. During this period they reported improvement in their relationship and they felt they did not at that time want to continue with any more therapy.

Case Example: Couple 2 — David and Sarah

David and Sarah had been married for eight years when they consulted. During that period David had been diagnosed as having a bipolar affective disorder and had had three severe hypomanic episodes. During the last of these, which followed a reduction in lithium dosage, he had behaved in ways which had provoked Sarah into leaving him. At the time of their consultation they were together again; David was depressed and was resisting and postponing a number of life tasks in and out of the home and Sarah was angry, impatient and uncertain about the future of the marriage.

David came from a family in which achievement was the main concern; his mother was a somewhat self-effacing woman and his father remote. He was at boarding school from the age of 9 and hated it; in his later adolescence he had abused drugs. His career was precarious due to the alternation between his high phases, marked by original and ambitious projects, and his subsequent phases of exhaustion, depression and infinite postponements. Sarah came from a high achieving, warm, quarrelsome, exciting family; she herself was a spontaneous, energetic and warm person, little aware of the less happy aspects of her early experiences and currently angry and demanding in relation to David.

Reformulation was carried out using the reciprocal role charts (Figures 8.3 and 8.4) and the following prose reformulation was devised:

> This is an attempt to trace your patterns of relating to others in the past and in the present, and of the (connected) patterns of self-care and control.
>
> *David*: Your main early experience was of acceptance being conditional upon performance. This is now re-experienced in your pattern of self-demand and in your response to others whom you see as demanding. The choice is seen as *either* gloomy compliance, *or* passive resistance. A compensatory version of care, from the manically idealized self (and from Sarah when you first met) frees creativity in a way dangerously close to omnipotence. But Sarah is nowadays usually seen to occupy the demanding-parent role, to be gloomily acquiesced to or passively refused.
>
> *Sarah*: In the 'official account', your family is full of energy, directness, quarrels, forgiveness and excitement, and this sustains the almost manic energy and capacity to perform and generate which is characteristic of you. But I think this real source is also, to a degree, enlarged and idealized as a means of denying the negative side; you as the parental child looking after your depressed mother, you as the excited, rebellious daughter to your father. Those pains were solved by you leaving home early and only re-establishing contact later in an adult relationship. Somewhere, the sad and needy Sarah is concealed; maybe looking after the sad and needy David was a way of coping with this?
>
> So, to David, Sarah can be a manic confirmer, a caring parent or a demanding parent; her attempts to claim her own needs (more direct of late) are very easily conflated, for David, with her 'parental' demands, to be resisted. Despite the huge surface differences between you, we see in the charts strong correspondences in the basic structures, which account for the power of the relationship and for the painful locking into negative interactions. Individually, the basic dilemmas for each are similar, but the chosen poles are complementary:
>
> *David*: It is as if, in relationships, the choice is *either* to be

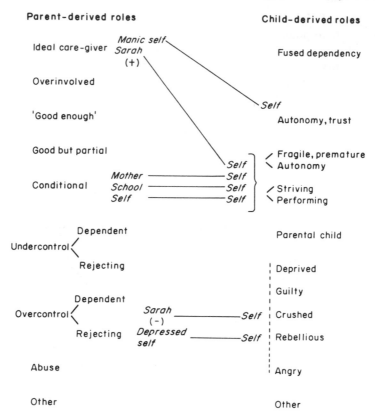

Figure 8.3 Reciprocal role analysis: David

powerfully (omnipotently) following my own enterprises (danger of hypomania), *or* facing inexorable demands from self and others, and responding with *either* gloomy compliance, *or* passive resistance (danger of depression).

Sarah: It is as if, in relationships, the choice is *either* to be powerfully performing or engendering, through parental-type care, chosen enterprises in myself or others, *or* (largely avoided) to directly acknowledge my own unmet needs. If this is risked and the needs are unmet, then I revert to the first option of cutting off (as I did by leaving home) rather than experience depression.

This couple were treated for six joint sessions followed by individual therapy, and benefited both individually and in terms of their relationship.

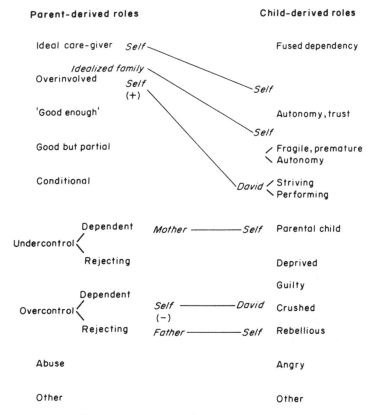

Figure 8.4 Reciprocal role analysis: Sarah

Case Example: Couple 3—Polly and Steve

Polly and Steve were a couple in their early thirties. They were referred from the child psychiatry department where they had attended in respect of their 3-year-old child who was not, however, considered to be in need of any individual treatment. The couple had a history of an unstable relationship for the past eight years, marked by numerous separations and recently by some episodes of physical violence, in one of which Steve had 'half-strangled' Polly, who had gone off to a women's refuge for a few days. Reformulation was based upon information gathered in three joint sessions by the registrar in child psychiatry and from two joint sessions of couple therapy. This reformulation was also based upon the couple each reading and marking the Psychotherapy File. They were asked to compare their two files, but this they had not done. The items scored as ++ by Polly were the following:

Traps

Avoidance, depressed thinking, social isolation and trying to please.

Dilemmas

2. *Either* spoil myself and am greedy, *or* deny and punish myself.
3. *Either* try to be perfect (feel depressed and angry), *or* don't try to be perfect (feel guilty, angry and dissatisfied).
4. If I must, then I won't (own and other's wishes are seen as too demanding and are resisted).

Choices About Self and Others

2. If I care about someone, then they have to give in to me.
3. If I depend on someone, then they have to do what I want.
5. *Either* involved and likely to get hurt, *or* uninvolved and lonely.
8. *Either* I stick up for myself and nobody likes me, *or* give in and get put on by others (feel cross and hurt).
9. *Either* a brute, *or* a martyr (secretly blaming the other).
10. *Either* look down on others *or* feel they look down on me.

Snags

(b) Feel limited by something inside myself.

Items scored ++ by Steve were as follows:

Traps

Trying to please (feel taken advantage of, angry, depressed, guilty — uncertainty about self is confirmed).

Dilemmas

1. *Either* keep feelings bottled up, *or* risk being rejected, hurting others or making a mess.

Choices About Self and Others

3. If I depend on someone, then they have to do what I want.
4. If I depend on someone, then I have to give in to them.

Snags

(a) Feel limited by fear of the response of others.
(b) Feel limited by something inside myself.

The reformulation reads as follows:

> You are both deep down very uncertain about yourselves, both vulnerable and expecting things not to go right, both bearing pain and anger which is also very much active between you. You both deal with the situation by being on the surface placatory, trying to win approval and acceptance from the other, and trying to convince yourselves and each other that you are 'good' by bottling up negative feelings and by forms of perfectionism. This, however, leads to smouldering resentment which in the end flares up, often inappropriately.
>
> Polly ultimately sees the choice for her as between that of being a 'good martyr' or a 'brute', and therefore chooses to be the martyr. Any anger she feels is so scary that she becomes disorganized, confused and ineffective, or it takes the form of passive resistance, not doing things for herself or Steve. Steve tends to inflate himself with unrealistic plans. This is coupled with a denial of his own childish weaknesses, seeing these as being exclusively located in Polly. The spiral that destroys the relationship starts here, overwhelming the confident and healthy adult parts of each. For both, emotional dependence is felt to be vulnerable and to depend upon the other is to feel controlled. This in turn leads to attempts to control the other, usually indirectly in the case of Polly, whose control is exercised largely by means of refusals, rejections and evasions. In the case of Steve, this is expressed by subtle and not so subtle bullying, noticeably by his adoption of a parental role, giving Polly good marks for good behaviour, dressing nicely and so on, and bad marks for failures. The more that Steve becomes critical and contemptuous of Polly in this way, the more Polly becomes a secretive, obstinate, withholding child, but also the more she feels that her earlier experience of loss and abandonments must have been in some sense her fault. Thus she concludes that she is a bad person and deserves this treatment and if she deserves it then she might as well die, hence the overdose taken after the first session here.
>
> I think both of you need to work hard on re-establishing your separate identities, reclaiming your individual strengths and acknowledging your individual weaknesses, difficulties and pains. This will be important for your own sakes and for that of your daughter.

You are both people who have managed many things, and survived many things, and there is something between you which has endured through eight years. I believe that if you can learn to understand and control the spiral I have tried to describe above, it is likely that you will try to stay together on better terms. If it turns out that you cannot stay together you will at least have tried to understand what has happened between you.

At a subsequent meeting a simple sequential diagrammatic reformulation was also offered (Figure 8.5). Although they both seemed to understand and get some control from the reformulation, the actual pattern of behaviour did not change very much over the first four or five sessions; indeed at the fourth and fifth sessions the spiral was re-enacted during the therapy session with Steve opening with a blast of contemptuous criticism of Polly's inertia and failures, and with Polly becoming incoherent and silent in response to

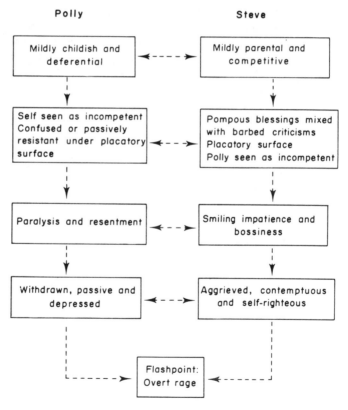

Figure 8.5 Sequential diagrammatic reformulation of a couple

this. These re-enactments were related to the reformulation, and in order to destabilize them some more directive methods were also used, namely allocating very clear areas of control and responsibility in order to block some of the ways into the spiral.

Joint therapy here produced some minor, perhaps only cosmetic, changes in Steve's behaviour, while Polly remained largely inaccessible, resisting all homework tasks and remaining vulnerable to Steve in the sessions. In view of this and of her own painful childhood and adolescence, during which both parents had died, joint work was stopped and Polly was started in individual therapy.

Conclusion

In describing how an individual organizes his acts and roles, the Procedural Sequence Model emphasizes how the sequence is constituted of inner mental events, of anticipations, of acts and of the perception of the consequences of acts. In describing the interaction between a couple one is identifying the interlocking of two sets of role procedures (in psychoanalytic terms, identifying the mutual projective identifications). Hence, the application of CAT to work with couples involves a straightforward extension of the underlying principles and methods.

In devising couple reformulations, clinical interview data, both historical and the observed interactions, can be usefully supplemented by other CAT techniques. The Psychotherapy File is probably particularly useful in identifying shared and complementary patterns. The reciprocal role charts provide a convenient way of summarizing individual histories and interactions and often, as in the first two cases described above, reveal unexpected similarities of patterning in couples whose temperaments are apparently opposed. Sequential diagrams of the repeated malignant interactions occurring in the relationship can serve as a basis for the therapist to pick up the pattern as it occurs during sessions, as in the third couple described above, and might enable the couple to carry out shared monitoring of their interaction, although this was not achieved in this case. Joint work on monitoring identified damaging interactions on the basis of mutually agreed reformulations could be linked with behavioural contracting or the use of other behavioural techniques aimed to replace or avoid such interactions.

CHAPTER 9

The Use of CAT in Various Clinical Settings

Prepared and edited by BEE J. BROCKMAN

In this chapter therapists describe their experience of working with CAT in different settings, namely as a counsellor in general practice, in a social work department, in forensic psychiatry services and in private practice.

CAT in General Practice

ANNALEE CURRAN

[Annalee Curran is a counsellor in a group general practice. She has also worked for ten years as an antenatal teacher and trainer for the National Childbirth Trust. She trained as a therapist in CAT in 1985 and now works as a supervisor.]

I had been working for some nine years in a medium-sized inner-London general practice when I joined the Guy's CAT project and later began to apply this approach to my work in general practice.

In this setting, I am a member of a primary care team which has a close and supportive working relationship. The patients whom I see are of diverse social backgrounds. Most are referred by the doctors or other health professionals in the team but many are self-referred. There is a wide age range (18–70 years) and men and women are seen in approximately equal numbers. Most present with neurotic and relationship problems, and a number with incomplete mourning reactions.

The advantages of working in this setting are that patients are seen in familiar surroundings, avoiding the stigma and effort of referral to psychiatric services, and that the GPs remain involved and are available to provide medical back-up.

These advantages carry some costs, however. The ease of referral can result in patients of low motivation being referred, and the fact that I am 'visible' and easily accessible to the patients can mean that appropriate boundaries can be hard to maintain. However, experience has led to more clarity on both these issues.

As in any service which offers more or less open access, the problem soon arises of over-referral, and the establishment of a waiting list reduces the advantages of the primary care location. For this reason, the introduction of CAT, with its time-limited and focusing elements, seemed highly desirable. When I began to use the method there were some patients who had been in long-term therapy to whom I offered a final 12 or 16 sessions using the CAT model. One such case is described below, in whom the changeover to CAT generated a much more active involvement in therapy. Another innovation introduced was to offer patients an initial contract of 1–4 sessions for assessment of their need for, and capacity to use, a course of therapy. When judged suitable for further therapy, these patients were given the psychotherapy file to read and were set appropriate self-monitoring tasks to carry out whilst waiting for the formal therapy to start.

Using the CAT approach in this setting has proved to be very effective. The high level of patient involvement and the explicit focusing process are acceptable to the patients and increase their active involvement in the process of therapy. This approach enables patients to begin to exercise more control over their symptoms and their lives and to avoid, or help them to move away from, the 'passive patient' role. Two illustrative case histories are presented.

Case Example: Margaret

Margaret, aged 24, was seen at her doctor's request for depression and bulimia nervosa. She was seen initially for more purely cognitive therapy, concentrating on the eating disorder. During this time she was late or missed appointments and seemed very unwilling to examine feelings. She was then given ten sessions of CAT. The reformulation yielded the four following TPPs:

1. In relationships I feel *either* close but out of control, *or* withdrawn but alone and empty.
   Aim: To feel that there are people I can get close to without losing the sense of myself.
2. With other people I must *either* keep my feelings bottled up, *or* express them and make a mess.
   Aim: To feel that it is all right to have my say without losing control and without driving people away.

3. The social isolation trap from the Psychotherapy File.
   Aim: To start believing in myself and to feel confident that I have something to offer the world and other people.
4. A cycle: when feeling lonely I give myself treats, usually food, which makes me feel guilty, I then make myself sick.
   Aim: To feel I can treat myself without feeling guilty and without having to punish myself.

The result of this CAT was that the patient became less depressed, less dominated by, but not free of, her eating disorder and quite a lot more positive and realistic about her future plans. She recorded some improvement on all four of the TPPs and was quite evidently more able to feel and express feelings by the end of the therapy than she had been at the beginning.

Case Example: Gudrun

Gudrun, aged 28, was referred by her GP for counselling because of anxiety and depression. She was suffering due to her inability to resolve the situation she was in. This consisted of her sustaining relationships simultaneously with two men, both of whom she loved, neither of whom she wanted to leave and neither of whom she wanted to hurt. In her family history she had been attached to both parents. The father, who was away frequently through her childhood, finally divorced the mother when Gudrun was aged 13. Gudrun spent much of her adolescence making sure that neither parent felt they had lost her.

Gudrun had met one boyfriend (William) while at college some seven years previously. She saw him as a stable secure person who was accepted by her family, and they had started living together after a short time. Three years later she had met Charles, with whom she had a number of ideas and interests in common and with whom she had intense discussions and an exciting sexual relationship. She had tried to resolve the situation by living on her own but she had soon returned to William's security, and not long after that began once more to see Charles in secret. That was the situation when she sought therapy.

Gudrun was seen for 18 months in once-a-week therapy, the theme of the sessions being her childhood and the continuing unresolved situation with her two men. Because no obvious resolution was taking place it was decided to revise the contract and to have a final 16 sessions along CAT lines. The effect of the change was that Gudrun became markedly more active in the therapy. She had always talked fluently about her experiences and her feelings, but she now seemed more thoughtful, particularly in relation to reading the Psychotherapy File, and from the second session onwards she was more overtly emotionally involved than she had been before. The Target Problem Procedures that were agreed were as follows:

1. I am *either* safe and contained and told what to do but feeling frustrated, *or* I am a free spirit getting food for the soul but feeling guilty.
2. The second dilemma, which related to the above and was called the 'Alice in Wonderland' dilemma, was: I am *either* being larger than life, feeling wild and free but insecure, *or* I am small and cosy and secure in a rabbit hutch.
   Aim: to be life-sized and to feel that my feelings are real.
3. The snag: feeling guilty about being myself I feel I need to compensate or pay for my life.
   Aim: to feel free to claim my own life and to feel able to give without feeling I am paying a debt.

Between the eighth and tenth sessions Gudrun became anxious and quite depressed in relation to the termination of therapy, and at the twelfth session she reported that, following the reading of some old diaries and the re-living of the pain she had felt about her parents' separation, she had become aware of a kind of abyss or black hole. This awareness was experienced directly during the session, as if it had opened up, and she broke down into convulsive frightened sobbing, clinging on to the therapist. At the thirteenth session she emphasized how important it was to face this abyss and begged that the therapy might be extended. An additional four sessions, making a total of 20, were negotiated at this point. In fact Gudrun became a lot calmer over the next two or three sessions; she could not really explain why this was, except that she felt more faith in her self and more able to be ordinary. Fearful feelings, which made her frightened about going mad, had been reported in the first phase of therapy; now, although still present, these were no longer frightening. By this time she had discontinued her meetings with Charles. The summary of the therapy, which was given to Gudrun at the end, was as follows:

> The main thing which has emerged from our time together is your discovery of a sense of yourself that is more real, more whole than you had experienced before. This is still quite fragile and new, but you seem to feel all right about going along with it, trusting it and not forcing it in one direction or another. I think you have realized that you haven't really found the answers or the solution but you have a bit more faith in yourself. As we explored things, it appeared that a possible reason for your not having been your real self was to do with the covering up of the frightening 'black hole'. By busily and actively moving from one side to the other, as in your movements from William to Charles, you had the illusion of something safe and solid over the hole, whereas in fact the entrance was always there, manifest from time to time as the frightening feelings which revealed that there was no solid island of your own

self. Perhaps the hole represented the lack of the real you. I think
that maybe you didn't allow yourself to be the real you because of
your childhood, especially your parents' separation and your feeling
that you had to make both of them feel that they hadn't lost you.
You seem more certain now about the relationship you had with
your mother, and no longer feel that you have to be the go-
between of your parents. I also feel that you don't have to protect
William or Charles so much from the possibility of losing you, and
you yourself seem more able to be real, calm, even ordinary,
without supernatural effort.

Losing people has never been easy for you but part of the idea of
this time-limited therapy was to help you experience losing me
while discovering that both you and I can survive, even if we both
find it painful. I think it is important to state that I feel *the
emergence of a more real you* which I trust in, even though it feels
fragile to you at times. It will take time to get to full strength but
you are standing on your own two feet now.

At follow up two years later, Gudrun was married to William, had a year-
old daughter and reported a continuing sense of being all right in herself.
The rating sheet completed during the CAT with Gudrun showed deterioration
in respect of her dilemmas and snag between the ninth and fourteenth
sessions, but a steady improvement to near the top of the scale between then
and the termination of therapy. This patient was treated before the development of SDR. It seems that the identified dilemmas and snags were related
to an underlying core of unmanageable feelings dating back to her parents'
divorce or perhaps earlier. Her ability to experience these feelings was
presumably the result of the safety experienced in the therapy, a safety
evidently only achieved following the introduction of CAT techniques.

CAT in a Social Work Setting

NORMA MAPLE

[Norma Maple is an experienced social worker who had worked for many years in
generic social work and in specialized mental health social work departments. She
received some psychotherapy training at the Tavistock Institute before being introduced to CAT during post-graduate training for her M.Soc.Sc. in mental disorder
studies.]

On my return to work in a social services department, subsequent to my
M.Soc.Sc. and CAT training, I proposed to the area team in which I was

working that I would investigate whether CAT was a useful model to implement in our work setting. At the time this was a short-staffed area fieldwork team in an outer-London borough which was providing support for a wide range of clients, a large minority of whom had originated from the Asian sub-continent. My main aim was to see if the model, which I had applied successfully in a hospital setting, could be used effectively in a less clinical, more generic, environment. I was also interested to see if some of the long-term work carried out by social workers, often involving statutory obligations and classified under various problem orientations, could in fact be re-defined as personal difficulties amenable to short-term focused therapy using the CAT model.

As with any new departure from the established practice in any organization, there were some incomprehensions and rivalries to be dealt with. Despite the explicit support given by both management and other colleagues, some referrals had the quality of 'treat that if you dare'. However, despite some difficulties an acceptable number of clients were successfully recruited from existing case loads or from new referrals to the 'duty desk', and these were offered CAT therapy. The presenting problems of these clients included family violence, disturbed behaviour in the children of the family, failure to cope with work or daily living, bereavement and alcohol abuse. One client was barely literate (see below).

The offer of therapy was made to identified individual members of the client families, but no pressure was put upon them to accept. Most of them had no prior experience of therapy and indeed had little concept of what they were committing themselves to. Where the department had a statutory commitment to the family, for example child-care supervision, appropriate strategies were developed to ensure that the statutory supervision was maintained by another worker during the period of therapy. Because of the limited educational attainments of many of the clients, a simplified version of the Psychotherapy File was developed. Some clients found it easier to tape their diaries rather than to write them, and reformulations were tailored to the particular client in the way they found most helpful. For example, one client preferred a diagrammatic description to the written one. One of the main advantages of the use of CAT in this setting was that it offered a focused reassessment of clients who had been receiving regular social work support for a long period of time. In many cases a major benefit of the intervention was that this long-term dependency mode of functioning was questioned, and many clients were enabled to accept increasing responsibility and independence during the period of therapy, and subsequently ceased to need care.

The emphasis on client participation, self-monitoring and self-help in the CAT model is of particular relevance to social work departments wishing to assist individuals to achieve independence and self-management and to take over care of their families. Even though many of the clients in this study showed marked levels of psychological disturbance and major social incapacity, many were able to make major changes. This was achieved despite the very real reluctance of most people to seek support from a social services department and despite the fact that their psychological difficulties were combined with quite major practical adversity. Moreover, therapy was being offered in an organization not geared to provide the basic requirements, such as appropriate accommodation and timetabling, which are needed to make the keeping of regular commitments possible.

In summary, therefore, my own experience suggests that short-term focused CAT offers social workers a method of psychological intervention capable of achieving change in some social work clients. It is also a model of work which is effective in avoiding or resolving unhelpful dependency by clients on workers. How such a therapeutic role for the worker can be negotiated alongside their statutory commitments is something requiring thought and experience from those responsible for running social work departments. [This project is more fully described in Maple (1988).]

Case Example: Louise

Louise sought help in order to regain the care of her daughter. The child was in the custody of other family members as a result of Louise's history of drinking to excess and a more general failure to provide reasonable care. Prior to starting CAT she had been receiving long-term case-work for more than eight years. The history of alcohol abuse and long-term dependency would normally be considered to be poor prognostic indicators in therapy. However, she completed a therapy focused on the following three dilemmas and a snag:

1. As if *either* a competent, caring but 'babied' daughter, *or* a resentful, lackadaisical mess.
2. As if *either* powerfully disarming, *or* murderous.
3. If I must, then I won't.
4. The snag. As if I can only have my life at my parents' expense.

Follow-up evaluation revealed several positive changes, which included successful completion of a training course and obtaining full-time employment. At a later date she referred herself back for further therapy in order to maintain and consolidate the primary therapy gains.

Case Example: Phillip

Phillip reported anxiety and a general lack of self-confidence since he had been rejected by his disabled wife. He suffered from deafness and could barely read or write. Despite these constraints he completed therapy, making considerable progress on his three TPPs which were:

1. The placation trap.
2. The social isolation trap.
3. The dilemma: As if I must *either* be alone *or* be a slave.

He rated himself to be 75% improved on the dilemma and 100% improved on the traps.

At follow-up he was noted to be able to take appropriate responsibility, had developed a wider social support network, and was looking for work in a more confident manner.

CAT in the Forensic Services

BEE J. BROCKMAN and JEANETTE SMITH

[Bee Brockman is now a consultant in forensic psychiatry, having previously played a leading part in the development of the CAT brief therapy project at Guy's Hospital. Jeanette Smith is a senior registrar in forensic psychiatry who has also had experience of applying CAT in a forensic setting. The work of both was largely carried out with patients attending out-patients, but some in-patients who were in regional secure units were also treated with CAT.]

In forensic settings the great majority of patients are of lower socio-economic status and have offended. Although a small number are self-referred the great majority are seen at the request of other psychiatrists, probation officers, social services, the courts, solicitors or GPs. A large proportion resist the idea of therapy. In this group of social and sexual deviants the underlying personality traits are commonly those of immaturity and inadequacies, often amounting to severe personality disorder with borderline structure. In these difficult cases it seems particularly important to follow-up the initial sessions with written material sent between appointments, prior to the full reformulation, as many of these patients have difficulty in retaining what has been said to them, and the establishment of a therapeutic alliance can be particularly difficult. As far as possible, patients were also encouraged to write accounts of their experience. The use of imagery and role-play was often effective with these patients.

The advantage of CAT for the psychiatrist in this setting was that realistic intervention was possible because of the clear time limit adhered to in most cases. The discipline of reformulation was also of value in preparing assessments for the courts, and in suggesting realistic therapeutic interventions which might be considered as alternatives to sentencing. For example, an individual who had repeatedly committed the same offence, but who, during the reformulation phase of CAT, came to understand in a new way the sources of his behaviour, could be seen to have embarked upon the process of gaining control over his behaviour prior to court disposal.

Forensic work imposes constraints upon the therapeutic relationship not often experienced in other therapy settings. Examples of these restraints are the issues of confidentiality, heightened patient resistance, and interruption of therapy through sentencing. Patients' resistance to therapy is obviously marked when they are attending for an assessment which they know will also be part of the evidence given in the court. In some cases this makes it impossible to make a therapeutic alliance, in others one has to take care that individuals who are 'wise' about court procedures do not use the interview in a manipulative way. Assessments usually have to be made prior to a court appearance, but therapeutic intervention is best left until the court has decided upon the future fate of the individual. This, however, is not always possible, which can create further difficulties for the therapist. For example, a 30-year-old homosexual man had waited six months for a Crown Court hearing in relation to a charge of assault and grievous bodily harm with intent to commit a sexual offence. He was referred by his probation officer whilst on bail because of the high level of distress and anxiety he was showing. The assault had taken place under the influence of alcohol after a period of considerable stress, and the problems underlying this stress needed to be addressed immediately. After six weeks of therapy the court heard the case, and he was sentenced to two years' imprisonment. Fortunately in this case it was possible to arrange to continue treatment with a prison psychologist.

In other cases the problem of confidentiality arises when patients, in the course of therapy, disclose information about undetected or unsolved crimes. In these cases, therapists have to encourage the patient to report the offence to the authorities. If this is not done, it is not possible to continue with the therapy. In cases of serious offending, confidentiality must be broken because of the therapist's continuing responsibility to the public at large; this potential problem of confidentiality is explained to the patient at the start of therapy.

A number of patients seen in forensic settings are severely damaged people who may need long-term support. Many of these patients are socially isolated to a degree which makes it difficult for them to work on problems between sessions. It is difficult to make long-term plans within this setting, but the reformulation of CAT provides a framework to define the needs and structure of the work to be done. An initial CAT intervention may achieve a clear redefinition of the problems and will provide a good measure of the patient's ability to use therapy. This allows the therapist to plan the use of intermittent further brief therapy or some other therapeutic programme if that is not appropriate.

In summary, in this difficult treatment setting the structured framework of assessment, reformulation and planned intervention provided by CAT benefits both patient and therapist.

Case Example: Albert

Albert was a young man in his mid-teens who, following arrest for theft, was referred by magistrates for a medical report. He had started to gamble with arcade machines, becoming addicted within a few months. He first stole from his mother, and then was arrested for stealing lead from a local church. The first interview revealed that his parents' marriage had broken down before he began to exhibit anger, anxiety and antisocial behaviour. Reformulation of the presenting problem was possible in this assessment interview. A four-session therapy involving monitoring of mood and behaviour, and one joint interview with mother, resulted in a dramatic shift in his relationships and behaviour. He was able to express emotions appropriately, relinquish his previous guilt for his parents' separation, and he ceased acting antisocially. Follow-up at one year demonstrated that the initial therapy gains had been maintained and he had not re-offended.

Case Example: Stanley

Stanley had pleaded guilty to repeated sexual exposure ('exhibitionism') and consulted on the advice of his solicitor, requesting a medical report to assist the court disposal. He was a graduate in his thirties, holding a responsible job, who had been in a stormy homosexual relationship for several years. His presenting problems were depression with marked anxiety; the latter had returned after he had exposed himself again. He experienced his desire to expose as an irresistible impulse, felt he had no control over his behaviour, and hated himself after each episode. He was appropriately worried about a possible prison sentence, as he had been prosecuted in the past.

CAT assessment and reformulation revealed a pattern of exposure that was triggered by events in his unsatisfactory relationship and delineated the procedural sequence culminating in offending. He made detailed use of the Psychotherapy File and carried out meticulous self-monitoring of a range of procedures. As a result, he was able to take charge of his behaviour, and express feelings appropriately, find effective modes of anxiety management and free himself from his destructively dependent relationship. Sufficient change had occurred in therapy prior to the court hearing for a recommendation to be made for him to be dealt with by a probation order with a condition of treatment rather than imprisonment. Follow-up over two years showed that his therapy gains were maintained, and revealed an unexpected spin-off from his improved assertion and confidence in the form of a job promotion.

Case Example: Winifred

Winifred, a middle-aged single care assistant, was admitted under the Mental Health Act for assessment after she had set fire to the old people's home in which she worked.

Assessment and treatment took place in the Regional Secure Hospital because of the potential risk to others of repeated fire setting, and to herself, as she had threatened suicide whilst in prison.

Assessment failed to demonstrate evidence of mental illness, but elicited a history of an atypical grief reaction following her mother's death some years previously. There was a life-long history of poor self-esteem, and feelings of guilt and inadequacy associated with placation. She had always been unable to express appropriate anger. She had lit the fire in a dissociated state the day after dismissal by her employers. At the time of her assessment it appeared that she was angry with herself, blaming her own behaviour for her loss of employment, and did not appear to bear any grudges.

The 16-session therapy was focused on her grief, poor self-esteem and associated placation, and the need to understand the fire-setting behaviour. In the course of therapy it emerged that the fire was her way of seeking punishment for herself, which she deemed necessary as she believed she was letting everyone down by her imminent departure from the old people's home. Her TP/TPP list (see below) shows that long-term issues were dealt with in the course of the therapy. By the end, she reported (on the TP/TPP rating sheet) 50–75% improvement on the three TPPs.

TPs

1. Fire-setting behaviour.
2. Guilt, underconfidence, loneliness, empty life.

TPPs

1. You live your life feeling guilty and worthless as if you had caused your mother's death.
   Aim: To work through your grief and recognize that the guilt is unnecessary and that you have a right to have your needs met.
2. In relationships you are *either* a lonely but safe hedgehog, *or* an intensely dependent child.
   Aim: To form adult mutual relationships, in touch with your emotions and other people but not childishly dependent.
3. In yourself you feel that you are *either* a bland placating pudding, *or* a volcano about to erupt.

Aim: To learn to assert yourself by both setting limits and recognizing your needs as well as accepting compliments and praise.

The court dealt with the case by way of a two-year probation order. Follow-up evaluation one year later demonstrated that her therapeutic gains had been maintained and generalized into other aspects of her life.

CAT in Private Practice

ELIZABETH MCCORMICK

[Elizabeth McCormick has worked in private practice since 1979. She is a clinical psychotherapist and counsellor with a background in humanistic and transpersonal psychology. She has applied CAT in a number of settings within the NHS and in private practice.]

Most patients seeking therapy privately are self-referred and are well motivated to make at least initial changes. The advantage of CAT in a private setting is that it enables busy people to have a focused look at their problems, and it is also of limited and predictable cost. I have found it to be a particularly effective model when working with people suffering from psychosomatic illness and with other patients who need to understand the links between behaviour and the onset of symptoms. This can be illustrated by the example of a typical group of patients who present with cardiac problems. Such patients may refer themselves for short-term CAT after a myocardial infarction ('coronary') because they recognize how much their self-defeating patterns of behaviour are impeding their recovery. Some coronary patients find it difficult to stop these repeated behaviours without experiencing a loss of self and associated depression and anxiety. Others feel that they are unjustified unless they are constantly in the service of others and, as a result, they are unable to take real care of themselves without feeling guilty and anxious. Some patients may seek a short-term therapy hoping to lower raised blood pressure. Such patients have often learnt early in life to hold their breath in case things go wrong. They have become terrified of any expression of anger in themselves or others, and hold themselves in, like an emotional pressure-cooker. Several female patients suffering from hypertension have described how they felt that unless they were 'super-woman', constantly trying to keep up perfectionist standards in everything they did—job, children, cooking, house, looks, holidays and hobbies—they did not exist. CAT intervention can make a great deal of difference to these patients, helping them to free themselves from exhausting strategies and unrealistic ideas of how they should be, and hence therapy can aid their physical recovery.

Because CAT engages the patients' thinking, and because it is an active therapy, particularly at the reformulation stage, these active and productive patients, who have previously only felt guilty and burdened by their physical symptoms and who often react to their illness by redoubling their efforts, come to understand clearly, often for the first time, the impact of their beliefs, attitudes and behaviours on their daily lives and on their health.

Compared to colleagues working within the NHS, I tend to use a greater number of sessions for assessment and reformulation, sometimes up to 10 sessions. This may be because mine is often the first psychological assessment the patient has had, so there are no referral notes from any source, while in hospital there is often a recorded psychiatric history.

I set the finishing date at the time of agreeing upon the TPPs, usually offering a further 10 or 12 sessions. It is important to work strictly within this framework, especially when other alternatives such as open-ended therapy are available; one is all to easily tempted to fall into the trap of colluding with the patient's fears of 'not getting enough' and so lose the force of time-limited work. At the follow-up date, which can be from six weeks after termination to three months, I reassess how the patient has used the interval. At this stage a few patients (often patients who would never have considered open-ended therapy earlier) decide to go into long-term open-ended therapy; others opt for a number of follow-up appointments spaced out at intervals.

Within the CAT framework a number of different skills and techniques can be used according to the patient's personality and requirements. As well as combining interpretive work with the CAT technique, I use active imagination, imaging, gestalt and psychodrama techniques to emphasize the nature of the patient's dilemmas, and to explore possible resolutions.

A session of CAT makes more demands on the therapist than does a session of long-term work; in addition, there is a need for active work to be done between the sessions. I find that I need to limit the number of my CAT patients to between four and six per week and feel it is reasonable to charge more per session for CAT than for long-term therapy. It is highly creative and stimulating work. Surprising and encouraging results often come right at the end, many issues being heightened and resolved in the last sessions before termination.

Case Example: Thomas

Thomas referred himself for a brief therapy because of his concern about his high blood pressure. He had limited financial resources and led a busy professional life as a research chemist, and hence welcomed the short-term contract.

He had suffered from hypertension for two years and had been treated with two types of medication in that time. His GP had suggested that 'stress' might be aggravating his physical problem so he decided to see if this was so. As he talked, I became aware of how often he held his breath in order to complete long, complicated sentences, and how he focused a non-blinking, determined stare at me; I also noted periods of hyperventilation. The only child of a single mother, Thomas had had to learn to fight to be heard by any adult early in his life, and even when heard he had been frequently criticized or corrected. His breath-holding, fixed gaze and over-breathing were symptoms related to his dilemma: It is as if unless I am super-vigilant and watch people's reactions all of the time or get my words out quickly and articulately, I will be rejected and then I have no one. This basic dilemma had established the conviction that he had to produce excellence at all times in order to survive. He was competitive in all areas of life, even with his wife and children, because of his basic terror of being 'rubbished', by-passed, or abandoned. We both became aware that the self-monitoring tasks and TPPs could themselves prove to be another hurdle that he had to jump over perfectly. At session five he realized that he could monitor either from his 'hawk-eye' self, which demanded super-vigilance, or from his 'vision' self, referring to his imaginative early life as a single child, when he would read, draw and imagine magical adventures. He expressed this part of himself with his own children but had not thought of applying it to himself anymore, as he had presumed it to be slightly shameful, 'only childish', and not of any use in a grown-up world. At this time, he developed his own meditation practices, based upon some active imagination work we had done on his 'vision' self. He monitored his hyper-vigilance and began to be aware of the number of times he had held his breath. Towards the end of the therapy he was able to let go enough to learn abdominal breathing which relieved him of his habitual hyperventilation. Analysis of blood pressure charts was inconclusive; the readings were erratic with no clear indication of any association between the raised readings and what was happening in his thinking, emotion or external life. One observation was that the readings were raised in the morning and went down at night. He spoke of waking up to 'fight the day', his anxiety starting before he got out of bed. In challenging the previous golden rule 'unless hyper-vigilant then rejected' he became aware of how difficult it was for him to express anger. We added another TPP which was: *If I get angry I will make a mess and be unlovable.* His aim was to begin to be aware of angry feelings (he had no awareness of feeling angry at first) and to use his 'vision' self to imagine what he would like to do with those feelings. Some of these ideas were acted out in the sessions, using the empty chair method of gestalt work and using cushions fired at the wall.

At three-month follow-up he was not taking medication. His blood pressure recording was still fluctuant but with fewer peaks. He felt he needed further sessions to look at anger and its management, both in himself and in other people.

It is frequently extremely difficult for patients with heart disease or other somatizing illnesses to let go of old defences. CAT offers a therapy which can attend immediately to the faulty learned thinking behind stress-maintaining procedures and allows use of other techniques, such as the teaching of meditation, breathing control, the use of gestalt and imaging techniques to release repressed thoughts and feelings and to give patients a new experience of themselves.

CHAPTER 10

The Theoretical Basis of CAT

The origin and basic theory of CAT were briefly described in Chapter 1 and the extensive examples of its practice given in subsequent chapters will have conveyed both the features constituting its specific practice and the flexibility open to therapists within those features. In the present chapter a rather more detailed consideration of the underlying theory will be presented. In the following chapters theoretical and practical comparisons with cognitive therapy and psychoanalysis will be considered.

Hidden Implications of Psychotherapy Theory

Scientific theories are formal attempts to model aspects of reality. As such, they do rigorously what every person does casually, for we all construct our relation to reality and rely upon abstractions of experience and rules to guide our actions. The most complicated of our systems of understanding and action are those concerned with ourselves and with our relationships with others. Patients seeking psychotherapy have problems in this sphere, which they have been unable to revise despite being aware of bad outcomes, and usually despite having received plenty of good advice. The psychotherapist, therefore, needs a theory which is more refined than the implicit ones which govern advising and persuading in the world at large, and one which provides her with an understanding of the neurotic person's failure to learn and which informs her interventions so that this failure can be overcome.

The problems besetting the theorists in this field are considerable, for the phenomena are extremely complex and the issues considered are bound up with popular beliefs and value systems. Moreover, the stamp of scientific approval is most readily granted to models that are accessible because they are simplistic and based on linear cause–effect relationships, but which are not appropriate to the type of interactions to be found in human higher-level mental and social functioning. An analogy is provided by the writings of Claude Bernard, who, facing the problem of providing scientific descriptions of physiological systems in the mid nineteenth century, argued eloquently

193

against falsely isolated observation on the one hand, and heady generalization on the other. Bernard pointed out that 'phenomena merely express the relations of bodies, whence it follows that, by dissociating the parts of the whole, we must make phenomena cease' but he also warned that 'if we gave ourselves up exclusively to hypothetical speculation, we should soon turn our backs on reality' (Bernard, 1957).

The tidy partial theories and sense of scientific rectitude of behavioural and cognitive therapy theorists exemplify the first of Bernard's dangers, for the simple causal chains hypothesized between stimuli, behaviours and outcomes, or between thoughts, emotions and actions, represent crude (but often useful) abstractions from the complex mental and interpersonal phenomena they set out to account for. Psychoanalysis, on the other hand, with its sprawling, infinitely debated jungle of metapsychological metaphors, stands for Bernard's other danger, that of infinite 'hypothetical contemplation', while simultaneously, in some respects, tending to reduce complexities to the simple resultants of opposed forces. It is a pity that Freud did not take note of the passage in Bernard from which the above quotations are taken, for it continues 'I am persuaded that the obstacles surrounding the experimental study of psychological phenomena are largely due to difficulties of this kind'.

As well as facing these intellectual difficulties and dangers, therapy theories can be distorting in ways which are morally risky to the enterprise of therapy. These risks are largely those of 'natural scientism', the 'error of turning persons into things' (Laing, 1967). The behavioural model allows no space to consciousness or choice (although behavioural therapists give evidence of experiencing the former and exercising the latter); in this respect behaviour modification could figure in nightmare utopias. It must be acknowledged, however, that in the real life of the clinic, it is likely that both therapist and patient accept the model as a usefully simple fiction. The 'natural scientism' of psychoanalysis is, perhaps, more dangerous, for it is embedded in a theory that seemingly aims to enlarge individual freedom. In classical psychoanalysis it is reflected in a mechanistic model of the 'mental apparatus', which explains human action as the resultant of conflicts between warring forces or institutions and which, in its preoccupation with mental events, can generate a kind of dismissive disregard for the patient's experience. In this respect, Miller's (1984) discussion of Freud's abandonment of the seduction theory (which placed the analyst in the role of one concerned to help his patient recover from the experience of violation in infancy or childhood) in favour of drive theory (in which fantasy generated by innate biological forces is the central concern), and the continuation of this latter emphasis in much contemporary analytic work, deserves serious consideration. Such 'natural scientism', in the context of the unequal relationship between therapist and patient, and especially where the induction of a regressed transference heightens this inequality to an extreme degree, exposes the patient to danger and places upon the analyst an enormous responsibility. The fortunate patient can remember and recover; the less fortunate, as Miller argues, may simply experience another violation.

There is, of course, no simple escape from this problem. Therapists are paid to educate and influence their patients, not to leave them unchanged. The word 'educate', from its derivation 'to lead forth', has come to have connotations of 'training' in order to develop 'some special aptitude, taste, or disposition' and the word 'influence' was first applied to occult powers and still implies an action 'of which the operation is unseen, except in its effects' (*OED*, 1933). Ideally, therapists do not wish to train or influence their patients, or at best would wish that the changes achieved through therapy should be those desired by the patient, but for many patients the problem is, at root, more an inability to know their desires or define their problems than a difficulty in visualizing the solutions. In this situation, the requirement upon therapists to respect their patients is a complex one.

The theoretical basis of CAT is intended to minimize the intellectual and moral dangers discussed above. The model offers a way of describing intentional, aim-directed action, and, as such, concentrates on those aspects of experience and action that are most specifically human. This does not, of course, imply that an individual's aims and intentions are fully known to him, or correspond necessarily to his account of them. The model itself is a cognitive one, interpreting 'cognitive' in a broad sense as meaning to do with higher mental functioning, including emotion, and of the organization of action, and by no means excluding from consideration unconscious mental processes. Behavioural and cognitive theories can be incorporated as subsets of the general theory. Psychoanalytic concepts are also incorporated as central to the model, but they are radically restated. It is to be hoped that this makes them more accessible and more compatible with other theories concerned with the psychology of human personal, social and mental functioning, while eliminating the pseudo-biological 'natural scientism' of some aspects of psychoanalysis.

The Procedural Sequence Model

The aim of the PSM is to understand neurosis and to guide psychotherapy. The basic descriptive unit is the procedural sequence (procedure for short) which describes intentional action in terms of a recurring modifiable repetition of sequences of mental processes and actions in the world. Such basic sequences seem to govern low-level motor skills, such as the child who sees, reaches for, grasps, conveys to the mouth and sucks an object, and the highest-level human enterprises, such as planning a career, organizing an institution or living a life. The higher-level procedures operate through an array of lower-level ones (sub-routines). Thus the model is both *hierarchical* and *sequential*. It should be noted that the distinction between higher and lower levels in this hierarchy are not to be interpreted as being similar to the distinction between conscious and unconscious. Individuals are often unaware of the higher-level processes that generate their lower-level activities. Moreover, the 'dynamic unconscious' of psychoanalysis is best understood as the result of the operation of the highest-level processes as Liotti (1987) argues.

The basic form of the PSM, as summarized in Chapter 1, is as follows:

1. Define aim (which may be a response to an external event).
2. Check the aim for congruence with other aims and values.
3. Evaluate the situation and predict (a) one's capacity to achieve the aim and (b) the likely consequences of achieving it.
4. Consider the range of means available (sub-procedures, goals, etc.).
5. Act.
6. Evaluate (a) the effectiveness and (b) the consequences of the action or role.
7. Confirm and revise (a) the procedure and/or (b) the aim.

This sequence is maintained and may be revised by a continual process of anticipation and feedback. The maintenance of unrevised or neurotic procedures (dilemmas, traps and snags) is described in relation to the basic model in Chapter 1. However, the question of how intentions are formed and the role of emotion require some further consideration. As regards intentions, the choices an individual makes represent the end results of largely unconsious mental processes reflecting the whole complex system of procedures governing his or her life. Consciously held intentions may reflect or may conceal or distort the aims expressed in action. Conflicting aims, however, are often resolved consciously, and such conflicts may be marked by emotion. In other cases, the aim or the emotion accompanying it may be repressed (see Mandler, 1988).

As discussed more fully in the next chapter, primary emotional responses are now considered to be processed rapidly, unconsciously and by a partially separate affective processing or appraisal system, which scans the environment for events with personal significance. Our emotional response to events such as facing an uncaged tiger are presumably very similar to those triggered in other primates, but the majority of emotional responses in humans are to threats or possibilities only comprehensible as such in terms of what has been learned socially. Direct emotional response in this context must be mediated by learned structures of meaning. These appraisal processes, in turn, will have been developed through the earlier elicitation, amplification or suppression of primary emotional responses in the social context. This complex interplay between appraisals, reflecting knowledge, socially created meanings and values, and primary emotion will form the basis of an individual's response to events and will influence his way of choosing between and judging his array of aims and intentions. In that sense, each procedure can be seen as the means of enacting the intentional implications of feelings and meanings.

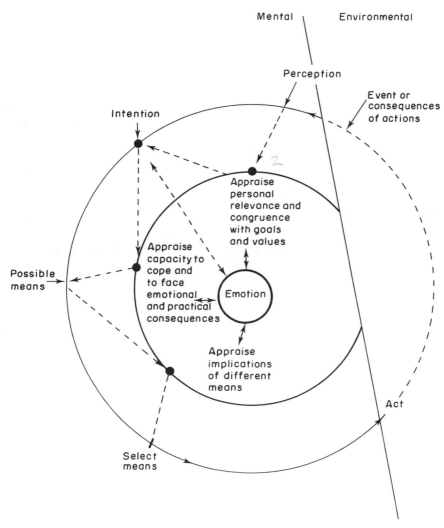

Outer circle – Perception, intention, organization of action
Middle circle – Appraisal
Inner circle – Emotion

Figure 10.1 Procedural sequence model of intentional action

This system of meaning will be applied to the initial perception and to making sense of events and situations; it will make memory selective, it will indicate how far aims are congruent with other values, it will operate in the evaluation of possible sub-procedures and influence which one is selected, and it will colour the perception of the consequences of any action. In short, the basic PSM, presented primarily in terms of the organization of action, must be understood in relation to a system of appraisal and emotion. Just as there is no emotion without an 'action tendency' (Lang, 1987), so there are no actions and no feelings that are not shaped by appraisal.

Oatley and Johnson-Laird (1987) suggest that this integration is necessary in view of the complexity involved in organizing behaviour in the face of competing aims and plans, and on the basis of incomplete information. The role of emotion in this situation is seen to be that of initiating transitions between competing plans. Leventhal and Scherer (1987) propose a sequence of 'stimulus evaluation checks' which parallels the first part of the sequence proposed in the PSM, namely: (1) a novelty check; (2) a check for intrinsic pleasantness; (3) a check for relevance to goals and plans; (4) a check for ability to cope; (5) a check for the compatibility of events or intended actions with the self-concept. The work of Lazarus and Smith (1988) described in the next chapter extends the consideration of the nature of the checks (appraisals) carried out.

This somewhat more elaborate form of the PSM is summarized in Figure 10.1. This model, to be read anticlockwise, represents the inner mental stages in the sequence as involving three parallel interconnecting processes, the outer circle being concerned with perception, knowledge and the planning of action, the middle with appraisal and the inner with emotion.

The Procedural Sequence Model, Vygotsky and Object Relations Theory

A crucial but seldom considered attribute to psychological theories is their chosen unit of observation. Wertsch (1985) in reviewing work in the Vygotskian tradition, including his own, concluded that the appropriate unit was 'tool-mediated, goal directed action', and suggested that such a unit was capable of being what Vygotsky had hoped for, namely 'a microcosm of consciousness' incorporating at the molecular level issues expressed in the molar level. Tool mediation in this respect includes language and the whole field of semiotics developed largely after Vygotsky's death. In so far as the procedural sequence model is concerned with intentional action, and in so far as its essential form can be applied to understanding simple or highly complex activity, the PSM can be seen to be based upon a similar unit of observation, and in this respect it is differentiated from behavioural, cognitive or psychoanalytic theories. The restatement of object relations theory presented in Chapter 5, with its emphasis on the early learning of discrete reciprocal role procedures and their later more or less satisfactory integration, and with its recognition of how intrapsychic structure is derived from early interpersonal experience, is entirely compatible with the Vygotskian emphasis on the origin of intrapsychological processes in interpsychological ones. The emphasis on tool mediation in learning can be seen to be reflected in the practice of CAT, with its use of verbal and diagrammatic reformulation as central tools of therapeutic change. Finally, the requirements for the transition from inter- to intrapsychological learning in the child are enumerated by Wertsch in terms which are parallel to what occurs between therapist and patient in the conduct of CAT. These are listed as follows with the CAT equivalents in italics:

1. The child's cognitive readiness.
   CAT: The recruitment of the patient to the task.
2. The adult's willingness to transfer strategic responsibility to the child.
   CAT: The therapist sharing the tools and concepts with the patient.
3. The provision by the adult of reflective assessment of the child's acts.
   CAT: The therapist's focused attention on the therapeutic task.
4. The adult giving explicit directives.
   CAT: The therapist's careful checking of the accuracy and precision of reformulations and of task instructions with the patient.
5. A level of language development enabling the child to master intrapsychologically the dialogic structure of the interpsychological functioning.
   CAT: The aim being that the patient internalizes the new understanding and evaluations fashioned in the conversation with the therapist.

By reflecting to some degree both the Vygotskian tradition of developmental psychology and the object relations school of psychoanalysis, the PSM represents the preliminary move towards what might well prove a very fruitful synthesis. CAT expresses in its practice the Vygotskian emphasis on the interpersonal learning of higher-level functions, and in this is sharply contrasted with the practice of psychoanalysts with their emphasis on the induction of more dependent regressed and less integrated states. In applying understandings derived from object relations, CAT offers the possibility of higher-level interpersonal learning but also must recognize the pre-verbal origins of what has become embedded in the patient's psychological structure.

The Self

The self as a concept has been largely neglected by psychoanalysis until the last two decades, during which time it has become a divisive issue, particularly in the USA where the debate between self-psychology proposed by Kohut (1971, 1977), the more object relations views of Kernberg (1975) and more classical traditions remains active. While accepting the therapeutic value of Kohut's emphasis on the analyst's mirroring role and on the value of exploring 'empathic failures' in therapy, which are both pursued, although in a very different way, through the reformulation process of CAT, the idea of 'self-objects' put forward by Kohut does not seem to me to serve any particular function. Object relations theory offers a more comprehensive structural theory; perhaps one could say that accurate mirroring should aim to reflect the understanding offered by object relations theory. The effects of incomplete integration of early reciprocal role procedures and the phenomena of splitting and projective identification related to these, and the understanding of the underlying links between intra- and interpersonal procedures, derived from object relations theory, can be described in terms of the PSM and seem of considerable value. These understandings inform the process of reformulation, through which the link between historic and current relationships and the transference and counter-transference interactions with the therapist are made explicit. The sequential diagrams represent a model of the structure of a poorly integrated self, which is also linked to object relations theory.

A theory of the higher levels of self organization is not made explicit in object relations theory and is surprisingly missing from psychoanalytic self-psychology. In making such a theory, a distinction needs to be made between the self-organization, representing the higher-level procedures governing the significant enterprises of an individual's life, and the individual's relationship to, or implicit theory of, that self. The latter represents another tier of procedures developed in order to explain and maintain the 'executive self' (see Epstein, 1973). A great deal of psychotherapy, perhaps most explicitly cognitive therapy, is directed towards this latter tier, identifying faulty or ineffective 'theories' of the self. It could be argued that even in behaviour therapy it is the self-observation of change and of the consequences of action rather than reformed reflexes that constitutes the therapeutic process. Psychoanalysis, however, regards psychopathology as the result of disorders in the lower levels due to excessively strong impulses or excessively rigid control, especially those not recognized in consciousness, and makes of these the main therapeutic targets. Even though integration is the aim, it receives little attention, being seen to emerge from the analyst's 'processing' of the patient's projections. In CAT the therapeutic emphasis is put most strongly on strengthening the higher levels, in particular through reformulation, which modifies appraisal processes and promotes active self-observation.

Generalized anxiety, depersonalization, and many other neurotic symptoms represent the effects of a loss of the high-level integrative functioning, and the breakthrough of unintegrated, inappropriate or excessive emotions occurs as a result of the loss of this integrative function. Negative self-attitudes and self-sabotage may continue to undermine a person's sense of value and coherence, largely through the repetition of active harmful procedures which, once recognized, can be modified. The implications for therapy of this view of self-organization are therefore evident in the practice of CAT, which emphasizes the need to respect and strengthen the patient's capacity for conscious self-observation, to fashion with him tools of self-observation and to identify with him, and to help him modify, procedures serving to maintain negative states and negative self-attitudes. In patients needing longer-term psychotherapy this same basic approach can be maintained, forming the basis of the treatment alliance, through which transference and counter-transference and other manifestations of irrational or incompletely recognized impulses or intentions can be identified and worked on jointly with the least possible loss of self-respect for the patient.

The impact of reformulation, the application of the new understandings encapsulated in the TPPs to daily life and to the therapeutic relationship, and the patient's exposure to new situations and the attempting of new behaviours all serve to modify Target Problem Procedures. In this process therapists are intervening at various points of the procedural sequence and at various levels in the procedural hierarchy and may influence knowledge, skills, appraisals and emotions. The most difficult therapeutic problems are those where major failures of integration have occurred. In these patients there is usually a complex core state of primitive conflicted emotions, some never directly experienced, some inappropriately mobilized. These individuals' main procedures are concerned with avoiding these feelings or with trying through ineffective means to express and meet some of their needs. The sequential diagrams of such patients clarify their structures and sometimes result in surprisingly quick improvements in integration, as has been described. There are, however, patients who need a long-term relationship with a therapist before they can fully risk entering the painful and confusing state expressed in the diagrams as the core state. Profoundly negative appraisals of emotional closeness may need prolonged and repeated contradictory experiences in therapy before they are modified, although even here, as suggested in Chapter 7, reformulation can be of value to both therapist and patient.

In the next two chapters converging developments in CAT and cognitive therapy will be considered, and the relationship of CAT to psychoanalysis will be more fully discussed. Before proceeding, it may be helpful to consider the following comments by Erdelyi (1988):

> The problem of terminology in Psychology is that, typically, the adopted vocabulary subliminally co-opts an implicit analogic

system ... if *Psychodynamics* is taken to mean 'the play of forces in the mind' (Freud, 1917) in a literal sense of either 'force' or 'play', we would be saddled with an absurdist position ... on the other hand, if we defined psychodynamics as the phenomena of mental 'interactions and counteractions' (Fenichel, 1945), it would be hard to understand in what sense any 'cognitive' process is not inherently 'psychodynamic'.

CHAPTER 11

Developments in Cognitive Therapy and CAT

The relation of CAT to the cognitive therapies and of the procedural sequence model (PSM) to some cognitive and behavioural theories was considered in some detail in an earlier book (Ryle, 1982). The theories considered included Rehm's (1977) behavioural theory of depression, Roth (1980) on learned helplessness, Beck's (1976) cognitive therapy, Rotter (1978) on generalized expectancies, Forsterling (1980) on attribution theory and Bandura (1977) on self-efficacy. With minor translations these models could all be aligned with the PSM and are in that sense compatible, but all, while being important contributions to the field, were restricted in their range of interest. There was, for example, a general failure to consider the self in detail; although appearing variously as 'the object of negative behaviours, the object of negative evaluations, as the more or less effective executor of acts or as a proper object of monitoring and control' no serious attempts to construct a model of self-organization was evident in these approaches to psychotherapy. Linked with this, the phenomena described as defences in psychoanalysis were scarcely considered despite the availability of a cognitive account of these phenomena in Haan (1977); indeed, the issue of cognitive structure was dealt with in an elementary way in theory, and apparently ignored in diagnosis and treatment.

CAT, as described at that time, was also deficient in certain ways, notably in the elementary consideration given to mental structure and to emotion. In this chapter, recent developments in CAT and in the field of cognitive therapy will be considered.

Developments of CAT

I owe to my friend and colleague Mikael Leiman of Helsinki a clearer recognition of the differences between the PSM and prevalent cognitive theories. Leiman had recognized in the PSM an emphasis on the circularity of thought and action which was familiar to him through the work of Vygotsky (1962, 1978), a writer with whom I was only very sketchily acquainted. In the cultural-historical theory developed by this author and his followers, man's relation to his environment and to others is seen to have a uniquely social component. The perception of and action on the environment characteristic of humans involves the use of culturally developed tools. The environment and these tools are represented by the words, signs and images which become, in due course, the tools of internal psychological activity. A child's environment and activities are, right from the beginning, organized by adults and hence the origin of the child's thinking is essentially social, not simply instrumental. The intrapsychological grows out of the interpsychological; the implications of this view for therapy are nicely encapsulated in Vygotsky's (1978) observation that what a child does with assistance today she will do by herself tomorrow. In CAT, the therapist, by sharing explicitly and shaping jointly the tools of understanding and control, enables the patient to work independently during and after therapy.

This recognition of the essentially active, tool-mediated and social nature of human thought has been reflected in CAT by the development of increasingly precise modes of reformulation, and this has reinforced confidence in the value of involving patients fully in the formulation and application of these tools. This development of more complex and precise forms of reformulation arose out of greater experience with personality-disordered patients treated with CAT, and was aided by a systematic attempt to restate the developmental and structural ideas of the object relations school of psychoanalysis in terms of the PSM (Ryle, 1985). This aspect of psychoanalytic thought, with its emphasis on the interpersonal sources of the structure of the individual's personality, is close in emphasis to Vygotsky. The development of SDR in particular seems to do adequate justice to the complexity of structure and also provides a base for understanding state shifts, in line with the emphasis on sequence which is central to the PSM and offering a powerful and accessible new tool to patients and therapists. For many people the use of a visual rather than a verbal means of description seems especially powerful.

A third area in which CAT was poorly developed was in the description of the relation between emotion and cognition. The then current assumption among cognitive therapists that 'cognitions precede affects' was accepted and the relation between knowing, attributing meaning and feeling was only incompletely considered. This is an area of considerable current interest marked by the appearance of the journal *Cognition and Emotion* devoted solely to this topic and by much ongoing interesting work. The integrated view proposed by Greenberg and Safran (1987) seems to offer a satisfactory account of the present situation in which existing knowledge from many sources, including both cognitive and psychoanalytic, is adequately accounted for in relation to a central theoretical stance. Theoretical models of emotion have focused on four main areas, namely: (1) cognitive arousal; (2) the evolutionary-expressive model, concentrating on the way in which expressive emotional behaviour functions as communication in social animals; (3) the social-psychological model, emphasizing the influence of culture; (4) the physiological, concerned with the bodily changes accompanying emotion. Woven together, these strands form a model which attends to internal physical and mental processes on the one hand, and to social and environmental events on the other, the resultant fabric representing tacit knowledge through which events are given personal meaning.

According to Greenberg and Safran, emotion is best regarded as a partially separate special 'type of information processing about the self in interaction with the environment'. The characteristic of this affect processing system is that a very wide range of sense data are rapidly and unconsciously scanned and processed (hence the 'given' quality of emotional experience) from which are selected, through structures of meaning, aspects of relevance to the self. These aspects are selected in a way which links them directly to an action tendency, that is to say, emotion is always about doing something.

The relation of cognition to emotion is further clarified by Lazarus and Smith (1988). These authors emphasize how knowledge and appraisal have been inadequately discriminated by many workers in the field, and suggest that appraisal, whereby actions and events, whether experienced or anticipated, are judged for personal relevance, always precedes emotion. The old cognitive therapist's slogan that cognitions precede affects should be revised to take account of this; it is cognitive appraisal that is the key to the understanding of emotions. These authors see appraisal as taking place (a) in relation to the perception of events in which their relevance to the self and their congruence to aims and values is considered and (b) in relation to the individual's anticipated capacity to cope *practically and emotionally* with the situation (repression, for example, can be understood as the result of an appraisal of a situation as being emotionally unmanageable, or of an action as being incongruent with other values). The affective processing system is, therefore, a rapid self-referent appraisal system through which appropriate emotional responses are aroused. This suggested model was applied to the development of the procedural sequence model discussed in the previous chapter.

This system of appraisal, which clearly operates both in and out of consciousness, and is linked with conscious and unconscious judgements and anticipations, encapsulates the individual's personal values and meanings which have been acquired throughout his life and which reflect the cultural influences he has been exposed to. Therapy needs to attend to both the consciously accessible erroneous beliefs identified by cognitive therapists and to those appraisals, conscious or not, which lead to restricted, stereotypic or avoidant responses to experience.

The understanding of this partially separate system is of particular importance in therapy where misconnections between cognitions and feelings may be a central therapeutic issue. Safran and Greenberg (1988) reviewed therapeutic strategies used in such cases. Where affects remain unacknowledged, therapists may need to do more than suggest their existence and permissibility, though this alone often helps. In CAT, reformulation, by identifying and naming the feared consequences of expressing feelings and by offering greater security through self-understanding, often frees hitherto unexpressed feeling. Beyond this, the therapist's own feeling responses, his concentration on the feeling and meaning implied by the patient's words, images and gestures, and his elicitation of direct feelings by empathy, provocation or by enactments in psychodrama or gestalt work, may all be used to help the patient achieve the direct experience of feeling.

Developments in the Cognitive Psychology Field

The distinction between tacit (holistic, synthetic, emotional, right hemisphere) as opposed to explicit (logical, analytic, left hemisphere) knowledge is an essential component of one recent major attempt to develop an adequate theory of the self of use to cognitive therapists, that of Guidano (1987). This author describes how the sense of self is developed by means of a hierarchical structure in which are merged together the two sub-systems of tacit and explicit knowledge. An individual's personal cognitive organization (PCOrg) bears the marks of his individual history, with characteristic nuclear themes. In relation to these, Guidano attempts to identify patterns characteristic of particular diagnostic groups. However, his account of early development is sketchy; he pays little attention to established developmental theories, and represents early learning as starting with the 'mere physical bonds' of infancy and continuing through imitation and identification in a 'tangle of endless mirror reflections'. This seems to be an extreme example of a common fault of cognitive theorists, that of describing learning and knowing in primarily passive ways with a corresponding neglect of the role of activity in learning and a neglect of the organization of behaviour.

This criticism can be applied also to the developments of the personal construct field. As Jahoda (1988) points out, Kelly's contribution was to provide a coherent model uniting the traditionally separate fields of cognition, conation and emotion. Work in the Kellyian tradition has continued to be influential in this way. But, as is implied in the title of the theory, the focus remains on construing and only secondarily on doing, and some personal construct theorists write as if the purpose of life was to extend the construct system rather than to live it. Neimeyer and Neimeyer (1987) have collected recent work done by themselves and others in psychotherapy in the personal construct tradition, much of which is interesting and the variety of which is a tribute to the openness of the theory. However, if, as I believe, we learn by acting upon the world, then a psychotherapist needs to understand that his patient's cognitive system is not so much a map as an operating manual, a recognition which leads to a wider range of therapeutic interventions.

To a greater or lesser extent other writers in the cognitive psychotherapy field continue the relative neglect of the importance of early interaction with others and of the organization of action, and hence fail fully to accommodate in their theories the importance of activity and its perceived consequences in the maintenance of cognitive structures and procedures. This seems true of schema theory (Pace, 1988) and of cognitive therapy in the Beck tradition, although the latter now pays more attention to restructuring deeper level schemes, to affective arousal techniques in therapy and to the transference relationship (Young, 1987). Mahoney (1985), who says 'conceptually, I sleep with the motor theories, but I keep an eye open', does suggest that 'a promising direction for research and intervention strategies may involve a shift away from what the therapist does *to* the client, and towards what the client is actively involved in *doing* to and with himself'. I would claim that CAT has made that shift.

Mahoney and Gabriel (1987), in reviewing the differences between 'rationalist' and 'constructivist' cognitive therapies, characterize the latter as having a more positive attitude towards emotion by emphasizing the need for emotional experience and behavioural change in therapy and by valuing the therapeutic relationship as a safe learning situation; they also regard relapses and regressions as opportunities for further learning. So here too a cautious welcome is extended to 'the motor meta-theories'. The constructivist position is clearly close to that of CAT in many ways. Resistance, in the constructivist view, is a self-protective process, guarding against excessively rapid core change. This view was elaborated by Liotti (1987), who regards resistance as representing the preservation of high-level integrative meaning structures, contrasting this with the psychoanalytic view that disturbing impulses have to be contained. In this, and in his emphasis on the hierarchically organized cognitive—emotional—behavioural system, Liotti comes close to the position put forward in CAT; however, he does not follow through these ideas as far as has been done in the CAT model with the emphasis on the circular sequence of mental and behavioural processes.

In CAT, understandings of resistance and of the role of higher-level integrated structures are reflected in the act of reformulation, which both describes these processes and initiates their revision.

Another restriction prominent in the cognitive therapy field and particularly dominating cognitive therapy research is the concentration on a given symptom, usually depression, and on examination of its intimate antecedents and consequences, with little concern being expressed for longer-term antecedents or for associated psychological factors. Thus depression is seen as being maintained by the cycle: impaired performance leads to depressed thinking leads to depressed mood leads to impaired performance and so on. Cognitive therapy addresses this depressed thinking cycle by trying to modify behaviour and by challenging depressed thinking, and research shows this can be successful and that correlations between changes in depressed thinking and changes in depressed mood can be demonstrated (although it must be said that the measuring instruments use rather similar items to evaluate thinking and mood). This model is helpful, of course, and explains why pharmacological, behavioural or cognitive treatments may all be effective in reducing the level of depression. In clinical practice, however, it is rather rare to see a pure 'case of depression', but very common to encounter depressed people and to find, in the latter, complex personality and historical factors connected with their liability to depression. Prominent among these factors will be a negative self-evaluation and the proneness to self-sabotage and a tendency to set up relationships with others on damaging terms. In short, in depressed individuals assessed for CAT, there are usually relevant procedures identified as needing change. It is of interest that one major worker in the field of cognitive therapy and depression has recently proposed that the propensity for negative thinking to be activated in ways deepening and prolonging negative mood states may reflect 'global negative characterological evaluations of the self' or may result from a tendency, presumably based on past experience, to view experience as 'highly aversive and uncontrollable' (Teasdale, 1988).

This last comment could be seen by many therapists as an example of the rediscovery of the wheel, but I think it is an important indication of changes taking place in the cognitive psychotherapy universe even though the focus of attention remains on beliefs rather than on procedures. As well as more attention being paid to influencing implicit beliefs and deeper-level schemata that are not accessible to introspection there is also a growing interest in the more action-oriented approaches. The question of mental structure is beginning to attract attention and emotion is being seriously studied. Linked with this, some use and understanding of transference phenomena is beginning to be incorporated. Largely despite themselves, and maybe without knowing it, cognitive psychotherapists' preoccupations are beginning to converge with the agenda of psychoanalysis. In CAT and the PSM can be found the matchmaker capable, I believe, of encouraging this desirable union.

Some of the obstacles to change in cognitive theory may be attributed to the nature of commonly held beliefs expressed within those theories. Dorner (1982), for example, argued eloquently against common distorting simplifications, in particular what he calls the 'operator doctrine' whereby (laboratory based) psychologists were prone to describe action-planning as consisting of the construction from elementary 'operators' of a bridge between a starting point and a goal. He points out that, in real life, thinking is embedded in a total living process, is linked always with emotion and is characterized by simultaneous, often conflicting, goal states. He further suggests that self-reflection is a largely neglected topic. Real thinking shows oscillations between levels of representation and often becomes ineffective by virtue of excessive generality, which misses important differentiations, or by virtue of excessive narrowness in which the point gets lost in the details. The loss of the sense of subjective competence leads to anxiety and this is often defended against by what he calls 'flight tendencies', many of which are observable in the work of scientists. These flight tendencies include returning to well-understood areas, creating verbiage which gives the appearance of control, moving to soluble problems rather than facing difficult and important ones, or indulging in simple two-dimensional 'woodcut' thinking. He notes that one important accompaniment of the anxious loss of subjective competence is a reduction in self-reflection.

Dorner's comments provide an indirect validation of aspects of CAT, which aims to enhance subjective competence through the development of precise, appropriately aimed reformulations, which hold the patient to the task of addressing his actual important problems and which explicitly build up the patient's skills in, and practice of, self-reflection.

CHAPTER 12

CAT, Psychoanalysis and Psychoanalytic Psychotherapy

The theoretical and practical differences between CAT and psychoanalysis, already indicated in the descriptions and discussions of earlier chapters, will now be considered more systematically, in particular by discussing some key psychoanalytic concepts such as 'the unconscious', defence, transference and counter-transference, resistance and the status of the self. This discussion will focus in particular on the differences between CAT and psychoanalysis, so at this point it is worth reiterating the ways in which CAT can be seen to represent an application of psychoanalytic ideas. The key understandings of how infantile experience shapes adult personality, the recognition of how far the mental processes which control our lives takes place outside our awareness, the frequently contradictory and conflicted nature of our desires and our ways of protecting ourselves from this fact, and the frequent recapitulation in the transference of elements of the individual's life problems are all incorporated in CAT. That these understandings are restated and revised in unfamiliar language, that the importance of action and high-level self-reflection are emphasized and that the patient's capacity to participate in her therapy is granted a more central importance in the therapy are all true, but do not, I believe, essentially contradict psychoanalysis, however heretical they may seem to the orthodox.

The Scope

Psychoanalysis, although developed in the clinical situation, has from its earliest years been taken out of this context and applied to the criticism and understanding of art, literature, history and politics. It is a strange cultural phenomenon that a body of knowledge derived from the study of the individual and emphasizing the power of the biological should have been so extended. Many such applications are essentially trivial, consisting of little more than the recognition of common themes such as the Oedipus complex

210

in the lives and works of painters, writers or historical figures, as if the description of what is claimed to be universal could eliminate what is particular and as if in some curious sense such knowledge were *deeper* than that provided by a study of the works of the artists, writers, historians or cultures. Clearly CAT has no pretensions to address these wider issues.

Within the clinical sphere, psychoanalysis has become, over time, progressively longer, patients commonly being seen four or five times weekly for many years. Clearly work of this duration and intensity must claim to make a more fundamental impact than brief interventions. As a practical response to human suffering this can have little relevance, as only a minute proportion of people can afford the time or money involved. It is also still true that the efficacy of full-scale psychoanalysis compared with briefer or less intensive methods has never been satisfactorily demonstrated. Other reasons may be advanced, however, for pursuing full-scale psychoanalysis. There are obviously many people who believe that unique gains in self-knowledge are to be made in this way and many who pursue it as a condition of their training.

The appropriate comparison with CAT is not with psychoanalysis, but with the applications of psychoanalytic ideas to less intense forms of therapy, say once or twice weekly, and to brief or time-limited psychoanalytic psychotherapy. In so far as issues of mental structure are addressed and the power of the therapeutic relationship is acknowledged and used, CAT should itself be seen to be an example of applied psychoanalysis; in common with brief psychoanalytic therapies the basic technique does not rely on the patient's 'free associations'.

Time-limited Therapy

Most psychodynamic therapists work on a once-weekly basis and expect to see their patients for one or more years. In practice, a very large proportion of patients drop out from treatment after only a few sessions, many of them having derived some benefit. Over the last 70 years, from Freud onwards, there have been a number of attempts to reduce the duration and intensity of treatment in order to meet the demands for therapy in those unable to afford long-term intense care. These time-limited approaches have seldom been well regarded by the psychoanalytic establishment, even where their claims have been modest and where their use has been confined to relatively healthy patients. Many of the arguments in favour of a form of time-limited work are cogently advanced by Alexander and French (1946) as the following quotation illustrates (page 338):

> The standard psychoanalytic technique is only one — and not in every case the most suitable one — of the many possible applications

of fundamental psychodynamic principles ... every therapy which increases the integrative functions of the ego ... should be called psychoanalytic, no matter whether its duration is for one or two interviews, for several weeks or months, or for several years.

In the 1960s and 1970s a renewed interest in brief therapy was apparent, in particular in the work of Sifneos (1972) in the USA and of Malan (1963, 1976a) in Britain. The former advocated 'Short Term Anxiety Provoking Psychotherapy' (STAPP) to carefully selected patients; the latter developed an approach in which the therapist selected a limited focus for interpretive work, linking historical family issues to current problems and to the transference. Following Sifneos, Davanloo (1980) developed an aggressive confronting approach to 'break down the defences' from the very first interview with the patient. My own response to a one-day lecture and video presentation by this author was one of profound distaste. For a more-or-less sympathetic account see Molnos (1986). Of these writers, only Malan has attempted research evaluation of brief therapy (Malan, 1976b) and there are problems of validity in the methods used (DeWitt, Kaltreider, Weiss and Horowitz, 1983). Mann (1973) and Mann and Goldman (1982) developed a strictly time-limited approach of 12 sessions and applied it to a less selected range of patients. Alone of these writers the focus of Mann's work was explicitly shared with the patient in a statement about the 'central issue' of the therapy; this described the patient's 'chronically endured pain' and linked this with the patient's continuing difficulties. Mann described a rapid and intense engagement in therapy achieved with this approach which is, of all those discussed above, the most similar to CAT. CAT and Mann both utilize a short time limit and a shared focus; CAT differs in having a more explicitly collaborative approach, in the use of written materials and of self-monitoring both of symptoms and, after reformulation, of identified procedures. A research comparison of the two methods (Brockman *et al.*, 1987) showed similar success rates as regards symptomatic relief and self-reported improvement. A greater cognitive restructuring, as indicated by repertory grid measures, was found in the CAT sample.

Selection of Cases for Therapy

In comparison with psychoanalytic brief therapies, CAT has been applied to almost any pattern of neurotic or personality disorder. The active collaboration of patients from the earliest sessions, combined with the time limit, makes such interventions safer and often more effective than purely interpretive or open-ended therapy. The patients are not required to be 'psychologically minded', it is in fact the therapist's job to make them so. In this respect, the indications of who is suitable for psychoanalytic psychotherapy listed by

Coltart (1988) seem extreme, requiring, as well as intelligence, a degree of 'ethical reliability' and money, a range of psychological capacities which would exclude the vast majority of those seeking psychological help in public service contexts. As regards brief analytic therapy, the exclusion criteria described by Malan (1976), which include a history of suicide bids, convinced homosexuality, a history of long-term hospitalization, more than one course of electroconvulsive therapy in the past, chronic alcoholism, incapacitating phobic or obsessive states and destructive or self-destructive states, would rule out many of the patients seen in NHS practice. CAT has proved applicable to patients meeting most of those exclusion criteria. A history of suicide bids is common, committed homosexuality is irrelevant, long-term hospitalization and electroconvulsive therapy often reflect psychiatric practice as much as patient pathology, phobic and compulsive states may need prior behavioural treatment (or these may be integrated within CAT), and destructive states are urgent indications for therapy. Chronic alcoholism (but not intermittent abuse) and current use of addictive drugs are exclusion criteria however. CAT has been used effectively with patients of all social classes and many different ethnic groups.

In summary, therefore, CAT in its scope and its aims is more modest and mundane than psychoanalysis, from which it does in part derive. As therapy, on the other hand, it would claim to be more widely applicable, more effective and more relevant to the needs of the ordinary population of neurotic and personality-disordered patients than are purely psychoanalytic approaches. We will now proceed to consider in more detail some of the theoretical and practical differences.

'The Unconscious'

The use of the term 'the unconscious' is widespread even among those critical of Freud's reifications of mental processes. This endurance must signify a recognition of, or comfort in, the idea of forces which determine our actions but which are beyond our knowledge or control. In our individualistic era, it provides a more acceptable (pseudo-scientific) metaphor than the unreliable gods of Greek mythology; though 'the fault lies not in our stars but in ourselves', it lies in a part of ourselves for which we can disclaim responsibility. A part, moreover, which Freud peopled with personifications like Eros and Thanatos, or heroes such as Oedipus, thus acknowledging their earlier external location. In unveiling these mythic forces, which are by definition unknowable, the analyst observes and interprets visible evidence, for the interest in 'the unconscious' is based, in the end, on its manifestations. The patient is listened to and watched, what he does or does not do or say is noted, how far he acknowledges what he physically expresses, or how far what he expresses matches his self-descriptions, will be explored. His dreams and fantasies and slips of the tongue may provide glimpses of unacknowledged or forbidden aspects of his nature. From such evidence, as it unfolds in the evolving transference relationship, the analyst constructs a model of the form and contents of this particular patient's 'unconscious' on the basis of which he offers interpretations to the patient. The model he builds will differ widely according to the school he adheres to, but the aim will always be to point out how memory, experience and desire are being erased or distorted by hitherto unacknowledged, unknown forces.

In CAT, these phenomena are differently described. Moreover, it is emphasized that the ways in which we do not know aspects of ourselves because they are dynamically repressed ('in the unconscious') blend into other forms of not knowing which are neglected in psychoanalysis. Procedures required for self-description are learned ones (as Brutus says to Cassius — 'the eye sees not itself but by reflection in some other thing'). What is learned about the self, and the capacity to reflect upon what has been learned, that is to say the level of development and the particular bias of the observing self, are the products of an individual's culture and history, both in the local family and in the more general sense. The work of Luria (1976), comparing pre-literate and part-literate people, showed that a whole range of conceptual capacities, particularly those to do with abstraction and gener-alization, were dependent on exposure to communal social living and to some formal education. This was true even in relation to how colours were classified and was markedly true as regard the person's ability to describe the self. Illiterate peasant mountain dwellers had almost no power to reflect on their own psychology, although while in their familiar culture they were personally and socially fully competent. Even within our own culture people's ability to give an account of themselves is very unevenly developed. Individuals remaining in a familiar and stable context do not have a large need for such a capacity, but in the modern world few people avoid social change. The extent of their adjustment or anxiety will reflect how adequately they can understand and control their lives and it is here that the absence of high-level self-reflective capacities will increase vulnerability. In our culture, individuals who are able to give an accurate account of the details of their daily lives and their everyday relationships are often quite unaware of the strategies which are manifested in these detailed events. This absence of higher-level self-descriptive concepts is a very important form of 'uncon-sciousness', little addressed in psychodynamic therapy. The procedural de-scriptions elaborated with the patient in CAT can be seen as contributing to a higher level of self-consciousness and therefore as producing a change in the individual analogous to the change from a pre-literate to a post-literate culture. With this change, enhancing understanding and control, the level of anxiety falls and the need to repeat destructive, defensive or self-damaging procedures diminishes.

In CAT, therefore, the exploration of the dark continent of 'the unconscious' will not be the central activity of therapy. Reformulation, with the development of new tools of self-reflection, offers, in most cases, the possibility of rapid change, mediated by practice and sustained by self-observation at a conscious level. This, in fact, also results in a rapid lessening in the intensity of the restrictive 'ego defences' (which represent diminished access to the world and the self), with the recovery of forgotten memory, increased dreaming and freer behaviour. It is as if the 'ego', when supplied with good conceptual tools, feels less beleaguered and can dispense with the fortifications of the 'dynamic unconscious', or, put plainly, it seems that people who have to shut out aspects of themselves and of reality because of anxiety, feel safer and more in control when helped to understand what is going on.

Once a hitherto unrecognized assumption or action is described and scrutinized it cannot be disowned and the extent of the patient's responsibility is henceforth more accurately defined. Moreover, in working with procedural descriptions the therapist has no need to withhold what he knows. Ill-timed interpretation of feared 'unconscious impulses' may disturb the patient, but devising an accurate and relevant description of his procedures is like 'holding' and is seldom experienced as disturbing except in so far as patients are often unhappy to realize how self-limiting they have been.

Defence

The analysis of defence is central to psychoanalytic therapy. In CAT, the potentially perjorative word 'defence' is usually avoided, it being considered that these often represent strategies that were once appropriate and necessary and which are now maintained by the obstacles to learning described as traps, dilemmas and snags. The emphasis is placed on the description of the strategies and the exploration of apparent alternatives. For example, a patient with 'repressed anger' is more helpfully described as someone who, faced with situations normally responded to in an angry manner, uses alternative procedures; for example, placatory behaviour, the development of a secondary emotion like anxiety, or a physical symptom. He may, in turn, 'choose' this alternative procedure because he sees his possibilities in the form of a dilemma, whereby the alternative to his behaviour, namely assertion or aggression, is seen as dangerous to the other or to himself. This, in turn, may be an aspect of an overall snag, whereby any powerful expression of self is avoided, as if forbidden or dangerous. In such a patient, repression is seldom complete; there may be half-acknowledged or denied bodily changes such as clenching of the jaw or flushing, which are witnesses to the fact that the affective processing system has been activated but has not been integrated with the conscious cognitive processing system.

The repression of memory is also better understood as a complex process of editing (Erdelyi, 1974), often involving interpersonal and social as well as intrapersonal factors. For example, the attention given to childhood sexual abuse in the media in recent years has enabled many people to remember their own experience of it; before, they may have acted *as if* they remembered, for example by seeing the choices in close relationships to be 'either abuser or abused', but the source of the dilemma was not known to them, and must often, in the past, have remained unknown even after extensive therapy.

The general position in CAT is therefore one in which the operation of the restrictive 'defences', whereby aspects of reality or of the self are 'edited out', will be dealt with by description and demonstration in the same way as other procedures. The aim will be to help the patient to recognize clearly what he is doing, and that description will include the exploration of what the (not necessarily consciously) perceived alternatives to his repeated actions are, or what the predicted consequences of the avoided action might be. The accuracy of the perceptions and predictions may be challenged or explored. This range of description is indicated by the Procedural Sequence Model; it is usually misleading to consider just one part of the sequence in isolation.

Defensive editing out of awareness is not an all-or-nothing phenomenon; one may have an entirely blank memory, or one may recall an experience but attach no meaning to it, or one may remember but with diminished or distorted affect. In the course of therapy it is important that this separation of knowing and feeling is overcome. In most cases the safety offered by the therapist's understanding presence, by the reformulation and by modifying appraisal processes, permit recollection or allow the new direct experience of feeling, either with the therapist or in some other context. In some cases, however, the recollection and understanding remain limited to cognitions only and in such cases gestalt or psychodrama techniques may be effective. An example is provided by the case of an intelligent young woman locked in depression in relation to an incompletely mourned (and uncompleted) end to a relationship. The lifelong personal strategies responsible for this state were worked out in her reformulation but she remained essentially no better until, following a weekend psychodrama workshop, her therapist employed the 'empty chair' technique. The result was a powerful but manageable flood of feeling and satisfactory further progress. An opposite problem is presented by patients suffering from excessive and uncoordinated feeling. As described earlier, the integrative task of therapy is aided in these people by the use of sequential diagrammatic reformulation as a basis for their own self-observation and as a help to the therapist in making sense of their powerful and inconsistent feelings.

In summary, in CAT 'defence' is seen to be the result of inadequate higher-order, integrative functions and is dealt with by strengthening those functions through reformulation in the context of the therapeutic relationship. In some cases the appraisal of emotional closeness as dangerous or confusing can only be modified by the repeated experience of trustworthiness offered in long-term therapy.

Interpretation and Reformulation

The central tool of psychoanalytic therapy is interpretation. What is interpreted are signs from 'the unconscious' which become manifest in the particular context of the psychoanalytic relationship. The relative passivity of the analyst is seen to allow the 'gathering of the transference', so that attributions and expectations, of which the patient may not be fully aware, become focused upon the therapist. The word 'interpretation' means 'to expand the meaning of, to render clear and explicit, to take in a specified manner' (this and the following definitions come from the *Oxford English Dictionary*, 1933). Freud described interpretation more directly as 'attributing meaning to'. In its full form, psychoanalytic interpretation will offer a link between the patient's current transference behaviour, his current life difficulties, his unconscious conflicts and his developmental history. The power of such interpretations lies in their immediacy; as Freud originally observed, rather than dealing with the history of the patient's past and current outside life, the therapist is working in the present.

However, the power of an interpretation may not be related very closely to its accuracy, and the act of interpreting always involves offering or imposing a particular version of the subject matter and implies that the interpreter is in possession of greater knowledge or wisdom. Both pupils and patients may grant this power to their teachers and therapists; in the case of patients, their relative helplessness and neediness will heighten this tendency, however far the analyst seeks to involve the patient in the task. Beyond this, the induction of a regressed transference further highlights the inequality, an inequality which is still further emphasized by the fact that the analyst's comments focus chiefly on presumed unconscious forces, that is to say on what the patient *does not* know about himself, often challenging or paying little attention to what the patient *does* know about himself.

When to all these factors is added the central one, namely, that the object of the interpretation is the person receiving it, the potential for imposing persuasive explanations and the possibility of reducing the patient's confidence and capacity for self-understanding can hardly be denied. This is not to say that interpretation, especially of transference behaviour, may not make useful sense to the patient, and may not in practice combine subtle descriptions and demonstrations with explanation.

In CAT, interpretation is seen as only one element of therapy and the form and the context in which it is employed are different. Essentially it is always preceded by the process of reformulation which implies *description* followed by *demonstration*. To describe is to 'give a detailed or graphic account of, to represent, to picture or portray'. In the written reformulations,

TPPs and diagrams presented in earlier chapters, the reader will have seen many examples of this process. There is, of course, an active component of selection and emphasis in this process of representing or portraying; the therapist's skill will be to work with the patient to make those selections which best highlight what troubles the patient and what needs to be changed. The process of demonstration, which means 'to point out and indicate or set forth' takes place in CAT in two ways. The first is through the patient's self-monitoring and diary-keeping in relation to his TPPs, in which he uses the new tools of self-description and demonstrates *to himself* how and when these described procedures are enacted. Secondly, the same descriptions are applied by therapists both to the patient's account of his life outside and to his behaviour during the session. In these ways, the patient experiences new ways of seeing himself and learns to identify their relevance and importance through these different repeated demonstrations.

Patients who take on board the understandings offered by reformulation are likely to remember and to dream more freely. The use made of dreams in CAT takes account of their condensed and many-layered meanings, but there is no attempt to demonstrate wish-fulfilment in every case. Essentially, patients construct the account they give of the images and thoughts they have constructed in their sleep. These accounts can include confusions, evasions, metaphorical battles between representations of opposing procedures, descriptions or solutions. Their meaning to the patient and their relation to the therapy can be considered jointly by patient and therapist in the same way as all the other communications of the patient.

Description and demonstration will confront the patient with experiences and behaviours which have been maintained without his conscious intention. The initial statement made by the CAT therapist will be along the lines 'Look how the way in which you think and act [i.e. your procedures] produces this result', whereas the dynamic therapist is more likely to point to presumed origins and postulated defence mechanisms, as in 'What you are doing with me suggests that you are re-enacting some of the unresolved anger you felt against your father, whom you attempted to idealize.' The insight aimed for in CAT is, therefore, more obviously present-and-future orientated rather than reconstructive, offering a clear identification of what needs to be changed. This does not mean, of course, that the CAT therapist ignores historical data, for the patient's life events, especially his early ones, are likely to be the source of his procedures. But history is only important now because of the structures formed and the conclusions drawn from it.

Transference, Counter-transference and Resistance

In the light of this general differentiation between the CAT and psycho-dynamic approaches we can see also how the use made of transference feelings and behaviours differs in the two methods. In CAT, as in psycho-dynamic therapies, transference and counter-transference events play an important part in the therapist's understanding and reformulation. Thereafter, in CAT the TPPs will be used equally to demonstrate the recurrence of neurotic procedures in the world and in the therapeutic relationship. While 'here and now' transference interpretation is subtle and immediate, the aim of therapy is to modify the everyday experience and acts of the patient. By accounting for both reported and 'in the room' behaviour by the use of the same descriptive TPPs, the transfer of what is learned in relation to the therapist to daily life is enhanced and the opportunities offered to learn in daily life are fully exploited. There is no rule against speculating on possible unconscious mental mechanisms at work in such cases, but such speculations should always be presented in the form of hypotheses and are not, in fact, central to the therapy.

Resistance, when it does not simply mean the failure of patients to respond to ineffective therapy (or the therapist's unrecognized collusion with a neurotic procedure), is most often dealt with by demonstrating how it is a manifestation of a procedure described in the patient's TPPs. Such demonstrations of how TPPs are being re-enacted does not always stop repetitions. Within the safety provided by the reformulation, patients can usually make use of such understandings, but in some cases, when the procedures are firmly locking out new understandings, the use of behavioural tools or of paradox may be necessary. This is particularly the case with patients exhibiting the 'It is as if, if I must, then I won't' dilemma.

The Self

One of the legacies of Freud's wish to claim a biological and physical science basis for psychoanalysis, reflected in the still current term 'mental apparatus', has been the continuing difficulty in accommodating the person or the self within the theory. Kohut (1971), in attempting to redress this, and having rather wildly suggested locating the self in the ego, id and superego, finally built up a parallel account of development in terms of the (undefined) self. This theory is seen by most writers to represent a radical departure from classical psychoanalytic thought, although some would claim a degree of compatibility (Goldberg, 1988). As a theory, analytic self-psychology seems to me to offer a much less developed account of personality structure and personal interactions than does object relations theory, and CAT, as noted above, draws primarily upon the latter. In terms of clinical practice, however, the emphasis placed by the self-psychology school on the role of accurate empathic mirroring, and the definition of the aim of therapy as being the restoration of self-integrity, are clearly closer to the aims of CAT than are the more centrally interpretive methods of object relations analysts. In fact there is no essential opposition between the task of accurate mirroring and interpretation, provided the interpretation is accurate also. As argued above, the risk of inaccuracy is reduced if description and demonstration are the therapist's primary acts. Once the therapist begins to claim that he can explore and name what cannot be demonstrated, however, he is bound to draw upon theory. Different theories will dictate relatively different explanations so that it is hard to claim truth for any of them, even though they all may have some utility. However, whether useful or not, whether true or not, interpretations always establish a radical inequality in the therapist relationship which I believe can impair the patient's ability to change.

In CAT the idea of self is central and the first task of the therapist is to empower the patient by strengthening the self through human support and through the development of the highest possible level of self-reflection. The newly equipped patient will then be able to recognize more clearly his responsibility for his distress. This recognition will often involve him in noting ways in which his knowledge and actions have been distorted, limited or contradictory. In this respect, he can be seen to recognize the operation of 'the unconscious' and of 'ego defences'. He may do this in collaboration with the therapist and in so far as he distorts this collaboration, for example with inappropriate dependency or opposition, he will be invited to collaborate in understanding this distortion. Patients can often work on crucial themes in this way in the course of time-limited CAT. I believe the relatively opaque interpretive stance of the traditional dynamic therapists is experienced by many patients as unhelpful and that conducting therapy on such terms can prolong dependency and block change.

Conclusion

To conclude this comparison of CAT and psychodynamic therapy it can be seen that the aims of the two approaches coincide, namely to help the patient to a greater capacity for self-awareness and self-control or, in analytic terms, to extend the range of ego functions. The differences in method between the two treatment approaches are great, however, and this, combined with the different language used, may make it difficult for many dynamically oriented therapists to accept CAT as an example of applied psychoanalysis. The differences are, I believe, important, especially in time-limited work. Powerlessness, helplessness and denied responsibility are common features of patients seeking psychotherapy. Whether induced by social or familial forces or by a combination of both, they are maintained by these unrevised procedures. Our patients' first need is to regain a sense of personal efficacy, as Bandura (1977) emphasizes. This sense is developed in CAT by the patient's active participation in the task of self-description and self-observation. Reformulation often gives patients back the meaning of their past experiences by validating previously disallowed sadness or anger, and recruits them to active work. A personally witholding psychodynamic therapist, who confines himself to relatively sparse interpretation of 'unconscious material', while reliably evoking dependent and perhaps persecutory feelings, can undermine rather than enhance the fragile autonomy, competence and self-knowledge of the distressed patient, and can delay the generalization of what is learned in the sessions to the patient's daily life.

The reader of this chapter will have recognized my conflicting attitudes towards psychoanalysis. On the one hand I owe to it my most profound insights into the psychotherapeutic process; on the other hand I am impatient with many aspects of its practices and with the complacency, conservatism and self-absorbtion of its institutions. I believe that CAT represents a significant development in the practical application of psychoanalytic and other ideas. The goals of CAT are modest and mundane, namely to begin the process of change by removing self-defeating blocks to growth, rather than to participate in the long-term remaking of the personality. I believe that for most patients this is an appropriate and achievable aim and one served more powerfully by CAT than by conventional psychodynamic therapy. I hope this immodest claim will be challenged rather than ignored, preferably by research rather than through polemics.

CHAPTER 13

Teaching, Supervising and Learning CAT

Over the past eight years I have taught CAT to psychiatric trainees, to other health service professionals (nurses, occupational therapists, social workers, psychologists) who have had variable but often modest counselling training, and to students or practitioners of counselling or psychotherapy with varying other training experiences. Apart from the first group, these trainees have all been volunteers, the last group literally so, in the sense of not being paid, so a great deal of self-selection is apparent. Such self-selection is likely to yield committed therapists and hence enhance the general positive effects of therapy on morale and hope, as described by Frank (1961); moreover, the participation of therapists in research projects also has a positive effect. I do not regret the operation of these 'non-specific' factors, for I believe that all therapies depend on them in important and positive ways (see Chertok, 1988) and would hope to maximize such effects. But their power does make research into specific effects of specific therapeutic acts more difficult.

Selection and Basic Training of Trainees

Working in the context of high demand and low provision has meant that virtually all volunteers for training have been accepted, provided they have one of the above primary professional backgrounds. The basic training programme begins with a two-day introductory workshop which provides an overall account of CAT and which offers small group practice in case reformulation. In addition to open workshops, many smaller workshops for particular local or working groups have been organized. Those wishing to gain CAT experience are then supervised while treating patients in the method. To complete training as a CAT therapist, a trainee will be expected to carry eight patients under supervision, to write up one case in detail, and to attend further workshops. (The address from which to obtain details of training facilities in the UK is given at the end of this chapter.)

Trainees are accepted as long as they have, or are obtaining, a basic professional qualification in medicine, psychology, social work, nursing, occupational therapy, counselling or psychotherapy. Prior psychotherapy or counselling experience has varied in practice from very little indeed, to full training in psychoanalytic or cognitive psychotherapy. Only a minority of trainees have had personal psychotherapy and this is not considered a requirement, although a number of trainees have sought and undergone a course of CAT themselves. This unselective entry would not be a safe procedure were it not for the fact that close supervision is offered, but it is also the case that the CAT treatment framework is one in which therapists can work according to their own skills, and up to the level of their own competence and confidence. The dangers of inexperience in psychotherapy are largely those of collusively responding to patients' transference pressures (for total care, for rejection and so on). The reformulation process, with the clear spelling out by way of the TPPs of the probable transference 'invitations' is a major safeguard against this. Personal therapy is a reasonable requirement for the full-time therapist, although its effectiveness remains unproven (Macaskill, 1988) but most therapy is not carried out by full-time therapists. For all trainees, whether they have personal therapy or not, supervision remains an absolute necessity.

Supervision

Supervision in the CAT programme is provided in groups of four to seven, although three or four would be ideal. Group supervision has the advantage of offering a more extensive exposure to case material and the chance of learning from the skills of other members of the supervision group. The role of the supervisor is twofold. The first function is to ensure that the process of history-taking and reformulation is carried out effectively. Once reformulation has been completed, supervision can usually be less intensive unless particular problems arise, and except towards the end when termination issues must be addressed. The second task in supervision is to attend to the transference—counter-transference, that is to say, to identify the patient's procedures as they are manifested in his attitudes, behaviours and 'invitations', and to note the therapist's reciprocations to these. The aim of reformulation will be to encapsulate descriptions derived from this therapeutic interaction as well as from other information and applicable in both situations. Supervision is particularly important where the therapist's response to a patient is very different from that evoked in previous interviews, or where patients present very different aspects of themselves at different sessions, or change radically during sessions. The recognition of borderline personality structure may be missed unless these experiences are understood. Working in an established supervision group offers close human support, and the matter-of-fact inclusion of transference—counter-transference considerations in relation to the reformulation process does not usually provoke personal anxiety in trainees. Being drawn into inappropriate responses, or modifying the treatment procedures for reasons that have not been thought through, often occur, of course; such events are often indications of unrecognized counter-transference and can be used to extend understanding. Once group members know each other, a given individual's normal repertoire becomes familiar and departures from this are quickly picked up and discussed. Often, as is familiar to psychoanalytically trained supervisors, the group or some member of it will pick up and resonate to aspects of the patient or to undercurrents in the therapeutic process which have not always been clearly defined by the therapist. In comparison with the supervision of psychodynamic psycho-therapy, the CAT supervisor with his more explicit, didactic 'how to do it' role, may be liable to provoke in those he supervises more dependence or more resistance. Ideally, however, the technical framework once mastered should free the trainee to develop a safe spontaneity in his interaction with the patient, and the supervisor should aim to achieve a parallel freedom in his supervision group.

The Scope of CAT Training

The aim of this teaching of CAT is to establish competence in this particular therapeutic method rather than to provide a complete psychotherapy training. For psychiatric trainees, the method offers an introduction to a range of therapeutic ideas, from psychoanalysis to cognitive therapy, and gives them experience in a form of therapy which is appropriate for the majority of patients seen in psychiatric settings. Some senior psychiatric trainees may, without taking up further formal psychotherapy training, gain some experience in CAT supervision in preparation for the fact that the reality of psychiatric practice, at any rate in the UK, is that assessment of patients and supervision of other professionals' treatment of them is the only way one can hope to meet the demand. Social workers trained in CAT have often incorporated CAT as one of their range of therapeutic responses, and nurses and OTs may apply CAT, especially in day hospital or mental health centre or inpatient settings. At present these workers are relatively unlikely to be clinically independent, but with the growth of interdisciplinary working, there seems every reason to hope that there will be increasing scope for specialized work of this sort for people with these professional backgrounds. The basic training of occupational therapists and nurses is, in many ways, a better preparation for the psychotherapeutic role than is a training in medicine, and better even than much training in psychiatry. There seems no reason why workers from these backgrounds should not become independent practitioners. For the clinical psychologist, professional counsellor or psychotherapist, CAT training offers an additional skill and provides a treatment framework within which methods learned in other training experiences can be effectively applied.

Trainees from Different Backgrounds

My experience of supervising workers from these different backgrounds is that, at least while they are working under supervision, the quality of work done by trainees does not depend upon their previous training. There are many natural therapists, people with good, accessible human skills, who are able to work within the CAT framework from the beginning in the absence of any previous counselling training. Several of the cases reported in this book are examples of trainees' first or second therapies. Prior training can, in fact, produce rigidities and anxieties which hamper the work. In the case of trainee psychiatrists, shifting role from the medical management of illness to the collaborative and personally exposing task of therapy can provoke anxiety, although, to their credit, this is an anxiety which most trainees are keen to experience. Social workers, on the other hand, are often familiar with this kind of work, at least on a long-term and supportive basis, but are often inclined to be reactive rather than active in their management of clients. Those who choose to learn CAT, however, are usually very pleased to have a model which recognizes and extends the client's capacity and responsibility. With the underfunding of services and the increasing pressures upon social workers in recent years, this group are often under enormous pressure to deal with statutory work and desperate social problems, and their own morale is helped by the opportunity to work in short-term thera-peutic ways. Such work, as Norma Maple has pointed out in Chapter 9, may also relieve the pressures engendered by ineffective long-term work. One social worker (J. Fosbury) discusses her experience of starting CAT as follows:

> I wanted to develop my interest and understanding of psychotherapy in a way that was not elitist and was adaptable to various patient and client groups. Personal experience of prolonged and protracted unfocused work and of unstructured therapeutic social work place-ments, had left me frustrated in my search for an in-depth way of working that suited me. Working as a social worker with different client groups with varying problems, from emotional to practical, I felt attuned to the integrationist approach inherent in CAT. I am often, for example, both Welfare Rights Officer and Counsellor to the same patient, and this can require my integrating monitoring, measuring, planning, containing, reflecting, and interpreting. When I read the introductory CAT document it made sense, especially because of the emphasis on the focusing of work with patients. I understood the TPPs more fully when I completed the Psychotherapy File for myself and in the course of this completion, I saw how clearly one's life dilemmas could be arranged in a meaningful,

non-threatening way. So I felt at ease when requesting my first patient to complete the file and welcomed the patient's participation in this and in self-monitoring. I felt the relationship became comfortably balanced in terms of the work and power relations. By the time I took on my first case [Marjorie in Chapter 2], I felt I had got to grips with the central themes of CAT. Reformulation diminished my nervousness because it prevented nebulousness on my side in the sessions and I felt comfortable in bringing my patient back continuously to the central dilemmas and pains of her life, finding this provided a continuing understanding for me and for her of how she perpetuated her negative experiences, in this case through self-sabotage. I found writing the prose reformulation extremely difficult; I felt desperate to get it right, mainly for my own benefit to use it as an anchor, but reading it out to her was a watershed in the relationship, and it felt as if from this point on the therapy really started to move. I felt all our cards were on the table, what I knew, she knew, and vice versa. I feel more comfortable working in this above-board active way, with things being said in this powerful, yet contained, way; and I saw how my patient changed in the course of her therapy.

I attended an introductory CAT workshop after I had completed my first patient. Many of the people I met in my group were critical of the time limit saying, '16 weeks, what can you do in 16 weeks?' As a social worker, with *massive* time restrictions, often forced to do shallow work as a consequence, I said and I believe (which I feel helps), '16 weeks, I can do anything in 16 weeks.' Well, that won't always be the case, I know, but to me to be able to work with a patient in this way for 16 weeks was a great luxury.

Clinical psychologists in the UK are usually well trained in cognitive-behavioural methods and only a small portion are trained psychoanalytically. Those who choose to train in CAT do not, in general, find the transition difficult, in so far as patient participation, forms of reformulation and active focused work are familiar to them. The value of CAT for them is in the understanding it offers of transference and counter-transference issues and in its relevance to the management of patients who fail to achieve or maintain improvements with cognitive-behavioural intervention. I also believe that the psychoanalytically derived concepts of personality structure incorporated in CAT and made operational in the reformulation, especially the SDR, are made accessible to psychologists without analytical backgrounds.

The nurses and occupational therapists who have sought the CAT training have done excellent work; I believe that one extension of the approach might be with group and therapeutic community settings, where such workers are usually the main resource available to patients. I would hope that nurses and occupational therapists trained in CAT would be recognized in the same way that behaviourally trained nurse-therapists are now established.

The most difficult group to train in CAT are those who are involved in, or who have completed, psychoanalytic training. This is understandable for two reasons; in the first place psychoanalytic rules about what therapists do or do not do are repeatedly broken in CAT, and this provokes doubt, guilt, anxiety and resistance. In the second place, psychoanalytic training is based upon a personal experience of analytic therapy, usually at least twice weekly, and trainees themselves have often been expected to treat only a small or very small number of patients over long or very long periods. They feel, in consequence, that to offer only 16 sessions is to make a hopelessly inadequate response to the patient and that to work within that framework puts an impossible pressure upon the therapist. The requirement to reformulate in four sessions, the unfamiliarity of doing this in writing, the setting of written work, self-monitoring and other homework all feel desperately foreign. Some such trainees, after one exposure, gratefully return to the more familiar and less strenuous psychoanalytic model, others, however, bite the bullet and continue training in CAT to discover that it works. These trainees are often able to bring what they have learnt about themselves and about transference–counter-transference work into the CAT framework and become very effective.

The Trainee's Experience of CAT

To conclude this chapter, some of the opinions expressed by trainees of their CAT training experience will be given. I am grateful to one of them (John Field) for the following, which is based upon work done for his MSc.

I sought the opinions of about 20 practitioners of CAT, interviewing each for about an hour, allowing time to express their attitudes to the approach and to describe how they used it. My sample consisted principally of trainee psychiatrists (and one consultant), but also included psychiatric social workers, therapists in private practice, and an occupational therapist.

Inevitably, I spoke to enthusiasts, members of a group that had grown up around the experiment in brief therapy at Guy's and St Thomas's Hospitals; they met frequently in supervision groups and at two-day workshops. Not surprisingly, then, they often expressed similar views. Four such commonly held opinions will be illustrated.

1. The CAT approach is accessible to beginners, while readily utilizing the experience of more seasoned practitioners

To start practising CAT one simply attends a two-day, introductory workshop and then joins a weekly supervision group. After a month or two one takes on a patient. Part of the approach's accessibility follows from the integrative nature of the theory that supports it, which assimilates the insights of different established approaches but which expresses these in its own terms, terms which are generally drawn from everyday usage. For example, in a recent supervision group, a psychiatrist with previous experience of psycho-analytic work reported a patient's eating difficulties. On some occasions, it appeared, she felt strangely repelled at taking foreign matter into her own body; at other times she was reluctant to destroy the attractive arrangement of food on her plate. The significance of her difficulty, in specifically Kleinian terms, which had struck the psychiatrist and had led him to a particular line of questioning, may only have occurred to half the group. But everyone was able to see the reported symptoms as an instance of a 'preemptive metaphor' (Bruner, 1966) which had been seen in CAT terms, in this case, as a dilemma. This dilemma incorporated other, previously described, inhibitions displayed by the patient, none of them to do with food.

A young psychiatrist, P., compared CAT with the model through which he had originally been introduced to psychotherapeutic work:

> I was given a patient to do some so-called 'long-term psychotherapy' on. And I must say I found the whole thing fairly confusing. I didn't really have a model which I felt comfortable working in. The supervision was quite practical, but again I wasn't really aware of the model that the supervisor was using, either. Now and again 'castration anxiety' or 'penis envy' was brought up, or something like that. In this particular case, it was a woman, so it was penis envy, so—but I mean, that didn't seem to make very much sense. And so I went through that experience in a mild state of confusion. I read Anthony Storr's *The Art of Psychotherapy* and various other texts, trying to make sense of it, but not having any useful model. And I had been to courses where psychotherapeutic theory was expounded, but psychotherapeutic theory being what it is, consisting of a number of different sorts of models, it was very difficult to know what to settle on and what to use and what was practical.

When he joined a CAT group, he found the approach helped him relate to a patient's distress more directly:

> ... having just encountered various things like classical Freudian theory and American post-Freudian and Kleinian stuff, and so on and so forth—I mean, all these things did seem to be quite removed from clinical reality, and I felt that rather than describing things in terms of Oedipal problems or good breasts and bad breasts or whatever, but in fact explaining them in terms of relationships, did

seem to make more sense to me. Also that a more cognitive approach, looking at how the patients construe their relationships, did seem to be very practical and straightforward.

However, some years of working in the CAT mode and attending supervision seminars, in which there are frequent translations from and to languages of other models, has led to a retrospective clarification:

Looking at someone's relationships in terms of, say, repressing sexual desire for mother and identifying with father, just did not seem to make very much sense to me when I began. Now I can look back on it and see how one can reformulate difficulties in that sort of way.

CAT's theoretically-based catholicity attracted another psychiatrist, A., who discussed his reaction on first hearing a lecture about CAT:

Now what I remember very clearly was that not only I, but also several other junior psychiatrists, felt enormous relief after the talk, because the truth was that most of us had, because of the pressures of work as a hospital junior and so on, actually fallen into mixing models, but always felt uncomfortable and guilty about it.

N., who had come to psychotherapy through social work and had had a great deal of psychodynamic and other therapy herself, said:

My major method of work within CAT, I would say, reflects my massive Kleinian background: I work with the transference, first and foremost, but I do use a lot of other techniques, for example gestalt techniques and a lot of behavioural stuff.

2. CAT appeals to those whose medical training has required them to base treatment on accurate diagnosis

Several of the psychiatrists mentioned this. B., whose first experience of doing long-term once-a-week therapy had been in a psychodynamic mode, said:

I think it forces you to clarify your thoughts about what's going on. Perhaps I'm more used to the idea of reformulation because of my psychiatric training, when you see someone for an hour and you expect to come out with a formulation—in more psychiatric terms, but nevertheless you come up with a formulation. I'm sort of

familiar with that approach, I suppose. Apart from my own feelings,
I think it's very helpful for the patients.

3. The CAT approach is easily grasped by patients, whom it treats caringly and with respect. It encourages a desirable candour between therapist and patient

Several subjects mentioned that, when working in the CAT mode, they
were not ashamed of showing the care they felt for their clients. In this
respect they rated it more highly than some psychodynamic approaches, in
which they had been encouraged to be more passive — and impassive. Sometimes, as patients themselves, they had experienced such forms of therapy as
uncaring and ungiving. N., for example, acknowledged:

> Well, my Kleinian therapist knows that I have been very envious of
> my clients, and I still am. Because I would have liked a hell of a lot
> more from her. I think that's very possibly why it felt so loving
> when I first saw how CAT worked. That, very soon into the
> therapy, this gift of the therapist's thinking is actually given over in
> a very overt sort of way, open to challenging — all kinds of things
> like that. It's a democratization of the therapy experience, unlike
> my Kleinian experience, I have to say.

C., a therapist in private practice, commented on the explicit reformulation
process as follows:

> I think it shows respect to the patient that you don't engage in
> some mystic psychic dance together. You actually lay your cards on
> the table and say, 'This is what *I* think is going on. Do you think
> there is a possibility this is so, and, in which case, shall we look at
> this together?'

But might this offer of shared responsibility be unwelcome to the patient?
Might he or she feel overburdened or embarrassed? B., already quoted,
went on to say:

> When I first started I was a bit anxious about how the patients
> would react. I thought, 'My goodness! They're going to think I'm a
> sort of schoolteacher, giving them homework!' You know, what
> with rating sheets and lists and homework, it's almost like marking
> out of ten, but not quite. I wondered 'Are they going to think this
> is treating them like children? And is it going to be a problem?'
> But actually I found the patients I had responded to it very well,
> and then I realized it was helpful to them, because the problem

with a lot of psychotherapy, I think, is that the patients find it terribly vague and full of uncertainty — they're not quite sure what they're supposed to be doing or saying. The passive therapist, I think, sometimes creates a lot of uncertainty and hostility in the patient.

4. The reformulation process, central to and possibly unique to CAT, has many advantages to therapist and patient alike

Of this, something has already been implied. C. described the essential elements of her reformulation of patients:

> what I'm trying to reach is this central feeling of the person, together with the strategy which has been making that a tolerable situation ... yes, it's the central feeling, the pain — the pain behind whatever the problem is — and the behaviour, the coping strategy that has maintained the defence against that central pain ... and the exit. So you've got the three things: you've got the central feeling of the person — their loss, their pain; something about how they're dealing with that, how they're coping with it, in order to defend against the pain and to cope with the external world; and also something about how they can get out of that, how they can actually make the change.

R., a psychiatrist, welcomed the way in which it reduced the initial apparent chaos of information provided by the client into a manageable, agreed-upon and mutually reassuring structure:

> It's what brings together the information gathering process at the beginning of therapy and what makes it manageable and workable upon, in terms of it being the patient's problem, for both the therapist and the patient. Because one finds a common language and a common way of understanding, something that can then be worked upon. And you can then measure the changes according to it, and you can refer back to it when you find yourself getting dug in somewhere, and I find that absolutely essential. I also find it the most fun way of therapy, as well. It involves the most thinking. Trying to order the chaos, if you like.

Thus, both the therapist and the client were felt to benefit; the former in understanding as clearly as possible what the therapist thinks, and having a chance to disagree and negotiate; the latter in being reminded of their full weight of responsibility for the movement of therapy. A put it this way:

The fact that we are supposed to determine the problem, present it to the patient and get patient feedback fits in very much with what I feel about therapy, which is firstly that if there is a failure of progress it is largely — well the onus is on the therapist. I do not approve of therapists who just attribute lack of progress to so-called patient resistance rather than to their own shortcomings. The fact that the patient has to understand and approve, or at least understand and accept and find useful, what we are presenting to them, makes it patient-centred and protects one from getting things too wrong, talking above the patient's head, or other obvious common mistakes that can happen in a less structured situation. It also prevents patients agreeing with one because they want to please. I find the insistence that one achieves some kind of re-formulation by the fourth or fifth session useful, because my own inclination is often to wait for more information and not stick one's neck out. However, in CAT the therapist is constantly having to stick his neck out, in a way that doesn't quite happen in other therapies, and one is actually quite exposed to criticism and to one's own failure which cannot be blamed on the patient's resistance.

The patient also benefits from having a record of what has been discussed and tentatively structured. As M., a young psychiatrist, pointed out, this common-sense advantage is generally overlooked in therapy:

I think that reformulation is an excellent idea. Not just for brief therapy, but, having had experience of therapy myself, I'm very well aware that there are times when you just wish you had some record or reference point. I mean, people actually do forget thera-pists between sessions, and its only later, when the pattern is repeated and the same point is gone over again and again, that one gets hold of it ... In brief therapy I think it's important for the process, to try and fill in the gaps, to try and increase the intensity, by giving patients something that can be taken away, so that they can look at it, think about it and see how it applies.

N. felt that, when skilfully composed, the reformulation could also convey what was *not* on offer — an important advantage with some extremely needy patients who begin with unrealistic fantasies of what they might receive:

The reformulation is a discipline, for a start, in making me be very clear about my thinking ... So I think in a four-week period — which I must admit sometimes gets to be six or seven, depending on who the client is, and sometimes how I am — the therapy experience has actually had a crystallization and we are in what I would see as a mutually agreed contract. And I think that, for the therapist, means that I've already addressed some of the wished-for, hoped-for expectations that are *not* going to be met.

This last observation may point to one of the contributory reasons why severely distressed patients are found to benefit from CAT, even when treated by relatively inexperienced trainees, provided, of course, that they are receiving supervision. Working within its clearly defined structure seems to engender a feeling of security, in spite of the rapid progress the model invites in the patient.

In commenting on the interviews he had carried out, John Field suggested that some of the enthusiasm for CAT reflected the context within which many of the therapists were working, mainly busy, under-resourced health service settings. He identified CAT with the 'problem-solving' therapies contrasted by Pentony (1981) with the 'person-changing' therapies, such as long-term psychodynamic work. He suggested that those attracted to CAT preferred the 'problem-solving' approach, while those rejecting it might do so out of preference for, or conviction of the superiority of, the slower psychodynamic 'person-changing' methods. I would agree with him that this perception may indeed operate, while personally believing that 'person changing' is usually best achieved by 'problem solving', provided that the problems solved are correctly identified in terms of the person's own procedures.

Training in CAT in the UK

Details of training opportunities in CAT can be obtained by writing to the author at:

Brief Psychotherapy Project,
Section of Psychotherapy,
Division of Psychiatry,
UMDS (United Medical and Dental Schools),
Guy's Hospital,
London Bridge,
London SE1.

CHAPTER 14

The Evaluation of CAT

Psychotherapy research is necessary for two reasons, firstly to try to understand better the process and secondly to justify the act in the face of its critics. It is perfectly reasonable for people paying for psychotherapy, whether individuals, insurance companies or health services, to require evidence as to its efficacy, even though such requirements are seldom put upon others with comparable roles, such as teachers, managers or parents. It is, in any case, clearly necessary for psychotherapists to provide this evidence, given the fund of prejudice which exists against the practice and given the current climate in both Britain and the United States in which decreasing value is granted to human need as opposed to human acquisitiveness. Without dispensing with the real argument for psychotherapy, that it is a profoundly humane activity, one must accept that, in any society, there is a need to show that it is provided in cost-effective ways. But in accepting that need, we must defend ourself against the temptation to demonstrate what is easily demonstrable, rather than what is important.

The need for good research is shown by the eagerness with which bad research giving negative outcomes is pounced upon by the opponents of psychotherapy. One such paper (Prioleau et al., 1983), based on the meta-analysis of only 32 research reports of which only five referred to patients seen in a psychiatric context, was granted prominence in a flurry of articles and editorials proposing the withdrawal of resources from psychotherapy in the UK. There are also dangers of misusing research into the easily demonstrable, positive effects of psychotherapy, for such research (commonly reporting behavioural techniques applied to visible symptoms, or research using a limited range of outcome measures, or research into the treatment of patients who are not very ill) might be read by politicians and managers to imply that only such therapies deserved funding.

The Problems of Outcome Research

There are numerous problems in conducting good outcome research. The clear definition of the patients treated, clear description of the therapeutic input, and the measurement of relevant change, are all hard to achieve. In the end, each patient and each therapeutic encounter presents highly complex individual problems. One solution is to mount large-scale studies, parallel in design to medical drug trials, in the hope that this would randomize individual features sufficiently to make overall judgements or comparisons of therapeutic inputs feasible. If the measures are sufficiently various and subtle and reliable, this type of research may yield one kind of useful data. A contrasting solution is to recognize the uniqueness of each therapy and to carry out '$n = 1$' studies, in which the patient serves as his own control, specific changes in relation to specific inputs being measured using the various designs described in Shapiro's (1966) classic paper. This approach is applicable to short-term interventions where compounding variables from other experiences are less likely to confuse interpretation.

The construction of satisfactory control conditions for psychotherapy research is also a difficult problem; a proper control condition should have equivalent input in terms of time, should arouse equivalent expectancy in the patient, and should not contain any ingredient considered possibly therapeutic. This is clearly an impossible set of requirements. A common imperfect solution is the waiting-list control, more correctly described as assessment-plus-expectancy, or the 'business-as-usual' control in which psychotherapy replaces or is added to existing practice. A third model is to compare two different psychotherapeutic inputs rather than to contrast with the no-treatment situation; this model may or may not be combined with a non-intervention control of some sort. A classic example of this is the study by Sloane *et al.* (1975) which showed a more-or-less equivalent outcome for time-limited behavioural and time-limited psychodynamic therapy, with a clear advantage for both over the waiting-list control conditions.

Despite a large body of research along these lines comparing therapeutic inputs, no firm data exists to indicate which therapies are in general better, or which are more appropriate for specific conditions. The reason for this failure, apart from the problems of design and the large volume of rather poorly designed research, may lie, as I suggested (Ryle, 1984), in two other causes. One is the powerful effect common to all therapeutic inputs on hope, morale and so on, and the other is the fact that any therapy modifying one part of a procedural sequence or one level in a procedural hierarchy will be assimilated by the patient into his whole system. Thus very differing inputs, for example interpreting guilt or reinforcing self-care, can produce indistinguishable outcomes. Despite obvious difficulties it should be possible to show that therapies which aim to produce particular changes do produce such changes, even though it is usually the case that other therapies produce the same changes and that the therapy in question produces other changes.

Attempts to standardize and accurately define therapeutic input are also fraught with difficulty. Variations in the therapist's personality, training, experience and style are inevitable. The recent fashion for trying to standardize cognitive therapy input by the use of therapy manuals predetermining responses, seems too great a distortion of the therapeutic process to be of interest. Probably only the very time-consuming analysis of video or audio recordings of sessions, linked with the use of therapists' and patients' reports on events in therapy, will begin to identify what actually goes on and what actually is related to change.

One approach which is perhaps more appropriate to the complexity of the therapeutic process is to study the effect of successively removing from the array of therapeutic inputs particular components. This 'dismantling' approach aims to discriminate those components, the removal of which significantly reduce the therapeutic effect. However, there are many elements in therapy, such as the therapist's presence and personality, that cannot be removed from the process.

One last point; research itself, through the influence of the person of the researcher, through the influence of the interviews and the tests undergone by the patient, and with the knowledge shared by the therapist and patient that the research is being carried out, undoubtedly influences the process and outcome of therapy. Moreover, the more closely the researcher attends to the complex human issues addressed in the therapy the greater this effect is likely to be. There seems no point in trying to escape from this problem by pseudo-objectivity. It is perhaps preferable to introduce the largely enhancing effect of research enquiry into all therapy. Both therapists and patients might benefit from the slogan 'No intervention without evaluation.'

With these general considerations in mind, the existing research into CAT will now be presented.

CAT Research

(a) Published Research

The first small research project (Ryle, 1980) reported the treatment of 15 patients with between 5 and 30 (mean 11) sessions of a style of therapy which subsequently developed into CAT. It was not a controlled or comparative study but aimed rather to demonstrate (a) that this intervention was effective in terms of symptomatic relief, (b) that changes in self-ratings on Target Problem Procedures would be accompanied by parallel changes in associated construct correlations in the dyad relationship grid completed before and after therapy, thus demonstrating 'the achievement of predetermined cognitive (dynamic) goals'. Scores on the General Health Questionnaire (Goldberg, 1972) fell for 8 of the 11 patients who completed both tests. Selected construct correlations, expressed as angular distances, changed in the predicted direction in relation to TPP formulations by a mean value of 10 degrees, although in 3 out of the 10 patients completing both tests there were small shifts contrary to prediction.

The second published paper (Brockman *et al.*, 1987) reported a comparative study in which patients received 12 sessions of either CAT or a focused brief interpretive therapy carried out on the lines described by Mann (Mann and Goldman, 1982). Mann's approach was selected because it represented the therapy model most similar to CAT, in that there was an explicit sharing of the focus with the patient. In this respect the study could be seen as an example of dismantling, the active homework and written tasks which form part of CAT being eliminated in the Mann condition. The patients were National Health Service hospital outpatients; the therapists were trainees in psychiatry, one trainee in a lay psychotherapy training programme, social workers and nurses. None had previous experience of working in brief therapy. Therapists saw patients in both conditions, the patients being allocated to therapists in rotation and the mode of the therapist's first treatment being determined randomly. Patients in both groups showed significant reductions in their symptom scores and in ratings carried out on Target Problem and Target Problem Procedure scales, formulated before therapy commenced by the researcher. Mean predicted changes in selected construct correlations in the dyad grid were significantly larger in the CAT sample, averaging 33 degrees, and thus considerably more than the first study reported above. The effect size (Smith and Glass, 1977) of CAT over interpretive therapy on this measure was a little over 0.5. Grid derived measures of changes in positive and negative self-attitudes were also larger in the CAT sample, with effect sizes, after matching for initial scores, of 0.53 and 0.38 respectively. The outcome of therapy in this study was independent of the patient's sex, educational level or the duration of symptoms, but was worse on some measures for older patients and for those with higher initial symptom scores.

This study demonstrated, therefore, that individual problems reflected in specific cognitive measures identified before therapy were modified to a greater degree by CAT than by a solely interpretive approach. The design of the study involved combining a number of measurements, some nomothetic (the symptom scores, the self-attitude scores derived from the grid) and some ideographic (the TP and TPP ratings and the grid prediction score). This approach meets, to some degree, the objection that can be made to either type of measure on its own. The different change measures used in this study turned out to be largely independent of each other. It is clear that the overall conclusions drawn from the study could have been quite different had only part of this range of measures been used.

(b) **Ongoing Research**

An intervention study (by Dr Jane Milton) is currently approaching completion, in which the efficacy of CAT in improving the diabetic status of poorly controlled, non-compliant diabetic patients is being assessed. Patients in this study were selected on the basis of having been poorly controlled for a year or longer, as indicated by a highly reliable biochemical marker, namely the percentage of haemoglobin A1. These are patients who had not sought psychotherapy and who were, by virtue of their selection, known to be non-compliant, and all had a history of at least a year and often much longer. Their non-compliance to their diabetic regime had occurred in the setting of a clinic (St Thomas's Hospital) which offers careful education and which encourages patients to be self-reliant and responsible for their own care as far as is possible. After interviewing and psychological testing, the patients were randomly allocated to one of four conditions, namely 12 sessions of CAT, 12 sessions of intensive instruction from a diabetic nurse, a combination of these, or 'business as usual'. The study therefore focuses on a single, highly objective outcome measure, but one which has powerful implications for the patient's future health. A clinical paper reporting the heterogeneous range of neurotic processes underlying this common end result is in press (Milton, 1989) and the trial will conclude sometime in 1989. Preliminary analysis shows that there are significant advantages to the group receiving CAT in terms of better diabetic control, but full analysis must await the completion of the study. These patients were also tested with the same methods as were used in the study by Brockman *et al.* (1987) which will permit comparison of the degree of psychological change achieved in this non-compliant population compared with neurotic outpatients. The nurse-instruction sample also constitutes a control group receiving a convincing parallel intervention, whose psychological changes can be compared with those occurring in the treated group. Preliminary analysis shows a significant effect for CAT, with or without education, on haemoglobin A1 levels.

In a second ongoing study, based at Guy's hospital, all patients referred to an inner-city catchment area psychiatric service, for whom psychological treatment is deemed appropriate (except those requiring purely behavioural interventions) are referred for assessment and psychological testing. They represent about one in three of all referred patients who attended for their first appointment. After testing, patients are randomly assigned to one of three conditions, namely (1) 16 sessions of CAT; (2) 6–8 sessions of CAT followed by two-month assigned homework based on the reformulation achieved, after which they are reviewed and needs for further therapy are considered; (3) a waiting-list control group who are given the Psychotherapy File and are reassessed at the end of a three to four month waiting period, at which time if therapy is required it will be offered. All groups are therefore retested some four to five months after first being seen and all will be clinically assessed at that stage as well as receiving psychological testing. A semi-structured interview will explore both the patient's perception of the change achieved and also the degree to which the CAT procedures were found helpful and were accurately recalled by the patient. The practical aim of the study is to seek to demonstrate the minimum effective psychotherapeutic input and see how far measures of change are related to the time spent in therapy.

A third ongoing study (Dr P. Cowmeadow) will investigate the value of brief or very brief CAT in patients seen in the accident and emergency department after admissions following deliberate self-harm. In a fourth study (Dr M. Marlowe), audio-tape recordings of psychotherapy sessions will be examined for evidence of state changes, which will be related in turn to sequential diagrammatic reformulation of patients who will be selected because they show evidence of borderline personality organization.

(c) Projected Studies

Plans are currently being drawn up (Dr P. McLaren) for another study of a life-threatened non-compliant medical patient sample, in this case patients with hyperlipidaemia, who are not observing their dietary rules. The application of CAT procedures to time-limited group therapy in which group members share their reformulations and SDRs, is currently being studied by Drs I. Duignan and S. Mitzman. A prospective study of the effect of CAT on personality-disordered patients is also planned.

Conclusion

The explicitly focused, time-limited form of CAT is helpful to the researcher, and the uses of measures specific to the individual as well as nomothetic instruments keeps the research activity close to the preoccupations of clinicians. None of the research projects described above are fully satisfactory, but together, I believe, they are building up an accumulation of data, which should convey the limits and extent of the therapeutic effectiveness of CAT. At some point, a joint project with a group practising a different time-limited approach, in which each might assess and measure the outcomes of the other group according to their own preferred criteria, might further clarify the strengths and weaknesses of the two approaches. This could be applied both to more purely cognitive and to psychoanalytic interventions.

Clinicians tend to be more influenced by anecdote and personal experience than by research evidence. This may to some degree reflect the clinician's temperament. It is also, I believe, the result of the fact that so much research has used methods and measures which do not seem to address the issues of concern to therapists or patients. CAT evolved in part out of impatience with that discrepancy, and remains a mode in which evaluation and therapy can go comfortably hand in hand. Research into, or more modest evaluations of, the effects of therapy are usually beneficial to both patient and therapist and serve to maintain curiosity and encourage innovation. Therapeutic procedures can easily become limiting and inappropriately rigid; research can give the therapist what the self-observation following reformulation gives to the patient, namely, an ability to recognize and revise his own procedures.

Afterword

When CAT began to take shape about 12 years ago, the main innovation was to add some extraneous features to the techniques of dynamic psychotherapy, notably the focusing on Target Procedures and the inclusion of cognitive-behavioural methods such as self-monitoring. Patient participation in the reformulation process was then extended through the use of the Psychotherapy File, but the aim was still to offer these methods of focusing and framing therapy rather than to develop a 'new' therapy. However, more recent developments, many of them evolving from innovations by trainees, have extended the basic CAT procedures, notably through the development of the prose reformulation and of sequential diagrammatic reformulation, through the more emphatic use of self-monitoring in relation to identified procedures throughout the post-reformulation phase and through the systematic use of goodbye letters, summarizing work done and indicating the continuing tasks facing the patient after termination. While this framework has continued to allow therapists to draw upon a wide range of discrete therapeutic techniques, the power of the central CAT methods of reformulation and TP/TPP monitoring, with early and continuing use of TP/TPP descriptions to give an account of the evolution of the patient—therapist relationship, has become more evident.

It now seems that CAT is, in many respects, a new therapy. Its distinctive method of collaborative forging of precise new tools for self-observation can, in most cases, recruit patients to the therapeutic task rapidly and effectively and can be surprisingly powerful in promoting personality integration. In this latter respect, it is of interest that a recent paper reviewing the treatment of patients with multiple personality disorder (Ross and Gahan, 1988) concluded that successful treatments always incorporated the following features: discussing the diagnosis and explaining it; stating that the goal of treatment was integration; mapping the system; negotiating and forming contracts. CAT, in working with patients with less dissociated personality structures, has clearly evolved a very similar range of methods,

241

although it does not usually incorporate other techniques used with multiple personality disorder such as abreaction.

The theoretical basis for CAT has also been developed, the PSM having been modified to incorporate the last decade's work on appraisal and emotion. The need for a theoretical integration of psychotherapy theory is widely acknowledged but attempts are often dismissed as premature. I believe that this book's attempt to relate CAT and the PSM both to object relations theory and to Vygotskian activity theory represents a position which can be fruitfully extended in the future.

The claim for CAT that it is an effective and socially relevant method rests on its capacity to help the majority of patients in a time-limited intervention. Because of its brevity it can reach the economically under-privileged, of whom there are many in a decade where consumerism and competition have become dominant values. Moreover, its method of working collaboratively with patients extends their autonomy, sense of effectiveness and capacity for mutuality, and serves to counter social pressures towards isolation and passivity.

At the time of writing, the CAT world is relatively small and most of its practitioners are those who have trained in the United Medical and Dental Schools of Guy's and St Thomas's Hospitals. Some of the more experienced of these now constitute a group of CAT trainers, many of whom are involved in training individuals and groups in other parts of the country. There are developed training programmes in Finland and developing ones in Greece. It may well be the case that experienced therapists will learn enough from this book to start working within the CAT model. It is to be hoped that all those working within the CAT parameters will become part of a loose federal structure and will keep in touch with the founding group (based at the Psychotherapy Section of the Division of Psychiatry, Guy's Hospital, London SE1), so that further developments of theory and practice and further research evaluation of the approach may be shared.

The Psychotherapy File

An Aid to Understanding Ourselves Better

We all have just one life and what has happened to us, and the sense we made of this, colours the way we see ourselves and others. How we see things is for us how things are, and how we go about our lives seems 'obvious and right'. Sometimes, however, our familiar ways of understanding and acting can be the source of our problems. In order to solve our difficulties we may need to learn to recognize how what we do makes things worse. We can then work out new ways of thinking and acting.

These pages are intended to suggest ways of thinking about what you do; recognizing your particular patterns is the first step in learning to gain more control and happiness in your life.

Keeping a Diary of Your Moods and Behaviour

Symptoms, bad moods, unwanted thoughts or behaviours that come and go can be better understood and controlled if you learn to notice when they happen and what starts them off.

If you have a particular symptom or problem of this sort, start keeping a diary. The diary should be focused on a particular mood, symptom or behaviour, and should be kept every day if possible. Try to record this sequence:

1. How you were feeling about yourself and others and the world before the problem came on.
2. Any external event, or any thought or image in your mind that was going on when the trouble started, or that seemed to start it off.
3. Once the trouble started, what were the thoughts, images or feelings you experienced.

By noticing and writing down in this way what you do and think at these times, you will learn to recognize and eventually have more control over how you act and think at the time. It is often the case that bad feelings like resentment, depression or physical symptoms are the result of ways of thinking and acting that are unhelpful. Keeping a diary in this way gives you the chance to learn better ways of dealing with things.

It is helpful to keep a daily record for 1−2 weeks, then to discuss what you have recorded with your therapist or counsellor.

Patterns That Do Not Work, but are Hard to Break

There are certain ways of thinking and acting that do not achieve what we want, but which are hard to change. Read through the list that follows and mark how far you think they apply to you.

Applies strongly ++   Applies +   Does not apply 0

Traps

Traps are things we cannot escape from. Certain kinds of thinking and acting result in a 'vicious circle' when, however hard we try, things seem to get worse instead of better. Trying to deal with feeling bad about ourselves, we think and act in ways that tend to confirm our badness.

Aggression and assertion

People often get trapped in these ways because they mix up aggression and assertion. The fear of hurting others can make us keep our feelings inside, or put our own needs aside. This tends to allow other people to ignore or abuse us in various ways, which then leads to our feeling, or being, childishly angry. When we see ourselves behaving like this, it confirms our belief that we shouldn't be aggressive. Mostly, being assertive — asking for our rights — is perfectly acceptable. People who do not respect our rights as human beings must either be stood up to or avoided.

Examples of traps

1. *Avoidance*
   We feel *ineffective and anxious* about certain situations, such as crowded streets, open spaces, social gatherings. We try to go back into these situations, but feel even more anxiety. Avoiding them makes us feel better, so we stop trying. However, by constantly avoiding situations our lives are limited and we come to feel increasingly *ineffective and anxious*.

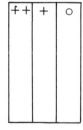

2. *Depressed thinking*

   Feeling *depressed*, we are sure we will manage a task or social situation badly. Being depressed, we are probably not as effective as we can be, and the depression leads us to exaggerate how badly we handled things. This makes us feel more *depressed* about ourselves.

3. *Social isolation*

   Feeling *under-confident* about ourselves and anxious not to upset others, we worry that others will find us boring or stupid, so we don't look at people or respond to friendliness. People then see us as unfriendly, so we become more isolated from which we are convinced we are boring and stupid — and become more *under-confident*.

4. *Trying to please (placation)*

   Feeling *uncertain about ourselves* and anxious not to upset others, we try to please people by doing what they seem to want. As a result (1) we end up being taken advantage of by others, which makes us angry, depressed or guilty, from which our uncertainty about ourselves is confirmed; or (2) sometimes we feel out of control because of the need to please, and start hiding away, putting things off, letting people down, which makes other people angry with us and increases our uncertainty.

++	+	o

Dilemmas (false choices and narrow options)

We often act as we do, even when we are not completely happy with it, because the only other ways we can imagine seem as bad or even worse. These false choices can be described as dilemmas, or either/or options. We often don't realize that we see things like this, but we act *as if* these were the only possible choices.

Do you act as if any of the following false choices rule your life? Recognizing them is the first step to changing them.

Choices About Yourself

I act as if:

1. *Either* I keep feelings bottled up, *or* I risk being rejected, hurting others or making a mess.

++	+	o

2. *Either* I feel I spoil myself and am greedy, *or* I deny myself things and punish myself and feel miserable.
3. If I try to be perfect, I feel depressed and angry; if I don't try to be perfect, I feel guilty, angry and dissatisfied.
4. If I must, then I won't (other people's wishes, or even my own, feel too demanding, so I constantly put things off, avoid them, etc.).
5. If other people aren't expecting me to do things, look after them, etc., then I feel anxious, lonely and out of control.
6. If I get what I want, I feel childish and guilty; if I don't get what I want, I feel angry and depressed.
7. *Either* I keep things (feelings, plans) in perfect order, *or* I fear a terrible mess.

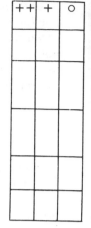

Choices About How You Relate to Others

I behave with others as if:

1. If I care about someone, then I have to give in to them.
2. If I care about someone, then they have to give in to me.
3. If I depend on someone, then they have to do what I want.
4. If I depend on someone, then I have to give in to them.
5. *Either* I'm involved with someone and likely to get hurt, *or* I don't get involved and stay in charge, but remain lonely.
6. As a woman, I have to do what others want.
7. As a man, I can't have any feelings.
8. *Either* I stick up for myself and nobody likes me, *or* I give in and get put on by others and feel cross and hurt.
9. *Either* I'm a brute, *or* I'm a martyr (secretly blaming the other).
10. *Either* I look down on other people, *or* I feel they look down on me.

Snags

Snags are what is happening when we say 'I want to have a better life but ...', or 'I want to change my behaviour but ...'. Sometimes this comes from how we or our families thought about us when we were young; such as 'She was always the good child', or 'In our family we never ...'. Sometimes the snags come from the important people in our lives not wanting us to change, or not being able to cope with what our changing means to them. Often the resistance is more indirect, as when a parent, husband or wife becomes ill or depressed when we begin to get better.

In other cases, we seem to 'arrange' to avoid pleasure or success, or if they come, we have to pay in some way, by depression, or by spoiling things. Often this is because, as children, we came to feel guilty if things went well for us, or felt that we were envied for good luck or success. Sometimes we have come to feel responsible, unreasonably, for things that went wrong in the family, although we may not be aware that this is so. It is helpful to learn to recognize how this sort of pattern is stopping you getting on with your life, for only then can you learn to accept your right to a better life and begin to claim it.

You may get quite depressed when you begin to realize how often you stop your life being happier and more fulfilled. It is important to remember that it's not being stupid or bad, but rather that:

(a) We do these things because this is the way we learned to manage best when we were younger;
(b) we don't have to keep on doing them now we are learning to recognize them;
(c) by changing our behaviour, not only can we learn to control our own behaviour, but we also change the way other people behave to us;
(d) although it may seem that others resist the changes we want for ourselves (for example, our parents or our partners), we often underestimate them; if we are firm about our right to change, those who care for us will usually accept the change.

Do you recognize that you feel limited in your life:
(a) for fear of the response of others;
(b) by something inside yourself.

Difficult and Unstable States of Mind

Indicate which, if any, of the following apply to you:

++	+	o

1. How I feel about myself and others can be unstable; I can switch from one state of mind to a completely different one.

	++	+	○

2. Some states may be accompanied by intense, extreme and uncontrollable emotions.
3. Others by emotional blankness, feeling unreal or feeling muddled.
4. Some states are accompanied by feeling intensely guilty or angry with myself, wanting to hurt myself.
5. Or by feeling that others can't be trusted, are going to let me down or hurt me.
6. Or by being unreasonably angry or hurtful to others.
7. Sometimes the only way to cope with some confusing feelings is to blank them off and feel emotionally distant from others.

Personal Sources Questionnaire

Description and Instructions

The purpose of this test is to explore the sources that you need in order to feel in tune with your values and good about, and secure in, yourself. People differ greatly in this respect and there are no right or wrong answers; the answers you give, which will be discussed with you, should be as accurate and undefensive as possible.

Thirty-eight possible sources are listed below. Go through this list taking time over each item, as you may not have thought explicitly about yourself in these terms before. When you recognize an item that applies to you, circle its number. You may add other sources that are important to you, in the blanks (39–42).

The second part of the test is an exploration of the costs and benefits of these various sources. First pick out the ten items that are most important to you. In judging importance consider how much effort you put into them, and how much it would matter to you if they ceased to operate. Then fill in the ratings that follow the list of sources, showing how you feel when each of these ten sources is operating.

The results of the questionnaire will be discussed with you by your therapist.

NAME: ....

DATE: ....

In order to feel good about myself I need, or tend, to:

1. Be a helpful and caring person.
2. Feel I am competent at my work.
3. Be tolerant and forgiving.
4. Avoid close emotional involvement.
5. Make certain I am not caught out.

6. Be loved by my family (i.e. parents, brothers, sisters, children).
7. Try to do what others want.
8. Be praised for what I do.
9. Behave badly in order to be reassured by the forgiveness of others.
10. Criticize or undervalue others.
11. Be a social success.
12. Be part of a group of friends giving mutual support.
13. Feel that I am sexually attractive.
14. Be placatory, avoid arguments.
15. Try to make up for what I feel is wrong with me.
16. Look good (e.g. clothes, make-up, etc.).
17. Disarm others (e.g. by weakness, sexuality, etc.).
18. Depend upon a stronger person.
19. Assert myself in work or social situations.
20. Think about what I hope to be or achieve.
21. Get intensely involved with people or activities.
22. Deprive or punish myself.
23. Know that I can make others want me sexually and/or emotionally.
24. Identify with and/or participate in something larger than myself (e.g. politics, religion, etc.).
25. Think about where I come from (e.g. family, class, country, etc.).
26. Give myself treats (e.g. food, comforts, presents, etc.).
27. Make others envy me.
28. Show I don't have to do what others want or expect.
29. Be active and productive all the time.
30. Control those I am emotionally close to.
31. Never show angry feelings.
32. Feel expert at the things that really concern me.
33. Feel properly valued and regarded for what I do.
34. Compete successfully with others.
35. Be loved by my spouse/lover.
36. Feel self-reliant.
37. Have others grateful to or dependent on me.
38. Be rejected or disliked by most people.
39.
40.
41.
42.

For the ten selected important sources, indicate how you feel when the source is available to you [e.g. when you *do* feel competent at your work (No. 2) or when you *are* depending on a stronger person (No. 18)] by putting a number 1−5 after each description.

> 5 = Applies very strongly   2 = Does not apply
> 4 = Definitely applies   1 = Very definitely does not apply
> 3 = May or may not apply

Source No.	I feel calm ___ I feel angry ___ I feel guilty ___ I feel strong ___	I feel hopeful ___ I feel depressed ___ I feel under stress ___ I feel free ___	I feel confident ___ I feel lonely ___ I feel childish ___ I feel happy ___
Source No.	I feel calm ___ I feel angry ___ I feel guilty ___ I feel strong ___	I feel hopeful ___ I feel depressed ___ I feel under stress ___ I feel free ___	I feel confident ___ I feel lonely ___ I feel childish ___ I feel happy ___
Source No.	I feel calm ___ I feel angry ___ I feel guilty ___ I feel strong ___	I feel hopeful ___ I feel depressed ___ I feel under stress ___ I feel free ___	I feel confident ___ I feel lonely ___ I feel childish ___ I feel happy ___
Source No.	I feel calm ___ I feel angry ___ I feel guilty ___ I feel strong ___	I feel hopeful ___ I feel depressed ___ I feel under stress ___ I feel free ___	I feel confident ___ I feel lonely ___ I feel childish ___ I feel happy ___
Source No.	I feel calm ___ I feel angry ___ I feel guilty ___ I feel strong ___	I feel hopeful ___ I feel depressed ___ I feel under stress ___ I feel free ___	I feel confident ___ I feel lonely ___ I feel childish ___ I feel happy ___
Source No.	I feel calm ___ I feel angry ___ I feel guilty ___ I feel strong ___	I feel hopeful ___ I feel depressed ___ I feel under stress ___ I feel free ___	I feel confident ___ I feel lonely ___ I feel childish ___ I feel happy ___

Source No.	I feel calm ___ I feel angry ___ I feel guilty ___ I feel strong ___	I feel hopeful ___ I feel depressed ___ I feel under stress ___ I feel free ___	I feel confident ___ I feel lonely ___ I feel childish ___ I feel happy ___
Source No.	I feel calm ___ I feel angry ___ I feel guilty ___ I feel strong ___	I feel hopeful ___ I feel depressed ___ I feel under stress ___ I feel free ___	I feel confident ___ I feel lonely ___ I feel childish ___ I feel happy ___
Source No.	I feel calm ___ I feel angry ___ I feel guilty ___ I feel strong ___	I feel hopeful ___ I feel depressed ___ I feel under stress ___ I feel free ___	I feel confident ___ I feel lonely ___ I feel childish ___ I feel happy ___
Source No.	I feel calm ___ I feel angry ___ I feel guilty ___ I feel strong ___	I feel hopeful ___ I feel depressed ___ I feel under stress ___ I feel free ___	I feel confident ___ I feel lonely ___ I feel childish ___ I feel happy ___

APPENDIX C

Therapist Activity Sheet

THERAPIST: ....

SESSIONAL RECORD

PATIENT: ....

Session No.:	1	2	3	4	5	6	7	8	9	10	11	12	13	14	15	16
History, patterns, feelings, meanings																
Rules, arrangements of therapy	*															
Assigning self-monitoring of any variable moods or symptoms	*	*														
Discussing self-monitorings and Psychotherapy File	*	*	*													
Formulating TPs/TPPs with patient				*												
TPP recognition homework assignment																
TPP homework discussed TPP/TP ratings done by patient					*	*	*	*	*	*	*	*	*	*	*	*
Other homework assignments																
Interpreting transference (± counter-transference) in relation to TPPs																

The fact and meaning of termination	*	*	*	*	*	*	*	*	*	*	*	*	*	*	*	*
Role-plays gestalt, etc.																
Other (specify)																

* Normal procedure should include this.

Rating Chart

NAME: ....

DATE OF FIRST CONSULTATION: ....

Rate each problem:

Describe problem:	Describe aim:	Aim achieved No change		
		Much worse		
Describe problem:	Describe aim:			
Describe problem:	Describe aim:			
Describe problem:	Describe aim:			

Date: ....

Session No.: .....

Relationship Test/Grid

The purpose of this form is to help in the understanding of the patterns of your relationships with others. It is part of an ongoing research project and a similar form has proved useful in identifying difficulties and clarifying the goals of treatment. You are asked to rate a number of relationships against a number of descriptions; some descriptions are provided and some relationships named, but there are also spaces for you to add your own. First decide which relationship you are going to add, listing these people in the numbered spaces below, giving their initials, their sex, and their relationship, e.g. boyfriend, female flatmate, hated male teacher, sister, etc.

	Initials	*Sex*	*Role in your Life*
1.			
2.			
3.			
4.			
5.			
6.			

Now choose at random any two of these and jot down, on scrap paper, descriptions of how they feel and act towards you, and of how you feel and act towards them, noting both similarities and differences. Repeat this with different relationships, and go on until you feel the important descriptions have been noted. Now turn to the rating grid; you will see that ten descriptions are provided and that a further six spaces are left blank. Write into these spaces the six most important of your own descriptions, leaving out any that are already provided. At the top of the form you will see the numbered relationships, these numbers correspond to your list above. Each relationship is rated against each description by allocating a score between 5 (very true) and 1 (not true at all). Fill in the form fairly quickly, rating all the relationships on each description in turn (i.e. fill in row by row, not column by column). After it has been processed we will discuss what can be deduced from the test.

NAME: ....

DATE: ....

Rating grid

Rate each relationship on each description with a number, scoring thus according to the degree to which the description applies.

Date:

5 = Very true
4 = True
3 = ±
2 = Not true
1 = Not true at all

	1. Looks after	2. Is forgiving to	3. Respects	4. Controls	5. Feels guilty to	6. Is dependent on	7. Gets cross with	8. Blames	9. Gives in to	10. Confuses	11.	12.	13.	14.	15.
Mother to father															
Father to mother															
Self to father at age															
Father to self															
Self to mother at age															
Mother to self															
Self to (1)															
(1) to self															
Self to (2)															
(2) to self															
Self to (3)															
(3) to self															
Self to (4)															
(4) to self															
Self to (5)															
(5) to self															
Self to (6)															
(6) to self															
Self to self															

Reciprocal Role Analysis

Parent-derived roles	Child-derived roles
Ideal care-giver	Fused dependency
Overinvolved	
'Good enough'	Autonomy, trust
Good but partial	Fragile, premature Autonomy
Conditional	Striving Performing
Undercontrol ⟨ Dependent / Rejecting	Parental child
	Deprived
	Guilty
Overcontrol ⟨ Dependent / Rejecting	Crushed
	Rebellious
Abuse	Angry
Other	Other

References

Alexander, F., & French, T.M. (1946). *Psychoanalytic Therapy: Principles and Applications*. New York: Ronald Press.

Bandura, A. (1977). Self-efficacy: towards a unifying theory of behavioural change. *Psychological Review*, **84**, 191−215.

Beck, A.T. (1976). *Cognitive Therapy and the Emotional Disorders*. New York: International Universities Press.

Bernard, C. (1957) (Trans. Green, H.C.). *An Introduction to the Study of Experimental Medicine*. New York: Dover.

Bowlby, J.A. (1969). *Attachment and Loss*. Vol. 1. *Attachment*. New York: Basic Books.

Brockman, B., Poynton, A., Ryle, A., & Watson, J.P. (1987). Effectiveness of time-limited therapy carried out by trainees: comparison of two methods. *British Journal of Psychiatry*, **151**, 602−610.

Bruner, J. (1966). *Toward a Theory of Instruction*. Cambridge, MA: Harvard University Press.

Chertok, L. (1988). Psychotherapy, suggestion and sexuality: historical and epistemological considerations. *British Journal of Psychotherapy*, **5**, 95−104.

Coltart, N. (1988). Diagnosis and assessment for suitability for psychoanalytic psychotherapy. *British Journal of Psychotherapy*. **4**, 127−134.

Davanloo, H. (Ed.) (1980). *Current Trends in Short-term Dynamic Therapy*. New York: Aaronson.

DeWitt, K.N., Kaltreider, N.B., Weiss, D.S., & Horowitz, M.J. (1983). Judging change in psychotherapy: reliability of clinical formulations. *Archives of General Psychiatry*, **40**, 1121−1128.

DiMascio, A., Weissman, M.M., Prufoff, B.A., Neu, C., Zwilling, M., and Klerman, G.L. (1979). Differential symptom reduction by drugs and psychotherapy in acute depression. *Archives of General Psychiatry*, **36**, 1450−1456.

Dorner, D. (1982). In (Eds) W. Hacker, W. Wolpert, and Von Cranach, *Cognitive and Motivational Aspects of Actions*. Amsterdam, New York: North Holland.

Edgcumbe, R., & Burgner, M. (1973). Some problems in the conceptualisation of early object relations. *Psychoanalytic Study of the Child*, **27**, 283−333.

Epstein, S. (1973). The self concept revisited. *American Psychologist*, May, 404−416.

Erdelyi, M.H. (1974). A new look at the new look: perceptual defence and vigilance. *Psychological Review*, **81**, 1−25.

Erdelyi, M.H. (1988). Issues in the study of unconscious and defence processes. In

M. Horowitz (Ed.) *Psychodynamics and Cognition*. London, Chicago: Chicago University Press.

Fairbairn, B.D. (1952). *Psychoanalytic Studies of the Personality*. London: Tavistock.

Försterling, F. (1980). Attributional aspects of cognitive behaviour modification: a theoretical approach and suggestions for techniques. *Cognitive Therapy and Research*, **4**, 28–37.

Frank, J.D. (1961). *Persuasion and Healing*. Baltimore: Johns Hopkins University Press.

Friedman, L.J. (1975). Current psychoanalytic object relations theory. *International Journal of Psychoanalysis*, **56**, 137–146.

Goldberg, A. (1988). *A Fresh Look at Psychoanalysis: The view from self psychology*. Hillsdale, NJ, London: Analytic Press.

Goldberg, R. (1972). *The Detection of Psychiatric Illness by Questionnaire*. Maudsley Monograph No. 2. London: Oxford University Press.

Greenberg, L.S., & Safran, J.D. (1987). *Emotion in Psychotherapy*. London, New York: Guilford Press.

Guidano, V.F. (1987). *Complexity of the Self: A developmental approach to psychopathology and therapy*. London, New York: Guilford Press.

Guntrip, H. (1961). *Personality Structure and Human Interaction*. London: Hogarth Press.

Haan, N. (1977). *Coping and Defending: Processes of self–environment organisation*. New York: Academic Press.

Holzman, P.S. (1978). In S. Smith (Ed.). *The Human Mind Revisited: Essays in honour of Carl Meninger*. New York: National Universities Press.

Horowitz, M.J. (1979). *States of Mind: Analysis of change in psychotherapy*. New York: Plenum Press.

Horowitz, M.J., Marmor, C., Krupnick, J., Wilner, N., Kaltreider, N., & Wallerstein, R. (1984). *Personality Styles and Brief Psychotherapy*. New York: Basic Books.

Horowitz, M.J. (Ed)(1988). *Psychodynamics and Cognition*. Chicago: University of Chicago Press.

Jahoda, M. (1988). The range of convenience of personal construct psychology — an outsider's view. In Fransella, F. and Thomas, L. (Eds.) *Experimenting with Personal Construct Psychology*. London and New York Routledge & Kegan Paul.

Kelly, G.A. (1955). *The Psychology of Personal Constructs*. New York: Norton.

Kernberg, O.F. (1975). *Borderline Conditions and Pathological Narcissism*. New York: Jason-Aaronson.

Kohut, H. (1971). *The Analysis of the Self*. New York: International Universities Press.

Kohut, H. (1977). *The Restoration of the Self*. New York: International Universities Press.

Laing, R.D. (1967). *The Politics of Experience and the Bird of Paradise*. Harmondsworth: Penguin.

Lang, E.J. (1987). Image as action: a reply to Watts and Blackstock. *Cognition and Emotion*, **1**, 407–426.

Lazarus, R.S. and Smith, C.A. (1988). Knowledge and appraisal in the cognition–emotion relationships. *Cognition and Emotion*, **2**, 281–300.

Leventhal, H., and Scherer, K. (1987). The relationship of emotion and cognition: a functional approach to a semantic controversy. *Cognition and Emotion*, **1**, 3–28.

Liotti, G. (1987). The resistance to change of cognitive structures: a counter proposal to psychoanalytic metapsychology. *Journal of Cognitive Psychotherapy*, **1**, 87–104.

Luria, I.A.R. (1976). *Cognitive Development, its Cultural and Social Foundations*.

Cambridge, MA: Harvard University Press.

Macaskill, N.D. (1988). Personal therapy in the training of a psychotherapist: is it effective? *British Journal of Psychotherapy*, **4**, 219–226.

Mahler, M.S., Pine, S., & Bergman, A. (1975). *Psychological Birth of the Human Infant*. New York: Basic Books.

Mahoney, M.J., & Gabriel, T.J. (1987). Psychotherapy and cognitive sciences: an evolving alliance. *Journal of Cognitive Psychotherapy*, **1**, 39–59.

Mahoney, M.J. (1985). Psychotherapy and human change processes. In M.J. Mahoney, & A. Freeman (Eds). *Cognition and Psychotherapy*. New York: Plenum Press.

Main, T.F. (1957). The ailment. *British Journal of Medical Psychology*, **30**, 129–145.

Malan, D.H. (1963). *A Study of Brief Psychotherapy*. London: Tavistock.

Malan, D.H. (1976a). The Frontiers of Brief Psychotherapy, London: Hutchinson.

Malan, D.H. (1976b). *Towards a Validation of Dynamic Psychotherapy*. London, New York: Plenum Press.

Mandler, G. (1988). Problems and directions in the study of consciousness. In M. Horowitz (Ed.). *Psychodynamics and Cognition*. Chicago and London: University of Chicago Press.

Mann, J. (1973). *Time-limited Psychotherapy*. Cambridge, MA: Harvard University Press.

Mann, J., & Goldman, R. (1982). *A Casebook in Time-limited Psychotherapy*. New York: McGraw-Hill.

Maple, N.A. (1988). Cognitive analytic therapy as part of a social work service provided by a social service team. *Social Services Research*, **2**, 18–28.

Menninger, K. (1977). *The Vital Balance*. Harmondsworth: Penguin.

Milton, J. (1989). Brief psychotherapy with poorly controlled directions. *British Journal of Psychotherapy*, **5**, 532–543.

Miller, A. (1984). *Thou Shalt Not Be Aware: Society's Betrayal of the Child*. London: Virago.

Molnos, A. (1986). Selling dynamic brief psychotherapy and teaching the patient: reflections on a symposium. *British Journal of Psychotherapy*, **2**, 201–207.

Neimeyer, R.A., & Neimeyer, G.J. (1987). *Personal Construct Therapy Casebook*. New York: Springer.

Oatley, K., & Johnson-Laird, P.N. (1987). Towards a cognitive theory of emotions. *Cognition and Emotion*, **1**, 29–50.

Ogden, T.H. (1983). The concept of internal object relations. *International Journal of Psychoanalysis*, **64**, 227–241.

Olds, D. (1981). Stagnation in psychotherapy and the development of active techniques. *Psychiatry*, **44**, 135–140.

Pace, M. (1988). Scheme theory: a framework for research and practise in psychotherapy. *Journal of Cognitive Psychotherapy*, **2**, 147–163.

Pentony, P. (1981). *Models of Influence in Psychotherapy*. New York: Free Press.

Pope, H.G., Jones, J.M., Hudson, J.I., Cohen, B.N., & Gunderson, S.G. (1983). The validity of DSM-III borderline personality disorder. *Archives of General Psychiatry*, **40**, 23–30.

Prioleau, L., Murdock, M., and Brody, N. (1983). An analysis of psychotherapy versus placebo studies. *Behavioural and Brain Sciences*, **6**, 275–310.

Rehm, L.P. (1977). A self-control model of depression. *Behaviour Therapy*, **8**, 787–804.

Roth, S. (1980). A revised model of learned helplessness in humans. *Journal of Personality*, **48**, 103–133.

Rotter, J.B. (1978). Generalised expectancy for problem solving in psychotherapy.

Cognitive Therapy and Research, **2**, 1–10.

Ross, C.A., & Gahan, P. (1988). Techniques in treatment of multiple personality disorder. *American Journal of Psychotherapy*, **40**, 40–52.

Ryle, A. (1967). *Neurosis in the Ordinary Family*. London: Tavistock.

Ryle, A. (1975). *Frames and Cages*. London: Chatto & Windus.

Ryle, A. (1978). A common language for the psychotherapies. *British Journal of Psychiatry*, **132**, 585–594.

Ryle, A. (1979). The focus in brief interpretive psychotherapy: dilemmas, traps and snags as target problems. *British Journal of Psychiatry*, **134**, 46–64.

Ryle, A. (1980). Some measures of goal attainment in focused integrated active psychotherapy: a study of 15 cases. *British Journal of Psychiatry*, **137**, 475–486.

Ryle, A. (1982). *Psychotherapy: A cognitive integration of theory and practice.* London: Academic Press.

Ryle, A. (1984). How can we compare different psychotherapies? Why are they all effective? *British Journal of Medical Psychology*, **57**, 261–264.

Ryle, A. (1985). Cognitive theory, object relations and the self. *British Journal of Medical Psychology*, **58**, 1–7.

Safran, J.D., & Greenberg, L.S. (1988). Feeling, thinking and acting: a cognitive framework for psychotherapy integration. *Journal of Cognitive Psychotherapy*, **2**, 109–131.

Schafer, R. (1968). *Aspects of Internalisation.* New York: International University Press.

Semner, N., & Freese, M. (1984). Implications of action theory for cognitive therapy. In N. Hoffman (Ed.) *Foundations of Cognitive Therapy, Theoretical Methods and Practical Applications.* New York, London: Plenum Press.

Shapiro, M.B. (1966). The single case study in clinical psychological research. *Journal of General Psychology*, **74**, 3–23.

Sifneos, P.E. (1972). *Short-Term Psychotherapy and Emotional Crisis.* Cambridge MA: Harvard University Press.

Slater, P. (1972). *Notes on Ingrid 72.* London: Institute of Psychiatry.

Sloane, A.B., Staple, S.R., Cristol, A.H., Yorkston, N.J., & Whipple, K. (1975). *Psychotherapy Versus Behaviour Therapy.* Cambridge, MA: Harvard University Press.

Smith, M.I., & Glass, G.V. (1977). Meta-analysis of psychotherapy outcome studies. *American Psychologist*, **32**, 752–760.

Sutherland, J.D. (1963). Object relations theory and the conceptual models of psychoanalysis. *British Journal of Medical Psychology*, **36**, 109–124.

Teasdale, J.D. (1988). Cognitive vulnerability to persistent depression. *Cognition and Emotion*, **2**, 247–274.

Vygotsky, L.S. (1962). *Thought and Language.* Cambridge, MA: MIT Press.

Vygotsky, L.S. (1978). *Mind in Society.* Cambridge, MA: Harvard University Press.

Winnicott, D.W. (1974). Fear of breakdown. *International Review of Psychoanalysis*, **1**, 103–107.

Wertsch, J.V. (1985). *Vygotsky and the Social Formation of Mind.* Cambridge, MA, London: Harvard University Press.

Young, J. (1987). In Ellis, A., Young, J. and Lockwood, G. Cognitive therapy and Rational–Emotive therapy: a dialogue. *Journal of Cognitive Psychotherapy* **1**(4), 205–256.

Index

265